ISSUES IN ACCOUNTING AND FINANCE

Issues in Accounting and Finance

Edited by
PETER ATRILL
LINDSEY LINDLEY
University of Plymouth Business School

Routledge
Taylor & Francis Group
LONDON AND NEW YORK

First published 1997 by Ashgate Publishing

Reissued 2018 by Routledge
2 Park Square, Milton Park, Abingdon, Oxon, OX14 4RN
711 Third Avenue, New York, NY 10017, USA

Routledge is an imprint of the Taylor & Francis Group, an informa business

A Library of Congress record exists under LC control number: 96079843

ISBN 13: 978-0-367-00150-6 (hbk)
ISBN 13: 978-0-429-44424-1 (ebk)

Contents

List of contributors

Magdy G. Abdel-Kader is a Researcher at Bristol Business School, University of the West of England.

Magda H. Abou-Seada is a Researcher at Bristol Business School, University of the West of England.

Abimbola Adedeji is a Lecturer in the Department of Accounting and Financial Management, University of Essex.

Peter Atrill is Director of Accounting Studies, University of Plymouth Business School.

John Bull is Professor and Vice Chancellor of the University of Plymouth.

Nick Carline is a Senior Lecturer at the Portsmouth Business School, University of Portsmouth.

Otto Chang is Professor of Accountancy, California State University-San Bernardion, USA.

Chee W. Chow is Vern Odmark Professor of Accountancy, San Diego State University, USA.

Juliet Cottingham is a Research Associate in the Bristol Business School, University of the West of England.

Fiona Dalton is a Senior Lecturer in the University of Plymouth Business School.

Sue Farrar is a Senior Lecturer in the University of Plymouth Business School.

Ann Hansford is Associate Senior Lecturer in the Bristol Business School, University of the West of England.

Roger Hussey is NWIS Professor of Financial Services at Bristol Business School, University of the West of England and Deloitte & Touche Fellow in Financial Reporting.

Bill Lee is a Senior Research Fellow in the Department of Accounting and Business Information Systems, University of Portsmouth.

Eddie McLaney is a Principal Lecturer in Accounting in the University of Plymouth Business School.

Peter Milford is Senior Lecturer in the Bristol Business School, University of the West of England.

Irvin T. Nelson is Assistant Professor, School of Accountancy, Utah State University, USA.

Audra Ong is Lecturer in Management at the University of the West of England and Bath College of Higher Education.

John Pointon is a Reader in Business Finance, University of Plymouth Business School.

Richard L. Ratliff is Arthur Andersen Alumni Professor, Utah State University, USA.

Jonathan Tucker Research Fellow at the University of Plymouth Business School.

Introduction

This book is based largely on selected papers from the South Western Regional Conference of the British Accounting Association held at the University of Plymouth Business School in September 1995. The book also includes, however, contributions from other sources. The book has been divided into four parts with each part containing chapters falling within a particular, broad area of accounting research.

Part One of the book contains two chapters which are concerned with issues in accounting education. Chapter One is part of the address to the conference by Professor John Bull, Vice-Chancellor, University of Plymouth. Professor Bull highlights the dearth of accounting research concerning the management and reporting of university finances and identifies a number of areas where research is much needed. Chapter Two examines a management tool which has received a great deal of attention in recent years - the balanced scorecard. The authors demonstrate how this management tool can be used as a means of achieving improvements to accounting education.

Part Two of the book contains three chapters which are concerned with issues in management accounting. Chapter Three is concerned with 'accounting lag' and the problem of existing accounting measures failing to reflect fully the advantage of new manufacturing systems. The authors examine the extent to which accounting and engineering practitioners can rely on professional journals as sources of information when seeking to overcome the limitations of accounting measures. Chapter Four considers the impact of accountability and market changes, which have been imposed by government in recent years, on general medical practitioners. The chapter employs models of professionalism to analyse the nature of general practitioner fundholding and Family Health Service Authority management. Chapter Five introduces the idea of control triggers and their role in organisational control systems. The authors argue that control triggers are particularly important in the context of world class operations.

Part Three of the book contains four chapters which are concerned with issues in financial accounting and auditing. Chapter Six reviews the literature on the auditor's use of confirmatory processes. The chapter also reports the findings of exploratory interviews with auditors to determine the factors which affect the use of confirmatory processes during evidence search and evaluation. Chapter Seven introduces grounded theory as a new methodology for accounting researchers. The author outlines the use of this methodology in related party disclosure research. Chapter Eight examines the legislative background to summary financial statements and investigates the reaction of private shareholders towards this form of reporting. Chapter Nine considers the problems of accounting for intangible assets in the food and drink industry. The author argues the case for a new corporate perspective in dealing with these assets.

Part Four of the book contains seven chapters which are concerned with issues in financial management. Chapter Ten reviews the literature concerning the evaluation of investments in advanced manufacturing systems and identifies new areas for research. Chapter Eleven examines the relationship between market beta and conventional accounting measures of risk. The author reports the results of an empirical study using data from 375 UK businesses over the period 1990-94. Chapter Twelve reports the results an international study of dividend policy. The authors identify a number of influences on corporate dividend policy and the variations which arise between countries. Chapter Thirteen outlines an optimisation model which has been developed for the simultaneous evaluation of leasing and purchasing options. The model's ability to make optimal decisions under differing inputs and assumptions is illustrated with a number of examples. Chapter Fourteen considers the impact of 'financial shocks' on the price of a security. The author develops a share valuation model which can be applied to companies subject to takeover or bankruptcy risk. Chapter Fifteen examines the influence of the macroeconomic environment on European corporate capital structure. The author reports the results of a study which identifies a number of significant macroeconomic influences on strategic capital structure. Finally, Chapter Sixteen considers the effect of simplifying decisions on an investment decision. The authors demonstrate that the simultaneous use of the year-end assumption and the working capital adjustment can have significantly distorting effects.

Part One
ACCOUNTING EDUCATION

1 Accounting research in higher education

Part of address 'Thoughts of a Lapsed Accountant' given by Professor John Bull, Vice-Chancellor, University of Plymouth

Introduction

It was perhaps my early upbringing in an arts sixth form that may have inadvertently led me into accounting. Why did Goethe regard accounting (book keeping) as 'the noblest invention of the human mind'? Did Cicero really believe his impassioned plea that 'there was no fraud, merely a misalignment of receipts and payments? Did Pliny really have such a low opinion of financial recording when he observed that 'the recognition that they (vineyard walls) decline in value over time unless they are properly maintained has merely given owners the opportunity to manipulate their profits? Perhaps it was the uncertainty whether accounting is to be regarded as some intellectual or moral touchstone or merely as a manipulation of figures to justify any - or almost any - desired outcome that made it so fascinating. It is this dilemma that has polarised much accounting research - from learned but esoteric theories of valuation and income measurement to the delirious excitement of reinterpreting the meaning of a standard cost variance.

Research is essential in any discipline, and for my part, I am particularly keen to encourage research in accounting that addresses problems that users of financial data want clarified, and the results of which can be generalised. Perhaps in this respect I speak as a Vice-Chancellor only too conscious that one of this country's major industries spending over £8 billion per year and with an asset base of around £12 billion - Higher Education - has attracted remarkably little attention as a field for financial research. The consequence, I believe, is that our financial decision making is not always as secure as it might be. Let me suggest a few areas of University finance that might repay more systematic research.

1. Resource Allocation

At both the macro and micro levels - Funding Councils and institutions - remarkably little work has been done to establish teaching resource allocation models. At the macro level, distribution is now a derivative of historic Funding Council policies (from fixed unit costs to market determined prices), and at institutional level distribution tends to be driven by tempered pragmatism. Can we really not establish in a more objective manner the relative costs of delivering teaching and research in different subject areas? Are we not able to establish a transfer pricing model ie inter departmental/faculty teaching that does not distort interdisciplinary activity? There is a need to explore issues related to full and marginal cost pricing for teaching activities and establish appropriate standard (as opposed to actual) costs, ensuring that the management accounting system can deliver variance analysis to managers in a user-friendly and cost effective manner,

2. Investment Decisions

It is estimated that over the next 10 - 15 years Universities will need to spend over £10 billion in renovating, modernising and improving building stock - a sizeable investment in any industry. A host of accounting and finance issues remain largely unexplored. What is the cost of capital in a University with no equity? What should be the appropriate asset valuation base? Are we properly evaluating the borrowing options - PFI, financial leases, BES schemes, escalating but cheap start mortgages? What are the risks associated with the increasingly elaborate VAT schemes associated with building projects?

3. Financial Reporting

The new SORP is now with us, and is generally to be welcomed. However, I still have conceptual problems with the treatment of depreciation and the mechanisms for drawing down the revaluation reserve established as a balancing figure for the fixed assets which appeared for the first time on University balance sheets. Are we not in essence treating an unrealised capital gain as income? What income concept is in fact being applied? The accounting treatment clearly impacts on conventional measures of performance, and impacts on borrowing capacity - important, given that Universities have already borrowed approaching £2 billion from the commercial market.

4. Joint and By-Products

Considerable attention has been focused upon the apportionment - allocation of costs between research and teaching - but are we costing joint or by-products? The issue is important not the least because Universities are exhorted by the NAO to ensure that the price charged for research/consultancy reflects the 'full cost'. There is, too, the view - justified or not - from the 'new' Universities that the teaching/research split identified by the 'old' Universities when HEFCE was established was not transparent, and the relative cost of teaching is the key parameter for the imposition of efficiency gains.

5. Behavioural Accounting

'Budgets affect people' is a well established truism, but I am not aware of much work being done on the budgetary game in the University sector. If you believe - as I do, strongly - that a University must be driven by its academic vision and constrained by finance, then the impact of financial and budgetary systems must be at the worst neutral and at the best supportive of the vision. I am not at all sure that is the case in all - dare I say, any - Universities, and we do need to do some research on the games academics play!

6. Human Resource Accounting

We are fond in saying that our staff are our most important asset, but we still seem to operate with reward and staff development systems that belie that assertion. I would very much like to see some fundamental research undertaken on human resource accounting in the education industry - it does have some particular features that are indeed unique.

Conclusion

So in conclusion, I would like to suggest that you apply your research efforts to what is indeed a major industry, the industry that employs you! I have outlined some areas which interest and concern me as a Vice-Chancellor responsible, as accounting officer, for the finance of a large business. When you are next considering a research topic please do not neglect your home base!

2 Using the balanced scorecard to stimulate and guide continuous improvement in accounting education

Otto Chang and Chee W. Chow

Introduction

In recent years, rapid advances in communication, data processing, and manufacturing technologies, together with the dismantling of trade barriers, have fundamentally reshaped the environment in which businesses operate. Change and ever-increasing levels of competition have become constants in this landscape. In response, companies are increasingly focused on satisfying their customers, as the latter are the ones who ultimately pay for their expenses and profit. Related to this, the dimensions of competition have expanded well beyond the traditional aspects of price and quality to include flexibility, speed, and continuous improvement in the ability to add value for customers.

What is true of the corporate world also applies, though probably to a lesser extent, to the business of accounting education. Increasingly, questions are being raised whether accounting education is meeting the needs of its customers. And who are the customers of accounting educational institutions and programmes? The group that most readily comes to mind is the students. But students really are only the output of accounting programmes. The customers - those who create the demand for accounting education in the first place - are the employers of accounting programme graduates. And just as business firms that fail to satisfy their customers will wither away under the assault of competitive forces, so will accounting programmess that fail to add sufficient value to their students.

Arguably the most noticed expression of concern for the current state of accounting education was the issuance, in 1989, of *Perspectives on Education: Capabilities for Success in the Accounting Profession* by the then-Big Eight international accounting firms. This document stated the opinion that accounting programmes were spending too much time teaching students technical rules that soon became obsolete, and too little time in developing communication skills, critical thinking and problem solving skills, interpersonal skills, integrative business knowledge, and the ability to become lifelong learners. In the U.S. and undoubtedly elsewhere, many accounting programmes have responded to this call for reform with efforts to revise their curricula and teaching processes. They were aided in no small part by such institutions as the American Accounting Association's Accounting Education Change Commission. Despite such efforts, there still remains a lot of room for change. In a survey conducted by the U.S. Institute of Management Accountants [Siegel & Sorensen, 1994], controllers from a majority of the U.S. Fortune 500 companies indicated that current accounting programmes were overemphasizing the preparation of certified public accountants at the expense of a broad-based need for management accountants. Many courses in the area of business analysis and management information are either ignored or curtailed to the extent that students after graduation require extensive on-the-job training in order to perform their assigned responsibilities.

Accounting educators and programmes can ill afford to ignore the concerns and demands of the marketplace. Increasingly, funding agencies, and even the public at large, are clamoring for accountability from educational institutions. On top of this, the business sector is developing alternatives to traditional venues of business education. Choi [1993, p. 428] has observed:

> (B)usiness schools as a whole will face increasing competition from their clients as well. Industry, dissatisfied with the products they are receiving from academe, are increasingly developing their own in-house educational programmess. Companies such as Motorola, Pepsi-Cola, General Electric, General Motors, Finland's Nokia, and many Japanese firms are examples in this regard.

For conventional educational institutions, the list of competitors can be expanded to include formal programmes offered by consulting firms, such as Arthur D. Little, as well as distance learning programmes, such as the U.K.'s Open University, which have been made possible by the increasing availability of INTERNET, worldwide web, and better and cheaper communication technology. Faced with increased public scrutiny and competition, accounting programmes that aim to survive and prosper will need to increase their responsiveness to the changing needs of their customers, and to ensure continuous improvement in their ability to do so. The purpose of this paper is to suggest how a new management tool - the balanced scorecard - can help accounting programmes to initiate and sustain continuous improvement in their ability to increase the value-added of their services.

The balanced scorecard

The balanced scorecard is a set of integrated performance measures focused on key aspects of operations. These measures can be for an organization, a subunit, or even an individual. The scorecard is analogous to the instrument panel on an airplane. To fly an airplane to its destination, a pilot needs to know conditions both inside and outside of the plane during flight. The instrument panel provides information about these conditions. Similarly, in managing complicated corporate affairs, managers need to know a myriad of internal and external conditions. The function of the balanced scorecard is to provide management with a holistic view of what is happening inside and outside the organization. In many organizations, there is a tendency to keep adding performance measures as long as somebody makes a suggestion. The result is a mountain of reports that hinders rather than helps. A major advantage of the balanced scorecard is that it provides management with key and interrelated indicators without the problem of information overload.

While the idea of using combinations of financial and nonfinancial performance measures is not new, the balanced scorecard represents an innovative way of packaging such measures. Robert Kaplan and his associate from the business sector, David Norton, deserve much of the credit for increasing understanding and awareness of this approach through a series of articles in the *Harvard Business Review* and a recent book (Kaplan and Norton, 1992, 1993, 1996a, 1996b).

At the organizational level, the balanced scorecard involves identifying several key components of operations, establishing goals for these, and then selecting measures to track progress towards these goals. The number of components can be expected to vary depending on the nature of the organization, though it is reasonable to expect that most organizations would have at least the following four:

(1) Customer perspective: How do customers see us?
(2) Internal business perspective: What must we excel at?
(3) Innovation and learning perspective: Can we continue to improve and create value for customers?
(4) Financial perspective: How do we look to providers of financial resources?

Since a number of articles already have expounded on the balanced scorecard approach and its application in the for-profit sector (e.g., Hoffecker, 1994; Newing, 1994, 1995; Maisel, 1992), we will not discuss each component in detail. Suffice it to say that the customer perspective tracks how well the organization is meeting the expectations of its customers; the internal business perspective focuses on the organization's operations as they relate to satisfying customer demands; the innovation and learning perspective emphasizes the organization's ability to sustain and increase its capability to satisfy customers; and finally, the financial perspective tracks how well the organization is translating its operational results into financial well being. In the past few years, the balanced scorecard approach has steadily gained acceptance in the for-profit sector. For example, starting in October 1992, KPMG has restructured its business operation to cater to the specific needs of its clients in different industries. After restructuring, each division has developed its own balanced scorecard for monthly evaluation of its performance, particularly in the area of client satisfaction (Irvine, 1993). In January 1994, Ernst and Young started to provide consulting service to companies interested in implementing the balanced scorecard idea (Vitale, Mavrinac and Hauler, 1994). By October 1995, a considerable number of major corporations had experimented with the method. CFO magazine summarized the prevalent practice and illustrated the details involved in implementation by All State Insurance Company (Birchard, 1995). Even though application of the balanced scorecard is still in the takeoff stage, Kaplan and Norton (1996a) suggest that there already is evidence of several major benefits:

(1) It promotes the active formulation and implementation of organizational strategies;
(2) It makes organizational strategies updated and highly visible;
(3) It improves communication within the organization;
(4) It improves alignment among divisional or individual goals and the organization's goals and strtegies;
(5) It aligns annual or short-term operating plans with long-term ; and
(6) It helps to align performance evaluation measurement and long-term strategies.

Using the balanced scorecard in accounting education

Even though discussions and applications of the balanced scorecard have been concentrated in the for-profit sector, its emphasis on strategic vision and linking performance measures to strategies should benefit not-for-profit organizations as well. As discussed earlier, accounting education (and business education in general) is facing serious challenges that require innovative and fundamental responses. We believe that the ideas embodied in the balanced scorecard approach can be of great help to accounting educators in creating more vibrant and value-adding programmes. In this section, we will first illustrate what a balanced scorecard may look like for an accounting programme. Then we will discuss how accounting educators can go about developing and implementing the balanced scorecard approach.

An illustrative balanced scorecard for an accounting programme

Table 1 presents an illustrative balanced scorecard for an accounting program. This scorecard is patterned after one shown in Kaplan and Norton (1992) and has four components, or perspectives. As we had suggested earlier, the most appropriate number of components would vary according to the organization's circumstances.

TABLE 1
An illustrative balanced scorecard for an accounting department

Customer Perspective	
Sample goals	Sample measures
Highly valued programme	Number of applications; percentage of accepted applicants enrolled
High quality instruction	Alumni and employer evaluation; student placement rate; external ratings
Service orientation	Student evaluations of staff
Flexible course schedule	Frequency of offering required courses; distribution of times of day and week courses are offered

TABLE 1 (continued)

Internal Business Perspective	
Sample goals	Sample measures
Specialized programme in systems	Number of specialized faculty; number of specialized courses
Optimal class size	Average class size
Quality instruction	Distribution of grades awarded; prerequisite enforcement rate; exit exam performance

Innovation and Learning Perspective	
Sample goals	Sample measures
Curriculum innovation	Number of new courses and number of curriculum revisions in past 5 years
Faculty research and creativity	Number of professional presentations and publications by faculty
Incorporating technology into teaching	Number of courses using new technology; expenditure per student for technology
Partnering with accounting firms	Number of joint activities; number of firms participating in joint activities

Financial Perspective	
Sample goals	Sample measures
Adequate funds for operations (survive)	Level of student enrollment; funding per student
Securing revenue sources (succeed)	Enrollment trend; test scores or GPA of incoming majors
Building surplus or capital funds(prosper)	Amount of external grants; contributions to endowment; annual giving to the department

Below, we briefly discuss each of the four perspectives. Before doing so, it is important to stress that the balanced scorecard links goals and measures to strategies, and as such, it is an integral part of the strategic planning process (Kaplan and Norton, 1996a). Further, acceptance of the balanced scorecard's importance is crucial to its successful implementation. Since acceptance is likely to increase with the degree of participation in its construction, all members of the department, from top to bottom, should be involved in the planning and communication process from the start. And because the whole process involves everyone in the organization and touches every major aspect of the organization's operation, its time requirements can be substantial. Yet this investment would be one of the most worthwhile that the organization can make, as the process of designing the balanced scorecard will stimulate thinking, discussion, and understanding of the organization's strategies and goals and what need to be done well to accomplish them.

Customer perspective

The quality of an accounting education programme probably is most directly reflected in how it is perceived by students and employers. Students' perception of an accounting programme is likely to depend on factors like the reputation of the programme, the quality of instruction, course availability and sequencing, tuition and fees, job placement and extracurricular activities. Employers are likely to focus on the skills of its graduates, the reputation of the institution, and the professional and community contributions provided by the institution. Table 1 shows how these considerations may be translated into four goals and associated performance measures:

(1) to become a highly valued programme, measured by the number of applications and the percentage of realized enrollment among accepted applicants;

(2) to maintain high qualify instruction, measured by opinions of alumni and employers, students placement rate, and external rating programme;

(3) to emphasize service orientation, measured by student evaluation of staff and;

(4) to have flexible course scheduling, measured by offering frequency required courses, convenience of course hours, and an even distribution of course offerings among weekdays.

In actual application, a variety of other possible goals and measures will likely be considered, such as high quality academic advising, measured by student to advisor ratios, percentage of faculty's time spent on advising, and student evaluation of advising; effective student placement service, measured by number of companies recruiting on campus; and active community service, measured by number of community activities sponsored and percentage of faculty holding office in external organizations.

Internal business perspective

To build a super image from the customer's perspective, an accounting programme must excel internally at curriculum design, quality of instruction, facility utilization, and human resource management. An accounting programme could, for example, distinguish itself by developing a specialized curriculum, increasing utilization rate and efficiency of personnel and facilities, establishing an optimal class-size mix to achieve quality instruction, establishing an active internship programme, and enhancing computer and library resources. Table 1 illustrates four potential goals and their associated performance measures in this area:

(1) to develop a specialized programme in accounting information systems, the progress of which will be measured by the number of faculty members specializing in the area and the number of courses offered in the specialized programme;

(2) to achieve an optimum class-size mix, measured by average class size in targeted courses;

(3) to assure quality instruction, evaluated by distribution of grade awarded, prerequisite enforcement rate, and student performance in an exit exam; and

(4) to establish an effective internship programme, measured by number of internships available and the number companies involved.

Innovation and learning perspective

To sustain and increase its ability to add value, an accounting programme needs to continuously innovate and improve. In addition to revising the existing curriculum at regular intervals, it also has to develop new courses that meet customers' changing needs. Even more important is continuous improvement in teaching. For example, incorporating computer and multimedia technology into the classroom can enhance both student interest and learning. Furthermore, what is taught in a classroom should be a reasonable reflection of what is done in practice. This would require faculty members to actively engage in professional growth by participating in continuing education and conducting research related to their fields of teaching. It also suggests a role for close interaction with industries in the form of joint research, faculty internships or use of practitioners as part-time instructors. Table 1 illustrates four goals and their related performance measures for the innovation and learning perspective. These are curriculum innovation, faculty research and creativity, incorporating technology into teaching, and partnership with accounting firms. Progress in curriculum innovation is measured with the number of new courses offered and the number of curriculum revisions in the past five years. Success in faculty research and creativity is measured by the number of faculty publications and presentations in professional conferences. The degree to which technology is incorporated into teaching is gauged by the number of courses incorporating new technology and the expenditure per student on new technology, as compared to target. Finally, success in partnering with accounting firms is measured by the number of joint activities and the number of firms participating in joint activities with the programme. Again, these goals and measures are for illustration only. For example, an alternative measure for evaluating progress towards the last goal could be the percentage of faculty members' time spent in joint activities with firms.

Financial perspective

No matter how excellent an accounting programme is, it cannot continue without adequate financial support. Thus, to be truly successful, an accounting programme must ensure adequate resources for current operations, as well as for future expansion and growth. Table 1 illustrates three goals in this perspective:

(1) to have adequate funds for operations, measured by the relation between current inflows and outflows, as manifested in the level of student enrollment and the funding per student from state or other sources;

(2) to secure revenue sources, measured by enrollment trend and test scores or grade point average of incoming majors; and

(3) to build surplus or capital funds, measured by the amount of external grants, contributions to endowment, and annual giving to the department.

Balanced scorecards for individual department members

Since attaining the overall goals of the programme requires inputs from each member, balanced scorecards also need to be designed for individual department members. We see no reason why all individual scorecards need to be identical. The goals and needs of any accounting programme are many and varied, and skills, talents, and interests also vary across individuals. To attain the greatest success as a whole requires accounting programmes to exploit these individual differences and to seek and create synergies amongst its members. Thus, unlike a golf team, where the team score is simply the sum of individual team members' scores, an accounting department is more like a basketball team, where the team outcome depends on coordination and cooperation, in addition to specialization among team members. Accordingly, while individual balanced scorecards need to be consistent with the overall organizational strategies, goals and measures, there also needs to be flexibility in accommodating individual strengths and weaknesses.

Implementing the balanced scorecard in an accounting programme

We are not aware of any accounting programme having explicitly implemented the balanced scorecard approach. But if the experience from the for-profit sector (Kaplan and Norton, 1996a, pp. 78-79) is any guide, then the design and implementation process can easily take up to two years or more, with the following component stages:

Months 1-2

> A departmental strategic planning retreat involving everyone in the department is held to identify strategic issues and to discuss possible solutions. The purpose of this meeting is to form consensus among departmental members regarding the vision and strategic goals and objectives. A second retreat meeting is held if necessary.

Months 3-4

A strategic planning committee (preferably including the chairperson of the department) is formed with the charge to formulate objectives for each of the four perspectives in the departmental balanced scorecard.

Months 5-6

Using the balanced scorecard as a communication tool, the strategic planning committee seeks comments on and acceptance of the departmental balanced scorecard from members of the department.

Month 7

Based on comments from departmental members, the strategic planning committee revises the departmental balanced scorecard.

Months 8-9

The revised departmental balanced scorecard is communicated to the departmental members. Each member is required to develop individual balanced scorecards that support the departmental goals and objectives.

Months 10-11

The strategic planning committee reviews individual balanced scorecards, suggesting possible revisions of the individual as well as the departmental balanced scorecards.

Month 12

Based on finalized balanced scorecards, the department formulates a five-year strategic plan. The first year plan is expanded into the annual operating plan for the coming year.

Months 13-24

Individual and departmental progress are reviewed quarterly to identify areas that require attention and additional effort.

Months 25-26

Based on the individual balanced scorecards, the departmental evaluation committee evaluates each member's performance for the last year and makes recommendations relating to retention, tenure, promotion, salary increases or other rewards.

The strategic planning committee revises the departmental balanced scorecard and the 5-year strategic plan based on internal and external scanning of the department's conditions and changes in the environment. In helping to revise the strategic objectives on the balanced scorecard, the strategic planning committee identifies as many strategic issues as possible and for each of these issues, considers possible solutions that can be employed by the department.

Even if the process could be completed in a fraction of this time, the lead time between start of process and harvesting of initial results still would be considerable. Thus, accounting educators have little time to lose in evaluating and implementing the balanced scorecard or other approaches to promote and support change.

Summary

Rapid changes in the technological and competitive environment are posing serious challenges to accounting education. Meeting these new challenges will require accounting educators and programmes to undergo fundamental changes and to continuously seek ways to increase the value of their contributions. The balanced scorecard, which has received major recent attention from for-profit organizations, holds great promise as a means for accounting educators to effect and sustain continuous improvement efforts. As an integral part of the strategy formulation process, developing a balanced scorecard can improve communication and increase focus on the key success variables. As a system of performance measurement, it can provide timely feedback on the organization's success in attaining its goals. It is hoped that the discussion and illustration provided in this article will help accounting educators evaluate the applicability of this management tool and in its implementation.

References

Birchard, B., 'Making It Count,' *CFO: The Magazine for Senior FinancialExecutives* (October 1995), pp. 42-51.

Choi, F.D.S., 'Accounting Education for the 21st Century: Meeting the Challenges,' *Issues in Accounting Education* (Fall 1993), pp. 423-430

Hoffecker, J., 'Using the Balanced Scorecard to Develop Companywide Performance Measures,' *Journal of Cost Management*, Vol. 8 No. 3, (Fall 1994) pp.5-17.

Irvine, J., 'The Man with 20/20 Vision,' *Accountancy* (September 1993), p. 42.

Kaplan, R. S., and D. P. Norton, 'The Balanced Scorecard-Measures that Drive Performance,' *Harvard Business Review* (January 1992), pp. 71-79.

_____ and _____, 'Putting the Balanced Scorecard to Work,' *Harvard Business_Review* (September/October 1993), pp. 134-142.

______ and _____, 'Using the Balanced Scorecard as a Strategic Management System,' *Harvard Business Review* (January/February 1996a), pp. 75-85.

______ and _____, *The Balanced Scorecard: Translating Strategy into Action* (Boston, MA: Harvard Business School Press, 1996b).

Maisel, L. S., 'Performance Measurement: The Balanced Scorecard Approach,' *Journal of Cost Management*, Vol. 6, No. 2, (Summer 1992), pp.47-52.

Newing, R., 'Benefits of A Balanced Scorecard,' *Accountancy*, Vol. 114, No.1215, (Nov. 1994), pp. 52-53.

_____, 'Wake up to the Balanced Scorecard,' *Management Accounting*--London (MAC), Vol. 73, No., 3, (March 1995), pp.22-23.

Siegel, G. and J.E. Sorensen, 'What Corporate America Wants in Entry-Level Accountants,' *Management Accounting* (September 1994), pp. 26-31.

Vitale, M., Mavrinac, S.C., and M. Hauler, 'D.C.: The Chemical Division's Balanced Scorecard,' *Planning Review* (July/August 1994), pp. 17, 45.

Part Two
DEVELOPMENTS IN MANAGEMENT ACCOUNTING

3 Professional journals, accounting systems and engineers

Bill Lee and Nick Carline

Introduction

'Accounting lag' is a term that was used by Robert Kaplan (1985) and others in the course of the nineteen-eighties to suggest that the development of accounting systems lagged behind manufacturing developments. Two implicit assumptions in these claims led supporters of the idea of an accounting lag to argue that its occurrence was problematic for firms. Firstly, there was the suggestion that companies now existed in an environment where it was most beneficial for them to manufacture a wide range of goods in smaller batches. This was presented as in stark contrast with the past when firms manufactured large volumes of a limited range of products (see, for example, Clark *et al*, 1985; Jaikumar, 1984; 1986; Johnson and Kaplan, 1987; Cooper and Kaplan, 1987). The various forms of computer controlled advanced manufacturing technology (AMT)[1] that were becoming available would permit firms to respond to the changing environment and manufacture the range of products in the batch sizes required. However, the second assumption made by the proponents of the original accounting lag thesis was that accounting systems were pervasive. Consequently, when a company's staff views the new manufacturing systems through the anachronistic investment appraisal methods (Primrose, 1991), cost monitoring techniques (Jaikumar, 1984; 1986; Skinner, 1986; Hayes and Jaikumar, 1988; Jones and Scott, 1986; Jones, 1989; Jones, *forthcoming*) and overhead allocation tools (Johnson and Kaplan, 1987; Cooper and Kaplan, 1987), they fail to recognise the real benefits of AMT in the current environment. The outcome is that the firms concerned either fail to introduce the new and necessary work systems in the first instance, or they fail to exploit the real advantages of the systems once they have been introduced.

The argument that there has been a widespread change to an economy comprised of manufacturers producing a wide range of goods in small batches has been discussed elsewhere (Piore and Sabel, 1984; Zeitlin and Hirst, 1991; cf, Williams *et al*, 1987; 1992; Wood, 1989; Lee and Kelleher, 1995).

It is sufficient simply to state here that the authors' view is that while there may not have been a general shift away from mass production, the manufacturing environment in some firms is likely to have changed so that companies now want to either manufacture a wider range of parts than they did previously, or they want to reduce the levels of inventories that they carried (Lee, 1994).

The second assumption in the original accounting lag thesis has also been challenged by what may be described loosely as a second wave of accounting lag theorists who have accepted that accounting systems may lag behind other developments in some organizations. However, they question the pervasiveness of accounting systems and, by corollary, the detrimental impact that these have within the organization. Dugdale and Jones (1994; 1995; Jones and Dugdale, 1994) have argued that higher managers adopt a pragmatic approach to accounting information and often draw on a range of other data before making decisions. Lee (1994; 1996) has detailed how the decision of what new manufacturing system to invest in often starts with engineers. He reports that engineers have - and often take - the opportunity to contour accounting criteria to reflect novel dimensions of performance of new engineering and manufacturing systems, rather than allowing new systems to be assessed simply by traditional accounting measurements and criteria. Thus, while accounting systems at some firms may be generally anachronistic, individual decisions are taken according to more accurate criteria.

In contrast with the early writers on accounting lag, there is a clear inference in these latter theories that a firm's personnel derive information about the strengths and weaknesses of new engineering systems, etc., from sources other than their company's accounting system.

It is recognised widely (eg, Armstrong, 1985; 1986; Loft, 1986; 1988; Jones, 1995) that professional institutes play an important role for their members by defining a function for practitioners to perform, developing the techniques necessary for the performance of that function and then disseminating information to their membership on how to apply those techniques. An important means for that dissemination is the professional journal. The objective of this paper is to report the findings of an enquiry into professional journals' coverage of manufacturing innovations and to consider the extent to which this information serves as a counter to the detrimental impact of accounting lag on the process of technical change within an organization.

Rationale and method of study

Engineers and accountants are key agents who are likely to be affected by the phenomenon of accounting lag in the process of technical change in an organization. Engineers are responsible for designing products and processes and proposing ways of implementing them, including conducting the initial financial appraisal of a proposed system. Accountants' responsibilities include applying the possibly anachronistic accounting techniques to assess the financial merits of engineers' proposals and to monitor that the systems that are introduced realise the outputs that were claimed for them. The main organizations that represent manufacturing engineers and management accountants are the Institute of Production Engineers (IPE) - which changed its name to the Institute of Manufacturing Engineers (IME) in 1991 - and the Chartered Institute of Management Accountants (CIMA) respectively.

The respective journals of these organizations are *Production Engineering* - which changed its name to *Manufacturing Engineering* in 1991 - and *Management Accounting*. Given the role that professional institutes are supposed to play, it is to be expected that the IPE/IME would seek to publicise the new manufacturing systems that are available and to seek to make people aware of any new accounting techniques if it were to materialise that existing ones were discouraging the introduction and certain types of deployment of new work systems. It is also to be expected that CIMA would use their journal both to convey information about engineering change, so that their members are aware of any potential for existing accounting systems to misrepresent the benefits of new technology, and subsequently to convey information about any new accounting techniques that were developed to reflect the strengths of new engineering systems. The purpose of this study is to examine whether or not this is indeed the case.

The research reported here constitutes a pilot project that will precede a more in-depth analysis of articles in professional journals. As this is only the pilot study, sophisticated forms of discourse analysis (eg, Krippendorff, 1980; Van Dijk, 1988; Cooper and Puxty, 1994) have been avoided. Instead, the method chosen for the collection and analysis of the primary data is a simple quantitative one. A number of key developments in engineering systems, associated management techniques and complementary accounting methods were identified[2].

The different computer based machine tools that were investigated were numerical controlled (NC) machine tools, computer numerically controlled (CNC) machine tools, flexible manufacturing cells (FMCs), flexible manufacturing systems (FMSs) and flexible transfer lines (FTLs). These have the generic title of advanced manufacturing technology (AMT) or computer aided manufacture (CAM). A range of other innovations that draw on microelectronic technology have also been introduced in different parts of the enterprise. These include computer aided design (CAD) which this study has also investigated.

The collective name that has been given to all of the different computer controlled innovations when they are linked together into a total system that pervades the whole factory - ie, as opposed to being 'islands of automation' surrounded by conventional machinery - is computer integrated manufacture (CIM).

It is alleged that the flexibility in computer based systems allows companies to increase the range of parts that they manufacture. It is also claimed that as the machine tools may be re-programmed quickly to machine one part after it has finished machining another, it allows a company to reduce the levels of inventory it carries. In order to realise this last objective, companies often require associated scheduling techniques and inventory control systems. The techniques that were investigated as part of this research were materials resource planning (MRP) and manufacturing requirements planning (MRP2)[3], Kanban and just-in-time (JIT).

Different accounting techniques were also examined. Discounted cash flow (DCF) methods of appraisal were investigated because it has been argued that these are more suited for the introduction of computer based systems than payback (Primrose, 1991). Flexible budgets and target costing were investigated as methods of controlling costs because flexible budgets are suited to an environment where there is a need to vary costs in line with changes in quantity and product range, whilst target costing is considered to be suitable for companies that are constantly introducing new products. Finally, throughput accounting and activity based costing (ABC) were also investigated. The former was selected because it is considered to be suitable for controlling and allocating costs according to the time that it takes to process a given part and may, thus, be compatible with just-in-time production. The latter was investigated because it is considered to be suitable for allocating costs in an environment where a company manufactures a wide range of products that require different operations.

A scan was made of the content pages of the relevant journals between 1971 - 1992 to see the titles of articles contained therein. When a title indicated that the article addressed any of the key developments discussed above, the article was read and either included in our classification or excluded, depending on the article's content. The distribution of articles on the same topic in *Production/Manufacturing Engineering* and *Management Accounting* were then plotted side by side to establish whether or not there was a lag between when the different journals carried articles with headings that indicated discussion of a particular innovation.

The period 1971 - 1992 was chosen for two main reasons. Firstly, the period covers the alleged break from mass production (Meegan, 1988). Secondly, the period was also one when there were marked advances in both the knowledge and use of computer controlled machine tools (see below).

The reason why the study of the journals was halted in 1992 was a practical one. The IME merged with the Institute of Electrical Engineers at this point. *Manufacturing Engineering* then changed in nature from being a monthly journal that carried articles aimed primarily at practitioners to being a bi-monthly journal that carried longer detailed articles. Thus, it was no longer comparable with the monthly publication *Management Accounting* that was still aimed primarily at practitioners.

There are a number of limitations implicit in our choice of method and the reader should be sensitive to these before seeking to generalise the findings in ways not intended by the authors. Firstly, the study is primarily concerned with the journals of two institutions representing two professions. There is no reason to believe that all of the members of professions ever look at even the content pages of their journals or use only the journals of their own institute[4]. Thus, we are not seeking to imply that only these journals will have an impact or that any impact is general across all practitioners.

Secondly, no attempt has been made to discriminate between the different articles according to whether they are critical or supportive of the new systems. Thirdly, the investigation did not involve an exhaustive study of all articles in the different journals to see whether they covered similar developments to those discussed here, but which were being presented under titles of a different name, or in articles with headings that did not infer the introduction of a new technology. The authors are fully aware, for example, that two articles on target costing appeared in *Management Accounting* in 1989, but that their banners gave insufficient indication of the full range of their content (Morgan & Weerakoon, 1989; Sheridan, 1989). Thus, below we report that no articles with titles that indicate target costing appear in *Management Accounting* in 1989.

Nevertheless, we feel justified in pursuing this method as our intention at this stage is simply to investigate the extent to which the professional journals will draw the attention of new developments to even the most casual of readers - ie, those who will simply skim the contents page to see whether there is anything of relevance. Thus, by looking at the timing and the frequency of articles that are - and that have headings that suggest that they are - about new developments, we will be able to give some indication of the extent to which the professional journals are a counter to any inaccurate information generated by internal accounting systems.

Findings

Tables 1 - 17 in the Appendix provide a summary of the frequency at which articles about the stated innovations appeared in *Production/Manufacturing Engineer* and *Management Accounting.*

For the purpose of analysing the pattern of the distribution of titles about specific topics in the different journals, and to link these patterns to the concept of accounting lag, it is of value to pose a series of questions about the timing of articles in the journals. These are the following:

(1) What is the relationship between engineering change and the appearance of titles of articles about those developments in *Production/Manufacturing Engineer*?
(2) Is there a lag between when *Production/Manufacturing Engineer* carry articles with headings that infer an engineering innovation and when *Management Accounting* carry articles with titles that suggest coverage of the same development?
(3) Is there a period of lag between when *Management Accounting* carried articles with titles about engineering innovations and when the same journal carried articles with banners suggesting the existence of complementary accounting developments?
(4) Is there a lag between when *Management Accounting* carry articles with titles that suggest an accounting innovation and when P*roduction /Manufacturing Engineer* carry articles with headings that suggest coverage of the same development? A subsidiary question to this is that if it is some considerable time, is it correct or appropriate to discuss accounting lag?

These questions will be addressed in turn in the next four sub-sections of the paper.

The coverage of engineering innovations in *Production/Manufacturing Engineer*

If *Production/Manufacturing Engineer* is to provide an effective counter to any inaccurate information generated by anachronistic accounting systems, it should carry articles about the novel strengths of the new systems both when they are being developed and when they are being introduced. Whether or not this was the case will be considered here.

Tables 1 - 9 summarise the timing and frequency with which titles indicating engineering innovations appeared in *Production/Manufacturing Engineer* and *Management Accounting*. As may have been anticipated, articles about the different generations of computer controlled machine tools tended to be discussed in some semblance of the chronological order in which they were developed. Articles about numerical control (table 1) were appearing from the start of our study in 1971. The discussion of CNC started in 1973 (table 2). Discussion of the more integrated systems started later; in 1977 in the case of CAM, in 1979 in the cases of FMS and FTLs, or 1981 in the case of FMC (tables 3 - 6). Finally, the more integrated system of CIM start appearing in 1984 (table 9).

The general pattern is that a small number of articles will appear on the topic for a number of years, followed by a period when there are large clusters of articles with headings alluding to the development, and then a later period when the number of titles subsides to a lower level. The indication is, however, that articles about engineering developments tend to be carried in the journal when a new system becomes adopted more widely by firms, rather than when the innovation is being developed and is first known. This suggests that *Production/Manufacturing Engineer* is not an important source of information in the process of technological change for engineers at the most innovative firms, although it may be so at the least advanced firms.

The tendency for articles to appear in *Production/Manufacturing Engineer* only after the innovations are adopted by firms may be seen by considering the example of NC, FMS and CAD. The potential of applying NC to machine tools was first known in 1949 (Nobel, 1979: 23). However, widespread adoption of numerical control in Britain was delayed. As late as 1976 only 1.32% of metal cutting machine tools in Britain were NC (Iredale, 1977). It was only after this, between 1979 - 1983, when the cluster of articles on NC appeared in *Production/Manufacturing Engineer* (table 1).

A similar pattern exists with FMS. The first FMS system preceded the development of microelectronics and was introduced at Molins Ltd in the late 1960s (Williamson, 1968). However, due to its primitive computer system, this configuration was not commercially viable and was only ever used for demonstration (Jablonowski, 1985: 131).

The first FMS system of the modern generation was introduced into Britain at Colchester Lathe Company in 1977 (Scott, 1987) with about 80 or so others being introduced in the early - mid 1980s with the assistance of Government grants provided under the Government's FMS scheme (DTI, private correspondence, October 1987). It was in this period when clusters of articles about FMS appeared in *Production/Manufacturing Engineer* (table 4).

Comparable clusters of articles about CAD only appeared in *Production/Manufacturing Engineer* in the years 1982 - 1984 (table 7). Williams (1985; Williams and Steward, 1985) reports that this is when New Technology agreements were used widely to negotiate the introduction of these systems.

The assistance that a professional journal provides to engineers in the process of change is also likely to be affected by the frequency with which a particular innovation is discussed. Two factors appear to affect the regularity at which *Production/Manufacturing Engineer* carry articles with banners alluding to a specific development. The first factor is the frequency with which the new system is adopted by firms. The second factor is semantics.

The impact of the frequency of the introduction of systems on the regularity at which those innovations appear in the titles of *Production/Manufacturing Engineer* may be seen by considering the system that was discussed more often than any other, CNC (table 2), and two of the systems that were discussed least often, FMC and CIM (tables 3 and 9). CNC is a ubiquitous system. It may be used as a standalone machine tool. Additionally, it is a feature of more integrated systems such as FMC and FMS. Thus, it is more likely to be introduced into a larger number of companies, hence its regular coverage in *Production/ Manufacturing Engineer*.

By contrast, it is probable that the limited numbers of headings alluding to FMC and CIM is a consequence of the limited number of installations of these systems. Between 1977 and 1985, considerable Government grants were made available to firms that introduced FMS. It is probable that any firm that might otherwise have elected FMC, opted for FMS because the grant made larger and more integrated systems cheaper than the less sophisticated FMC alternative. The significance of grants for FMS affecting the deployment of FMC appears to be confirmed by the cluster of articles about FMC in *Production/Manufacturing Engineer* in the late 1980s. It is possible that firms started to introduce these cheaper and less complex systems in this period when these systems met their requirements because grants for FMS were no longer available.

To some extent, the existence of any banners alluding to CIM makes this system an anomaly as full CIM has yet to be realised. However, media coverage - eg, *The Economist* (1987) - has encouraged people to view installations such as FMS as components of CIM rather than the islands of automation that they are. Thus, some, albeit limited, discussion of CIM is to be expected.

The influence of semantics on the patterns of titles of articles in *Production/Manufacturing Engineer* may be seen by considering the cases of CAD and CAM (tables 7 and 6) and FTLs and AMT (tables 5 and 8). CAD and

CAM are markedly different from one another. The former is a term that describes a specific configuration that is employed for design purposes in the office. By contrast, the latter is a generic term that alludes to a wide range of configurations that are used for manufacturing in the factory. Nevertheless, CAD and CAM are often reported as CAD/CAM systems as if they are linked organically to one another. Not surprisingly, the pattern of frequency at which CAD and CAM are reported in the professional press resemble one another closely.

Production/Manufacturing Engineer's coverage of FTLs and AMT has probably been limited by the range of different names given to these systems. Although FTLs are markedly different from FMS in that the former is restricted by its deployment of a uni-directional conveyor (Warnecke, 1985: 4), FTLs qualified for Government grants under the Department of Trade and Industry (DTI)'s FMS scheme in the 1980s because (i) they contained more than one machine tool; (ii) that were linked by an automatic conveyor system; (iii) that were all under the control of a host computer (DTI, 1984). Thus, many firms considered themselves to possess a FMS system and conveyed this to the outside world. Consequently, there were likely to be fewer articles on FTLs in *Production/ Manufacturing Engineer*.

Similar reasons probably explain why AMT is not discussed to any great extent in *Production/Manufacturing Engineer*. AMT and CAM are often used interchangeably. As the term CAM has been popularised by the way that it has been linked with CAD, AMT appears to have been used less as a consequence.

The overall picture presented here is that articles about innovations tend to appear in *Production/Manufacturing Engineer* when firms start to adopt those systems, rather than when the systems are first developed. The more widely adopted is the system, the greater will be the number of headings about that innovation, although a factor that will affect this will be whether or not a given system is also known by other names.

The fact that articles about innovations tend to appear in journals only after those developments have been introduced by a number of companies indicates that, at these firms, the professional journal is not an important source of information to counter any wrong information that is generated by the internal accounting system. However, for engineers at companies that are not quick to adopt change, *Production/Manufacturing Engineer* may be an important source of information.

There is an important corollary to this. *Production/Manufacturing Engineer* tends to report most often those systems that are introduced most frequently. By doing this, the journal may be encouraging the adoption of some systems while not encouraging the adoption of others, even though the former may not be best suited to some companies' requirements. Consequently, the professional journal may sometimes be another source of wrong information for engineers.

The coverage of engineering innovations in *Management Accounting*

If *Management Accounting* is to provide an effective counter to the operation of accounting lag, it is to be anticipated that it would provide details of new engineering systems at the time when firms are considering purchasing them. It would also provide details of accounting techniques that complement these purchases at the same time. The appearance of banners on engineering and manufacturing innovations will be considered in this sub-section. Consideration of the pattern of titles on accounting developments will follow, below.

It is perhaps to be expected that as management accountants are employed in industries other than manufacturing and are concerned with dimensions of an organization's performance other than production, less articles will appear about engineering innovations in *Management Accounting* than appeared in *Production/Manufacturing Engineer*. This is indeed the case. With the exception of AMT (table 8), considerably more headings about engineering developments appeared in *Production/Manufacturing Engineer* than appeared in *Management Accounting* (tables 1 - 7 and 9). The reason why AMT does not conform with this pattern is probably due to the preponderance of the title, CAM, in *Production/ Manufacturing Engineer* - see above.

What is perhaps to be expected less is the time when the different banners first appeared. It has already been noted above that titles about engineering innovations appeared in *Production/Manufacturing Engineer* only after firms had started to introduce those systems. Yet headings about the same topics did not appear in *Management Accounting* until much later, indicating that the accountant's journal was not an important counterweight to any wrong information generated by the internal accounting system. *Management Accounting*'s delay in discussing novel engineering systems may be seen by considering the cases of CAM, CAD, FMS, AMT and CIM (tables 6, 7, 4, 8, and 9). Banners inferring these systems first appear in *Management Accounting* six years after they first appeared in *Production/Manufacturing Engineer*. Thus the first titles alluding to CAD and CAM were carried in *Production - Manufacturing Engineer* in 1983, but did not appear in *Management Accounting* until 1987. Articles with headings about CIM and AMT only appeared in *Management Accounting* in 1987 when they had started to appear in the engineers' journal in 1984 and 1985 respectively. FMS starts to appear in the banner of articles in the management accountants' journal in 1988. Articles with titles alluding to FMS had previously appeared in *Production - Manufacturing Engineer* from 1979.

What is an interesting feature of the distribution of articles on new engineering systems in the accounting journal is the preponderance of headings about microelectronic work systems that appear after 1987. This was the year when Johnson and Kaplan's seminal work *Relevance Lost: The Rise and Fall of Management Accounting* was first published. This is possibly the most widely read book that is known for its berating of management accounting systems for generating the wrong information in the new manufacturing environment. The appearance of articles at this time indicates that a key factor that influences the appearance of banners in professional journals is the state of academic thought and the extent to which a particular thesis captures the public imagination.

A slightly different pattern to the above is apparent when titles of articles about developments that tend to span engineering and accounting are considered. Kanban, JIT and MRP/MRP2 are all terms that have a common currency in both accounting and engineering circles as all tend to be concerned with manufacturing strategies. This perhaps explains why the evidence of a lag is much less. Headings alluding to Kanban and MRP/ MRP2 (tables 10 and 11) first appear in *Management Accounting* in the same year as when they first appeared in *Production/Manufacturing Engineer.* Apart from one article that appeared in *Production/Manufacturing Engineer* in 1981, there is an approximate co-incidence of banners about JIT in both *Production/ Manufacturing Engineer* and *Management Accounting.* The second article on JIT appears in *Production/Manufacturing Engineer* in 1985 while the first two articles appear in *Management Accounting* in 1986.

What is equally significant is that Kanban and just-in-time are associated with a process of 'Japanization' of industries. Titles about these systems appear in the journals from 1981. Yet it was in 1980 when the leading British-based firms, such as Ford (Elger and Smith, 1994: 1), started to embark on their Japanization projects. This tends to confirm the pattern witnessed above that professional journals tend to report innovations only after they have started to be implemented rather than while they are being developed. Thus, the professional journals are unlikely to be of use to innovators at the most advanced companies.

The general indication from the distribution of articles on engineering and manufacturing developments is that *Management Accounting* does not provide an effective counter to any lag in a company's accounting systems. Articles about new engineering systems are only carried some time after the innovations have been adopted, rather than when they are first being developed and considered by firms.

Management Accounting's coverage of accounting innovations that correspond with the new engineering systems

For *Management Accounting* to be a fully effective counter to accounting lag for management accountants, it would have to report developments in accounting techniques simultaneous to the corresponding developments in engineering and manufacturing. Moreover, it would have had to have carried articles that provided sufficient information for firms to be able to discriminate between when the adoption of new engineering systems necessitated the introduction of new accounting techniques and when they didn't. Our current data does not allow this second issue to be addressed. The first issue will, however, be considered here.

For the purpose of analysis, accounting techniques that are deemed to be complementary to the new engineering innovations may be divided into two categories. There are those that were known prior to the development of new production systems and the adoption of new manufacturing strategies and there are those that have been developed in response to these production ideas. DCF and flexible budgets fall into the first category while target costing, throughput accounting and - to a lesser extent - activity based costing fit into the second category.

Of the first set of techniques, there are only three articles on flexible budgeting in *Management Accounting*. One appeared in 1974 and two others were carried in 1992 (table 14). The fourteen headings alluding to DCF appear from 1987 onwards. The variation in the numbers of articles reporting existing innovations would appear to confirm the influence of academic thought on the appearance of banners in professional journals. Despite its name and its capacity to reflect different sums of money available to a department according to changes in the range of parts that are produced, the authors are unaware of many academic articles that link flexible budgets to the alleged new manufacturing environment. There is, however, a whole body of academic literature that links together the issue of the method of appraisal such as DCF and the potential introduction of new work systems (Primrose, 1991; Kaplan, 1985; Pike *et al*, 1989; Curry, 1989; Nixon and Logie, 1992; Slagmulder and Bruggerman, 1992).

What is of greater relevance to this discussion is that of the existing techniques that are considered to be appropriate for firms that observe new manufacturing principles, only one title alluding to flexible budgets appeared before the development of microelectronic based work systems, just-in-time strategies, etc.

All others appeared some time after. Thus, *Management Accounting*'s coverage of these issues are unlikely to have provided an effective source of information if a company's introduction of new engineering systems also necessitated the introduction of new accounting systems. Of the innovations that have been developed or re-invented in the context of the alleged new manufacturing environment, there were no articles with titles suggesting that they were about target costing (see discussion above), there were four articles with headings alluding to throughput accounting and twenty-five articles with banners referring to ABC in *Management Accounting*. The discussion of these techniques start in 1987 which is some time after the new manufacturing systems and production strategies were adopted by the most innovative firms. This tends to suggest that *Management Accounting* was not an effective means of disseminating information to practitioners at the most innovative of firms.

There are two inter-related interesting features of *Management Accounting*'s discussion of DCF, throughput accounting and ABC. First, the titles on these subjects tend to start at roughly the same time as the same journal started to discuss the more advanced manufacturing systems. Second this discussion starts in 1987 which was the same year that Johnson and Kaplan's *Relevance Lost: The rise and fall of Management Accounting* was published. Two potential interpretations may be read from this pattern. Firstly, even though *Management Accounting* did not promote awareness of new manufacturing systems when they first became available, it did carry articles about new accounting techniques that were complementary to the new environment, once these engineering developments were known to accountants. Alternatively, it may be that some authors that were writing in *Management Accounting* - eg, consultants - were using accountants' growing awareness of new technology to generalise a concomitant adoption of a new manufacturing environment and need for new accounting techniques. However, research has shown that for many firms, the introduction of microelectronic based work systems is suited to the continuation of existing manufacturing principles (Lee, 1996; Lee and Kelleher, 1995) when some extant accounting practices are still likely to be operable. If the articles in *Management Accounting* are generalising the need for new accounting techniques, they could be a new source of wrong information for management accountants.

The coverage of accounting innovations in *Production/Manufacturing Engineer*

Although *Production/Manufacturing Engineer* may not have been an effective means of disseminating information about engineering innovations to firms other than those that were slow to adopt new manufacturing systems, it might still have been an effective means of information if it were to report new accounting techniques for the benefit of those firms that needed them, prior to the installation of the engineering systems and the adoption of new manufacturing principles.

For the purpose of analysis, articles on accounting developments in *Production/Manufacturing Engineer* will be divided into the two categories of those that preceded *vis-a-vis* those that post-date the debate about the new manufacturing environment. Of the former, no articles with headings indicating a discussion of flexible budgets appeared in *Production/Manufacturing Engineer* while four articles appeared about DCF. Three of these appeared in the course of the 1970s, prior to the widespread adoption of AMT and *Production/Manufacturing Engineer*'s discussion of those engineering developments. The reason for this is probably related to DCF allegedly giving a more accurate indication of the value of an investment to a company and so it is well suited for any expensive work system, not just AMT. The appearance of these articles prior to the widespread adoption of AMT meant that they were potentially of assistance to practitioners at all firms, including the most innovative.

The appearance of banners about DCF and the absence of titles about flexible budgets is likely to be related in part to engineers being responsible for preparing the financial justification for new systems while they simply work within budgets. However, the significance of this explanation should not be overstated as *Production/Manufacturing Engineer* has discussed some of the new developments in accounting innovations that are used for ongoing cost control and overhead allocation (see below). The rest of the explanation is likely to be that neither academics, nor accounting practitioners have tied flexible budgets to new engineering and manufacturing systems.

Interestingly, no articles with headings alluding to target costing appeared in *Production/ Manufacturing Engineer.* One title alluding to throughput accounting appeared in 1991 in *Production/Manufacturing Engineer.* In the same journal, two banners referring to ABC appeared - one each in 1991 and 1992. This indicates that there is a lag between when engineers are made aware of developments in accounting, just as there is a lag between when accountants are made aware of innovations in engineering. Thus, unlike the articles on DCF, these articles were not likely to be of any benefit to practitioners at firms.

Concluding discussion

The purpose of this paper has been to report research into the extent to which the professional journals are important sources of information for accounting and engineering practitioners, when they seek to overcome the constraints that might otherwise have arisen from the wrong information provided by a firm's internal accounting system.

The research has found that the general pattern of reporting appears to be that titles alluding to engineering developments appear first in *Production/ Manufacturing Engineer* and latterly in *Management Accounting*. These articles in *Management Accounting* coincide with the appearance of articles about accounting innovations in the same journal. This is followed at a later period by articles about the same topics in *Production/Manufacturing Engineer*.

Two general factors lead to a variation from the general pattern outlined above. Firstly, the extent to which the developments were common to both accounting and engineering. Where this was the case, they are more likely to appear in both the engineering and accounting journal in the same general period. The second factor that affected the above pattern was whether the developments in accounting were known of before the engineering innovations. Some of the accounting developments, particularly DCF, preceded the development of micro-electronically controlled engineering systems. It is only these articles that are likely to have the potential to have a generally positive benefit for all practitioners who read them.

Whether or not the other articles will be of positive use to practitioners will be affected by two factors that were discussed above. Firstly, the time of their respective firms' adoption of new engineering systems. As already noted, articles on engineering innovations first appeared in professional journals only after those new systems had been introduced by the most innovative of firms. The articles would have had little benefit for such firms. The impact that the articles had on practitioners at the firms that were slower to adopt change was potentially greater. However, whether this was beneficial or detrimental to these companies is unclear. The indication is that the reporting of engineering developments in *Production/Manufacturing Engineer* tends to reflect the frequency at which the systems are introduced. Yet, any one new engineering system is unlikely to be suited to all companies (Avlontis and Parkinson, 1981; Bessant and Heywood, 1985). Thus, unless the articles on innovations that were reported regularly, were sufficiently discriminate in their description of the conditions under which the systems were useful to organizations, these articles in the professional journals may have been a source of incorrect information.

The second factor that will influence the impact of a journal's articles is whether or not a firm's introduction of new engineering systems is co-existent with their adoption of new manufacturing principles and a concomitant need for the introduction of new accounting techniques. *Management Accounting*'s coverage of new engineering systems tends to coincide with their coverage of new accounting techniques. However, microelectronic-controlled manufacturing systems are not necessarily indicative of the adoption of new manufacturing principles and the need for new accounting techniques (Lee, 1994; 1996). If the articles in *Management Accounting* are not discriminating sufficiently between when the introduction of new work systems necessitates the introduction of new accounting practices and when it does not, these articles may be an additional source of misleading information.

This suggests further avenues for this research into the usefulness of the professional journal as a counter to any detrimental impact that the lag in accounting systems has on information circulating within an organization. Our understanding of the potential impact of professional journals on the process of change within an organization could be enhanced by a detailed examination of articles on engineering and accounting innovations to establish: (i) whether the articles carried are generally supportive or critical of the new systems; (ii) whether individual articles link together developments of different types in an inappropriate way; and (iii) whether or not the articles discriminate between instances when these innovations are applicable and when they are not.

Notes

1. Also known as Advanced Manufacturing Systems.

2. See Avlontis and Parkinson (1981) for a discussion of the different manufacturing systems detailed here, and Drury (1992) for a description of the different management and accounting techniques that are discussed.

3. As these techniques are similar, no attempt was made to differentiate between the two for the purpose of this analysis.

4. The two different institutes do both have considerable memberships. The IME had 21,105 members as of June 1991. Of these, 4,664 were students (*Production Engineer*, 1992). CIMA had 35,788 members and 56,992 registered students at the end of December 1993 (*Management Accounting*, 1994). It is likely that some members of these institutes would at least look at the contents page of their respective journals to see whether anything of interest was reported in them.

References

Allen, J. and D. Massey (eds) (1988): *The Economy in Question*, London, Sage.

Armstrong, P. (1985): 'Changing management control strategies: The role of competition between accountancy and other organizational professions' in *Accounting, Organizations and Society*, Vol. 10, No. 2, pp. 129-148.

Armstrong, P. (1986): 'Management control strategies and inter-professional competition: The case of accountancy and personnel management' in Knights, D. and H.C. Willmott (eds) *op cit*.

Ashton, D., T. Hopper and R.W. Scapens (eds) (1995): *Issues in Management Accounting*, 2nd Edition, London, Prentice Hall.

Avlontis, G. and S. Parkinson (1981): 'The automatic factory dawns' in *Management Today*, May, pp. 74-77 and 156-157.

Bessant, J. and B. Heywood (1985): *The Introduction of Flexible Manufacturing Systems as an Example of Computer Integrated Manufacture*, Brighton Polytechnic, Department of Business Management.

Bruns *Jr*., W.J. and R.S. Kaplan (eds) (1987): *Accounting and Management: Field Study Perspectives*, Boston, Massachusetts, Harvard Business School Press.

Clark, K.B., R.H. Hayes and C. Lorenz (eds) (1985): *The Uneasy Alliance: Managing the Productivity-Flexibility Dilemma*, Boston, Massachusetts, HBS Press.

Cooper, C. and A. Puxty (1994): 'Reading accounting writing' in *Accounting, Organizations and Society*, Vol. 19, No. 2, pp. 127-146.

Cooper, R. and R.S. Kaplan (1987): 'How cost accounting systematically distorts product costs' in Bruns *Jr*., W.J. and R.S. Kaplan (eds) *op cit*., pp. 204-228.

Curry, W.L. (1989): 'The art of justifying new technology to top management' in *Omega*, Vol. 17, No. 5, pp. 409-418.

Drury, C. (1992): *Management and Cost Accounting*, 3rd Edition, London, Chapman and Hall.

DTI (1984): *Flexible Manufacturing Systems: Information for Applicants*, London, Department of Trade and Industry.

Dugdale, D. and T.C Jones (1994): 'Finance, strategy and trust in investment appraisal' in *Management Accounting*, April, pp. 52-56.

Dugdale, D. and T.C. Jones (1995): 'Financial justification of advanced manufacturing technology'in Ashton, D., T. Hopper and R.W. Scapens (eds) *op cit*.

Economist, The (1987): 'Survey: The factory of the future' in *The Economist*, 30th May.

Elger, T. and C. Smith (1994): 'Introduction' in Elger, T. and C. Smith (eds) *op cit.*, pp. 1-24.

Elger, T. and C. Smith (eds) (1994): *Global Japanization? The Transnational Transformation of the Labour Process*, London, Routledge.

Hayes, R. and R. Jaikumar (1988): 'Manufacturing's crisis: New technologies, obsolete organizations' in *Harvard Business Review*, September/October, pp. 77-85.

Iredale, R. (1977): *'Metalworking Production': The Fourth Survey of Machine Tools and Production Equipment in Britain*, London, Morgan Grampian.

Jablonowski, J. (1985): 'Reexamining FMS' in *American Machinist*, Vol. 129, No. 3, pp. 125-140.

Jaikumar, R. (1984): *Flexible Manufacturing Systems: A Managerial Perspective.* Working Paper 1-74-078, Cambridge, Massachusetts Division of Research, Harvard Business School.

Jaikumar, R. (1986): 'Post industrial manufacturing' in *Harvard Business Review*, Vol. 64, No. 6, pp. 69-76.

Johnson, H. and R. Kaplan (1987): *Relevance Lost: The Rise and Fall of Management Accounting*, Boston, Harvard University Press.

Jones, B. (1989): 'When certainty fails: inside the factory of the future' in Wood, S. (ed) *op cit.*, pp. 44-58

Jones, B. (*forthcoming*): *Technological Convergence and the Limits to Managerial Control*, Cmbridge, Cambridge University Press.

Jones, B. and P. Scott (1986): ''Working the system': A comparison of the management of work roles in American and British flexible manufacturing systems' in Voss, C.A. (ed) *op cit.*

Jones, T.C. (1995): *Accounting and the Enterprise: A Social Analysis*, London, Routledge.

Jones, T.C. & D. Dugdale (1994): 'Academic and practitioner rationality: The case of investment appraisal' in *British Accounting Review*, Vol. 6, No. 1, pp. 3-25.

Kaplan, R. (1985): 'Accounting lag: The obsolescence of cost accounting systems' in Clark *et al* (eds) *op cit.*

Knights, D. and H. C. Willmott (eds) (1986): *Managing the Labour Process*, London, Gower.

Krippndorff, K. (1980): *Content Analysis: An Introduction to its Methodology*, London, Sage.

Lee, B. (1994): 'No accounting for advanced manufacturing technology?' in *Proceedings of British Accountancy Association SWAG Conference, September 1994*, Accountancy Internet.

Lee, B. (1996): *The Justification and Monitoring of Advanced Manufacturing Technology: An Empirical Investigation of Twenty-one Installations of FMS*, in Management Accounting Research, 1996, 7, pp 95 - 118.

Lee, B. and M. Kelleher (1995): *Ford: On the Road to Where?* Paper presented to the 13th International Labour Process Conference, Blackpool, England, 5th - 7th April.

Loft, A. (1986): 'Towards a critical understanding of accounting: The case of cost accounting in the UK, 1914 - 1925' in *Accounting, Organizations and Society*, Vol. 11, No. 2, pp. 137-169.

Loft, A. (1988): *Understanding Accounting in its Social and Historical Context: The case of Cost Accounting in Britain, 1914 - 1925*, London, Garland Publishing.

Management Accounting (1994): 'As a matter of interest ... ' in *Management Accounting*, March, p. 12.

Meegan, R. (1988): 'A Crisis of Mass Production?' in Allen, J. and D. Massey (eds) *op cit*., pp. 136-183.

Morgan, M.J. and S.H. Weekaroon (1989): 'Japanese management accounting: Its contribution to the Japanese economic rationale', in *Management Accounting*, June.

Nixon, W. and A.A. Logie (1992): *Technological Innovation and Management Accounting Control: Some Survey Evidence From Thirteen Case Studies*. Paper ACC/9205, Dundee Department of Accountancy and Finance, University of Dundee.

Noble, D. (1979): 'Social choice in machine design: The case of automatically controlled machine tools' in Zimbalist, A. (ed) (1979) *op cit*., pp. 18-50.

Pike, R.H., J. Sharp and D. Price (1989): 'AMT investment in the larger UK firm' in *International Journal of Operations and Production Management*, Vol. 9, No. 2, pp. 13-26.

Piore, M. and C. Sabel (1984): *The Second Industrial Divide: Possibilities for Prosperity*, New York, Basic Books.

Primrose, P. (1991): 'The appliance of science' in *Manufacturing Engineer*, November, pp. 42-43.

Production Engineer (1992): 'Notes' in *Production Engineer*, January. Scott, P. (1987): *Craft Skills in Flexible Manufacturing Systems*. Unpublished PhD thesis, University of Bath.

Sheridan, T. (1989): 'Don't count your costs, manage them' in *Management Accounting*, February

Skinner, W. (1986): 'The productivity paradox' in *Harvard Business Review*, July/August 1986, pp. 55-59.

Slagmulder, R. and W. Bruggeman (1992): 'Investment justification of flexible manufacturing technologies: Inferences from field research' in *International Journal of Operations and Production Management*, Vol. 12, No. 7, pp. 168-186.

Van Dijk, T. (1988): *News Analysis: Case Studies of International and National News in the Press*, New Jersey, Lawrence Erlbaum Associates.

Voss, C.A. (ed) (1986): *Managing Advanced Manufacturing Technology*, Bedford, IFS Publications.

Warnecke, H.J. (ed) (1985): *Flexible Manufacturing Systems*, Bedford, IFS Publications.

Williams, K., T. Cutler, J. Williams and C. Haslam (1987): 'The end of mass production?' in *Economy and Society*, Vol. 16, No. 3, August.

Williams, K., C. Haslam and J. Williams (1992): 'Ford versus `Fordism': The beginning of mass production?' in *Work, Employment and Society*, Vol. 6, No. 4.

Williams, R. (1985): *Investigation of the Content of Technology Agreements*, Technology Policy Unit, Aston University, mimeo.

Williams, R. and F. Steward (1985): 'New technology agreements: An assessment', in *Industrial Relations Journal*, Vol. 16, No. 3, pp. 58-73.

Willamson, D.T.N. (1968): 'The pattern of batch manufacture and its influence on machine tool design' in *Proceedings of the Institute of Mechanical Engineers*, Part 1, 182, pp. 870-895.

Wood, S. (1989): 'The transformation of work?' in Wood, S. (ed) (1989) *op cit.*, pp 1-43.

Wood, S. (ed) (1989): *The Transformation of Work?*, London, Hutchinson.

Zeitlin, J. and P. Hirst (1991): 'Flexible specialisation versus post-Fordism: Theory, evidence and policy implications' in *Economy and Society*, Vol. 20, No. 1, February.

Zimbalist, A. (ed) (1979): *Case Studies on the Labor Process*, New York, Monthly Review Press.

APPENDIX

TABLE 1 - NUMERICAL CONTROL

Year	Production/ Manufacturing Engineer	Management Accounting
1971	1	1
1972	0	0
1973	2	0
1974	3	1
1975	0	0
1976	2	1
1977	4	0
1978	5	0
1979	7	0
1980	6	0
1981	7	0
1982	11	0
1983	8	0
1984	2	0
1985	4	0
1986	6	0
1987	0	0
1988	5	0
1989	2	0
1990	1	1
1991	0	0
1992	3	0
Total	79	4

TABLE 2 - COMPUTER NUMERICAL CONTROL

Year	Production/ Manufacturing Engineer	Management Accounting
1971	0	0
1972	0	0
1973	1	0
1974	3	1
1975	0	0
1976	2	0
1977	4	0
1978	4	0
1979	5	0
1980	2	0
1981	8	0
1982	20	0
1983	21	0
1984	20	0
1985	10	1
1986	5	0
1987	3	0
1988	12	0
1989	4	1
1990	6	0
1991	4	0
1992	7	0
Total	141	3

TABLE 3 - FLEXIBLE MANUFACTURING CELLS

Year	Production/ Manufacturing Engineer	Management Accounting
1971	0	0
1972	0	0
1973	0	0
1974	0	0
1975	0	0
1976		0
1977	0	0
1978	0	0
1979	0	0
1980	0	0
1981	2	0
1982	3	0
1983	1	0
1984	3	0
1985	0	0
1986	1	0
1987	0	0
1988	5	0
1989	4	0
1990	0	0
1991	2	0
1992	1	0
Total	22	0

TABLE 4 - FLEXIBLE MANUFACTURING SYSTEMS

Year	Production/ Manufacturing Engineer	Management Accounting
1971	0	0
1972	0	0
1973	0	0
1974	0	0
1975	0	0
1976	0	0
1977	0	0
1978	0	0
1979	1	0
1980	1	0
1981	4	0
1982	6	0
1983	12	0
1984	9	0
1985	8	0
1986	8	0
1987	2	0
1988	6	1
1989	4	3
1990	2	1
1991	1	1
1992	2	2
Total	66	8

TABLE 5 - FLEXIBLE TRANSFER LINES

Year	Production/ Manufacturing Engineer	Management Accounting
1971	0	0
1972	0	0
1973	0	0
1974	0	0
1975	0	0
1976	0	0
1977	0	0
1978	0	0
1979	1	0
1980	0	0
1981	0	0
1982	1	0
1983	0	0
1984	0	0
1985	0	0
1986	0	0
1987	0	0
1988	0	0
1989	0	0
1990	0	0
1991	0	0
1992	0	0
Total	2	0

TABLE 6 - COMPUTER AIDED MANUFACTURING

Year	Production/ Manufacturing Engineer	Management Accounting
1971	0	0
1972	0	0
1973	0	0
1974	0	0
1975	0	0
1976	0	0
1977	1	0
1978	0	0
1979	2	0
1980	2	0
1981	5	0
1982	9	0
1983	7	1
1984	13	0
1985	6	1
1986	5	1
1987	2	1
1988	5	1
1989	2	3
1990	2	2
1991	4	2
1992	7	1
Total	72	13

TABLE 7 - COMPUTER AIDED DESIGN

Year	Production/ Manufacturing Engineer	Management Accounting
1971	0	0
1972	0	0
1973	0	0
1974	0	0
1975	0	0
1976	0	0
1977	1	0
1978	1	0
1979	1	0
1980	3	0
1981	5	0
1982	8	0
1983	7	1
1984	19	0
1985	9	1
1986	6	1
1987	2	1
1988	8	2
1989	3	4
1990	2	1
1991	4	3
1992	10	2
Total	89	16

TABLE 8 - ADVANCED MANUFACTURING TECHNOLOGY

Year	Production/ Manufacturing Engineer	Management Accounting
1971	0	0
1972	0	0
1973	0	0
1974	0	0
1975	0	0
1976	0	0
1977	0	0
1978	0	0
1979	0	0
1980	0	0
1981	0	0
1982	0	0
1983	0	0
1984	0	0
1985	1	0
1986	1	0
1987	2	1
1988	1	1
1989	2	4
1990	0	2
1991	2	3
1992	1	3
Total	10	14

TABLE 9 - COMPUTER INTEGRATED MANUFACTURING

Year	Production/ Manufacturing Engineer	Management Accounting
1971	0	0
1972	0	0
1973	0	0
1974	0	0
1975	0	0
1976	0	0
1977	0	0
1978	0	0
1979	0	0
1980	0	0
1981	0	0
1982	0	0
1983	0	0
1984	4	0
1985	5	0
1986	6	0
1987	3	1
1988	3	1
1989	1	1
1990	1	2
1991	0	0
1992	4	1
Total	27	6

TABLE 10 - KANBAN

Year	Production/ Manufacturing Engineer	Management Accounting
1971	0	0
1972	0	0
1973	0	0
1974	0	0
1975	0	0
1976	0	0
1977	0	0
1978	0	0
1979	0	0
1980	0	0
1981	1	1
1982	0	0
1983	0	0
1984	1	0
1985	3	0
1986	0	0
1987	4	0
1988	2	0
1989	0	0
1990	0	0
1991	0	0
1992	1	0
Total	12	1

TABLE 11 - MANUFACTURING RESOURCE PLANNING/ MATERIALS REQUIREMENT PLANNING

Year	Production/ Manufacturing Engineer	Management Accounting
1971	0	0
1972	0	0
1973	0	0
1974	0	0
1975	0	0
1976	0	0
1977	0	0
1978	0	0
1979	1	1
1980	1	0
1981	1	0
1982	0	2
1983	1	1
1984	2	0
1985	3	0
1986	3	0
1987	4	0
1988	6	5
1989	2	2
1990	3	2
1991	7	1
1992	10	2
Total	44	16

TABLE 12 - JUST-IN-TIME

Year	Production/ Manufacturing Engineer	Management Accounting
1971	0	0
1972	0	0
1973	0	0
1974	0	0
1975	0	0
1976	0	0
1977	0	0
1978	0	0
1979	0	0
1980	0	0
1981	1	0
1982	0	0
1983	0	0
1984	0	0
1985	3	0
1986	0	2
1987	5	1
1988	7	2
1989	1	13
1990	3	7
1991	5	4
1992	7	4
Total	32	33

TABLE 13 - DISCOUNTED CASH FLOW

Year	Production/ Manufacturing Engineer	Management Accounting
1971	1	0
1972	0	0
1973	0	0
1974	0	0
1975	0	0
1976	1	0
1977	0	0
1978	1	0
1979	0	0
1980	0	0
1981	0	0
1982	0	0
1983	0	0
1984	0	0
1985	0	0
1986	0	0
1987	0	1
1988	0	1
1989	0	4
1990	0	2
1991	0	3
1992	1	3
Total	4	14

TABLE 14 - FLEXIBLE BUDGETING

Year	Production/ Manufacturing Engineer	Management Accounting
1971	0	0
1972	0	0
1973	0	0
1974	0	1
1975	0	0
1976	0	0
1977	0	0
1978	0	0
1979	0	0
1980	0	0
1981	0	0
1982	0	0
1983	0	0
1984	0	0
1985	0	0
1986	0	0
1987	0	0
1988	0	0
1989	0	0
1990	0	0
1991	0	0
1992	0	2
Total	0	3

TABLE 15 - TARGET COSTING

Year	Production/ Manufacturing Engineer	Management Accounting
1971	0	0
1972	0	0
1973	0	0
1974	0	0
1975	0	0
1976	0	0
1977	0	0
1978	0	0
1979	0	0
1980	0	0
1981	0	0
1982	0	0
1983	0	0
1984	0	0
1985	0	0
1986	0	0
1987	0	0
1988	0	0
1989	0	0
1990	0	0
1991	0	0
1992	0	0
Total	0	0

TABLE 16 - THROUGHPUT ACCOUNTING

Year	Production/ Manufacturing Engineer	Management Accounting
1971	0	0
1972	0	0
1973	0	0
1974	0	0
1975	0	0
1976	0	0
1977	0	0
1978	0	0
1979	0	0
1980	0	0
1981	0	0
1982	0	0
1983	0	0
1984	0	0
1985	0	0
1986	0	0
1987	0	0
1988	0	2
1989	0	2
1990	0	0
1991	0	0
1992	1	0
Total	1	4

TABLE 17 - ACTIVITY BASED COSTING

Year	Production/ Manufacturing Engineer	Management Accounting
1971	0	0
1972	0	0
1973	0	0
1974	0	0
1975	0	0
1976	0	0
1977	0	0
1978	0	0
1979	0	0
1980	0	0
1981	0	0
1982	0	0
1983	0	0
1984	0	0
1985	0	0
1986	0	0
1987	0	1
1988	0	0
1989	0	3
1990	0	8
1991	1	7
1992	1	6
Total	2	25

4 Markets and managerialism: Are GP's 'dancing with the devil'?

Peter Milford

Introduction

The government-imposed changes experienced by the National Health Service in the 1980s and 1990s have been the focus of much research activity across a broad spectrum of academic disciplines. These include accounting, economics, social policy, organisation behaviour and, to a limited extent, medicine. The focus of this paper is on accountability by and control of general medical practices. The paper draws on published evidence from a range of academic disciplines and from a continuing research project involving fourteen GP practices to analyse the impact of the changes.

Changes imposed on general medical practices

General medical practices have undergone more government-imposed changes than most other health care agencies in the past five years. These changes can be categorised into two broad areas, 'accountability' and 'markets'.

'Accountability' changes include the 1990 GP contract, new 'managerial' Family Health Services Authorities (FHSA's), medical audit and 'indicative drug amounts'. These changes were documented by Laughlin, Broadbent and Shearn in a study of the impact of the 1990 contract (Laughlin, Broadbent and Shearn, 1992) on a small number of practices in Sheffield.

The contract introduced new controls over the services provided by practices (Secretary of State for Health et al, 1989 [1]). It increased the target 'capitation' (ie payment for the number of patients on a practice list) percentage of the remuneration package for practices from 46% to 60% (Bain, 1991). There is evidence that this target has been achieved (Milford, 1993), and practices are now heavily reliant on list size for achievement of a profit level acceptable to the partners. In addition, it introduced health promotion 'target' and 'clinic' payments, together with a range of new fees. The government's intentions appeared to include making practice profits dependent upon 'workload', thereby reducing the relative importance to practice profits of payments for simply being a 'GP in practice' (Handysides, 1994 [1]).

Much resentment was expressed at the changes, particularly the new contract, for a range of reasons, but predominantly 'intrusion into professional autonomy' (Morrell, 1991; Laughlin, Broadbent and Shearn, 1992; Laughlin, Broadbent and Willig-Atherton, 1994). It has also been suggested that the resentment may have arisen from the perceived (by doctors) failure of the then Secretary of State for Health, Kenneth Clarke, to consult the medical profession properly (Glendinning, Chew and Wilkin, 1994). New FHSA's replaced the old Family Practitioner Committees in 1990, and were charged with improving the quality of delivery of family practitioner services in their localities (Secretary of State for Health et al, 1989 [2]). This new role entailed taking a 'managerial' perspective, as compared to the previous 'administrative' role. Other 'accountability' changes included the introduction of 'quasi-budgets' (indicative drug amounts) for drugs prescribed by practices and the development of arrangements for medical audit.

One of the principal 'market' changes was the introduction of the GP fundholding scheme, in which practices are given budgets, previously held by District Health Authorities, for a range of services. These services include drugs prescribed by the practice, diagnostic services (eg pathology) provided by local hospitals, some non-emergency inpatient and outpatient services. The budgets also include practice expense reimbursements (practice employee costs, rent and rates), which were previously controlled by FHSA's (Secretary of State for Health et al, 1989 [2]).

The other significant 'market' change is the government's attempt to introduce a 'consumerist' philosophy for NHS patients; this philosophy underpinned the Citizen's Charter initiatives. The Patient's Charter was issued as part of this initiative, being applied to general medical practices from 1992 (Smith, 1992; Department of Health, 1992 and 1995).

A key motivating force for these changes appears to have been the desire of the government to justify and, where possible, reduce public expenditure. A significant element in these changes has been the apparent 'attack' on 'professionalism' throughout the 1980s, in which professionals have been treated by the government as 'obstacles to change' (Harrison and Pollitt, 1994 pages 7-9).

This paper

The paper draws on published work from a range of academic disciplines to examine the impact of 'accountability' and 'market' changes on general medical practices. In addition, the author has been working with ten practices in one FHSA and with four practices in three other FHSA's. Collection of data from these practices is, however, at an early stage, and research activity is continuing. Examples from the preliminary findings of this research are used to illustrate arguments where appropriate.

Laughlin, Broadbent and Willig-Atherton regard the contract as the major change (Laughlin, Broadbent and Willig-Atherton, 1994). This paper contends that the 1990 Contract is now an issue of secondary importance. It is argued that GP fundholding, the 'managerial' role of FHSA's and 'consumerism' have had a much more significant impact on practices than the 1990 contract. It is central to the paper's argument that the government has changed radically the mechanism for rationing services to patients within primary health care, with the expressed objectives of securing 'more appropriate' (*not* necessarily 'equitable') services for patients and more 'value for money' in the use of resources by GP's (NHS Executive, 1994 [1] and [2]). It is proposed that GP fundholding has acted as the 'engine' for ensuring the success of this policy.

The paper argues that the government has created an 'illusion of freedom' for GP practices. It has, for example, claimed to create a 'stronger partnership between health authorities and GP's' (NHS Executive, 1994 [2]) whilst actually increasing accountability to 'constrain' their freedom of action (see Hopwood, 1989). The NHS planning system exemplifies the overt use of apparent freedoms for practices, whilst covertly attempting to control the way that they operate. FHSA's are heavily implicated in this drive for control.

The paper begins with a review of the forces driving the changes, and then focuses on five issues:

(1)	Professionalism:	which model of professionalism underpins the changes?
(2)	Rationing:	a transfer of 'blame'?
(3)	GP fundholding:	the engine for rationing health care in the 1990's.
(4)	FHSA management:	'illusions of freedom'.
(5)	Patients' charter:	'unleashing the consumer'.

Finally, the theoretical basis on which the changes may be analysed is discussed, followed by a conclusion.

Forces driving with the public

Public expenditure

Underpinning the changes is the public expenditure 'problem', with a neo-liberal government philosophy underpinning the use of 'managerialism' and 'internal markets' to solve the 'problem' of NHS spending (Humphrey, Miller and Scapens, 1993). As Paton noted:

'The Prime Minister (Margaret Thatcher) saw the NHS as a black hole swallowing funds without trace or evidence of result' (Paton, 1992 page 37).

Successive Conservative governments since 1979 have been elected to power on the basis both of close control over public spending and increasing 'privatisation'.

These two elements of 'expenditure control' and 'competitive markets' have been brought together, with the latter being regarded as a key method of achieving the former. The extent to which the focus of these changes has been a desire to control public spending ('economic rationality') or to introduce a particular view of the world ('political or social rationality') or both is, however, open to question (Gray and Jenkins, 1993; Ezzamel and Willmott, 1993; Pollitt, 1993). 'Competitive markets' are regarded by elements in the conservative tradition as ethically and morally 'right' since they allow individuals to express unfettered freedom of choice without government interference.

Family practitioner service expenditure was viewed as a particular problem by the incoming conservative government in 1979 because spending by GP's was 'open-ended' and 'demand-led'. Any increase in expenditure by GP's led to unintended increases in overall public expenditure or pressures to reduce spending elsewhere. Family practitioner services are still not fully cash limited, although the web of financial control tightened in 1986 with the introduction of the limited list for drug prescription. This meant that GP's became unable to prescribe on the NHS drugs outside the limited list. Further constraints were achieved by government in 1990 with the introduction of cash limits for expense reimbursements to practices. The tap for expanding services in GP practices was being slowly turned off.

One major difficulty for government is that the NHS is held in high public regard. Any overt attempt to reduce expenditure on such a 'sacred cow' would be political suicide. A further problem is that GP's in particular have proved highly resistant to any attempts to control, whether financially or otherwise, what they do. The relative financial autonomy of GP's can be traced back to the inception of the NHS, when they managed to secure independent contractor status, whereas their hospital consultant colleagues became employees of the new NHS (Laughlin, Broadbent and Shearn, 1992).

Accountability

Gray and Jenkins define accountability as:

> _ _ an obligation to present an account of and answer for the execution of responsibilities to those who entrusted the responsibilities (Gray and Jenkins, 1993).

For the purposes of this paper, accountability means that GP's must answer for resources that they use to those who provided the resources. The provider is seen as the government or its agencies, as opposed to the patient or taxpayer. The government's stated aims of increasing accountability arise through an apparent concern to secure effectiveness ('appropriate interventions'), efficiency ('best practice') and value for money in NHS spending, with GP's expected to be:

> _ _ properly accountable for the services they provide and their use of resources (NHS Executive, 1994 [2]).

Demands for increased accountability have been made since the 1970's, but were made much more vigorously when the conservatives came to power in 1979. Cash limits were introduced for the secondary care (hospitals) sector in 1980, and further accountability 'initiatives' followed. These included the Financial Management Initiatives and Rayner Scrutinies, and ultimately the White Paper in 1989 (Secretary of State for Health et al, 1989 [2])

Doubts have been cast on the belief that 'accountability' can resolve perceived organisational problems (Humphrey, Miller and Scapens, 1993; Gray and Jenkins, 1993). Challenges to the apparent deterministic managerial orthodoxy implicit in the NHS reforms are rooted in scepticism at the ability of management control systems to deliver the requisite changes. The deterministic logic of 'accountability' relies upon bringing about changes in behaviour by those subject to new rules such as budgetary control. The potential failure of this deterministic logic as far as accounting systems of control are concerned has been highlighted elsewhere (see, for example, Hopwood, 1989, in which the mediating influence of organisation and culture is stressed).

Markets

'Quasi-markets' have been described as markets in which consumers' decisions are 'mediated through intervening agents' (Bartlett, 1991). In the new 'market driven' NHS, health authorities and fundholders act as purchasing agents for the 'consumer' (the patient). Fundholders purchase services from 'providers', who include NHS trusts and the private hospital sector.

The use of markets to allocate resources apparently derives from a belief that the 'market' will make rationing decisions more effectively than a 'top-down' approach (Laing and Cotton, 1994; Ezzamel and Willmott, 1993). The use of 'markets' for these purposes has been referred to as the 'theory of contestable markets' (Lapsley and Pettigrew, 1994). In this 'mixed market' model of health care provision, costs will be driven down by opening up the markets.

This has been criticised on the basis that the 'deterministic' logic of the market is underpinned by social relations which comprise cooperation as much as competition (Ezzamel and Willmott, 1993). The model may also be undermined by the problem of 'transactions' costs, such as 'bounded rationality' (Bartlett, 1991), in which the 'consumer' does not have the expert knowledge required to take health purchasing decisions.

Professionalism: What model of professionalism underpins the changes?

Models of professionalism

The changes imposed on GP practices cannot be discussed without first reviewing models of 'professionalism'. It is extremely difficult for government to influence professional behaviour. Professions are characterised by 'autonomy' and 'self-regulation', and do not welcome intrusion into their sphere of professional action. Doctors in particular have rejected interference, usually appealing to the sick 'patient' ('shroud-waving') when they feel threatened. The advertising campaign undertaken by the British Medical Association in 1989 against the then Secretary of State for Health, Kenneth Clarke, exemplified the use of this technique.

The government has approached accountability and market changes with a particular view of 'professionalism'. It has been argued that GP's could be perceived as having all the rewards of private practice, with none of the risks, in effect a publicly subsidised business (Huntingdon, 1993). This government view of professions as self-seeking and resistant to change has been documented elsewhere (Paton, 1992; Harrison and Pollitt, 1994). Harrison and Pollitt propose three alternative models of professionalism which are useful here:

(1) the 'functional' model, where professionals maintain occupational autonomy and self regulation to enhance standards and protect the 'client' from exploitation of the trust relationship with the professional. This model is noted by Goode, who refers to the esoteric knowledge base and service ideal of doctors as professionals (Goode, 1960). Freidson refers to clinical autonomy as control over the content of work (Freidson, 1970)

As suggested earlier, it has been argued that 'individual patient responsibility' and 'clinical freedom' have been used to enhance the power of the medical profession (Stacey, 1988; Ezzamel and Willmott, 1993). Furthermore, Armstrong argues that, within the 'functional' perspective, a lack of accountability by doctors has dangers, for the patient (the doctor who ignores their views) and for society (the doctor who allocates resources without control) (Armstrong, 1989, page 87).

(2) the 'control' model, where professionals are seen to maintain occupational barriers as a strategy to control rewards and working conditions (see Johnson, 1972). It is clear that this model accords closely with that used by the government.

(3) the 'illusory autonomy' model, where the state allows apparent autonomy, whilst effectively allocating 'blame' for rationing decisions. In the NHS, overall resources are allocated by the government, but individual spending decisions within these resources are made by professionals. It is in the government's interests for this to continue, because it can avoid 'blame' when rationing decisions have an adverse effect on members of the public.
It will be argued that the 'illusory' model also accords closely with the perspective used by the current government.

Clinical autonomy and management

Laughlin et al attribute resentment at the 1990 contract to 'intrusion' into professional autonomy (Laughlin, Broadbent and Shearn, 1992). The model of professionalism used to analyse this change is that proposed by Freidson, the 'functional' model of clinical autonomy (Freidson, 1970). It can be argued that intrusions into clinical autonomy may have existed anyway. The development of the primary health care team over the past twenty years has constrained clinical autonomy. Pringle refers to the tensions created between the desired autonomy of GP's and the need to work in a Primary Health Care Team (Pringle, 1992). As Handysides notes perceptively:

'It (the contract) is a convenient focus for the woes of general practitioners, but many of the woes existed before the contract' (Handysides, 1994 [2])

Furthermore, the distinction between doctors and managers has become increasingly blurred in recent years. Consultants have become 'clinical directors', and it has been suggested that GP's have become the effective managers of Primary Health Care Teams (Marsh, 1992). Furthermore, GP's employ and manage the staff within their practice, although this task is frequently delegated to a practice manager.

GP's as professionals and entrepreneurs

Apart from being drawn into the world of management, GP's have become exposed increasingly to the harsh realities and risks of self-employment. Two examples of this are increasing competition for dispensing practices and falling property values.

One rural practice that the author has worked with was dependent upon dispensing income to supplement profits from a small list. A pharmacist requested permission to move into the village and, after appeal to the Secretary of State, succeeded. It is apparent that the government has proved more amenable to such appeals in recent years, preferring to leave dispensing to 'market forces'.

Falling property values have hit GP's very hard. The most significant tangible business asset for any practice is its building, and the government has enticed many practices into building new premises through the cost rent scheme. The problem of 'negative equity' has become reality for many practices, and has led to tensions within partnerships, particularly when partners retire or are newly appointed.

Historically, GP's have traditionally been 'entrepreneurs of healing' (Stacey, 1988, page 82). Caines refers to the 'entrepreneurial spirit' of GP's (Handysides, 1994 [3]). The potential clash of the 'professional' ethic and the 'business' ethic is not new, but has, it will be argued, become more apparent as government has introduced the 'market' ethic into the NHS.

Reflections

The government has embarked on change in the NHS with a particular view of professionalism. It will be proposed that government is taking the 'control' perspective, in which GP's must be called to account for the resources that they use. It will also be argued that the 'illusory' model of professionalism is relevant, with government using apparent freedoms for GP's (eg fundholding, partnership with FHSA's) to bring them 'on board'. Irvine sees the changes as a move from:

> unfettered individualism to a managed health care system, with general practice as its foundation (Irvine, 1993).

These developments need to be viewed against the background of changes in clinical autonomy and the harsher business world in which GP's now practice.

Rationing: A transfer of blame?

The rationing decision - pre 1990

The overall level of resources allocated to the NHS has, from its inception, been set by Parliament. As noted earlier, allocations to the hospital and community care sectors were capped in 1980, with spending by the Family Practitioner Services (principally GP's) still being effectively 'open-ended'.

Services provided by GP's themselves were rationed before 1990, but in a very limited way. Consultations and any resulting drug treatments by GP's were rationed only by GP time available. It has been argued that 'time-induced' rationing has become more significant in recent years as a result of increasing patient demands (Marsh, 1992). In 1986, a further restriction was introduced by the 'limited list' of drugs available on prescription. Within these limited constraints, however, GP's could treat their patients personally without restriction.

With regard to hospital services, referrals for hospital treatment by GP's were rationed in a more obvious way. This was because hospital treatments were restricted through availability of physical resources, such as the number of beds, theatre space and staff time. Rationing decisions were made either through 'waiting lists' and juggling priorities within the lists or through use of barriers (such as age) for refusing treatment. The 'blame' for any perceived ill effects of these rationing decisions was not, however, allocated to the GP but to the hospital consultant and/or Health Authority.

The pre-1990 situation can be described as 'delegated micro-rationing', with GP's delegating blame for refusal of hospital treatment or delays in being treated to their hospital colleagues. GP's were free to refer their patients as they saw fit, with any consequent problems being passed to the hospital.

The rationing decision - post 1990

The advent of GP fundholding in 1990 has changed this position dramatically. The 'micro'-rationing decision for referring individual patients now becomes one for the individual fundholding GP to take, with all the potential 'blame' if treatment is delayed or refused. The practice has a budget for hospital referrals and the GP has to make explicit choices between clinical priorities within this budget.

The Government has also delegated 'macro'-rationing decisions on priorities for resource allocation to fundholding practices and Health Authorities. Paton refers to Health Authorities and fundholding practices taking the place of government at the macro level, with individual doctors rationing health care at the micro level on behalf of patients (Paton, 1993). Priorities for care (eg the elderly, childrens' services) are effectively set via the contracting process, when the purchasers decide what services to 'buy' over the next year.

In this way, government can make overall resource allocation decisions and take the credit for any apparent increases. The 'real' increase (ie after adjustment for NHS specific inflation) is usually significantly less than the headline percentage, but it is the latter that is seen by the general public. The impact of increases in demand arising from the rising elderly population and medical technology is also hidden within the headline increase.

A recent well publicised case involving refusal to treat a young girl with leukaemia provides a clear example of delegating blame. The Cambridge Health Authority refused to pay up to £75,000 for what it saw as unjustified treatment, arguing that it had to set priorities. Legal action to force the Authority to treat the girl was unsuccessful. The Appeal Court found that:

> Difficult and agonizing decisions over the use of limited resources had to be made (Independent Law Report, 1995)

The role of overall government resource allocation in this rationing decision did not appear to be an issue. 'Blame' was passed on to the clinicians treating the girl and to the Health Authority:

> Doctors don't like it, but they are being used as rationers. The health service reforms have shovelled the blame away from politicians and on to doctors (Mihill, 1995)

An alternative perspective would be that there is sense in allowing doctors to make explicit clinical choices within overall resource constraints because they know how to assess clinical priorities. The Cambridge Health Authority case outlined above could only have been managed in the way that it was with the explicit cooperation of the doctors responsible for the care of the girl concerned. Glennerster argues that, in the past, rationing decisions were made by professionals without public debate and that the contract system has made them more managerial and explicit (Glennerster, 1994).

Whether the new system of health care rationing is 'right' or 'wrong', it is clear that it has changed substantially as far as GP's are concerned. GP's are being forced to ration in their capacity as fundholders, and they can no longer 'delegate' micro-rationing decisions to their hospital colleagues.

Which model of professionalism applies here? Arguably, it is 'functional' because it is right for GP's to take such decisions, rather than managers with no knowledge of medicine or patient needs. Alternatively, it could be seen as 'illusory' because the government have avoided blame for the consequences of taking rationing decisions. Glennerster has argued that some GP's enjoy the power that fundholding has given them, and consequently the 'control' model may apply (Glennerster, 1994).

GP Fundholding: The engine for rationing health care in the 1990s?

Terms of reference

As outlined earlier, the government has introduced a 'market' for health care because it believes that the 'market' allocates resources more effectively than a 'top down' approach. In addition, there is an implicit belief that competitive forces will drive down transactions costs (Ezzamel and Willmott, 1993). It should be stressed, however, that the White Paper did not use the word 'market' (Secretary of State for Health et al, 1989 [2]; Appleby, 1992 page 19). If, however, it is accepted that there is now a 'market' for health care (or a 'quasi-market' as defined earlier), then the role of a GP fundholder is as one of the 'purchasers'. The effective rationer is the GP fundholder, who will not be able to overspend the practice referral budget, without finding matching savings elsewhere (see Lapsley, 1991). The fundholding GP has a potentially schizoid role in the internal market, acting as the agent for protecting patients' interests (Bevan, 1989) and, arguably, as the first stage in the rationing process.

Paton suggests a further perspective on the introduction of 'markets', in which the government is seen to be deflecting public debate about the NHS from financing to provision and reform (Paton, 1992 page 36). The mid-1980s had seen an increase in media criticism of the level of NHS funding through, for example, the bed crisis at Birmingham Children's Hospital. It can be argued that a government unwilling to increase the overall level of resources needed to be seen to be 'taking action', hence the 1990 reforms.

Evidence

Why fundholding?

Why, then, have GP's been willing to go fundholding? Reasons given by GP's include improved patient care, freedom to refer and improved management systems (Glennerster, Matsaganis and Owens, 1992). A survey in the Northern Region identified the 'opportunity to be independent' as the most common reason (Newton et al, 1993). All of the practices in these surveys were first wave fundholders, and it is noticeable that the reasons identified were largely 'positive'.

Of the fourteen practices currently working with the author, seven are fundholding (three of these in consortia). Of the non-fundholders, two are in alternative purchasing consortia. Only five have steadfastly refused to have anything to do with purchasing services. The central reason for becoming a fundholding practice given by each of the seven is a perceived lack of sensible alternatives (ie 'because we have to'). None of these practices are first wave fundholders, and it is possible that 'negative' reasons are more relevant to later waves of fundholding; further research in this area is clearly required.

It is noticeable that even the television GP practice in 'Peak Practice' is now fundholding, despite being ideologically opposed to fundholding in earlier episodes (Fundholding, 1994)! The reason given for becoming fundholding was also 'negative' in this case, being due to the presence of a competing fundholding practice in the same town.

How many?

The recent government statement of intention 'Developing NHS Purchasing and GP Fundholding; Towards a Primary Care Led NHS' confirms that GP fundholding now covers more than a third of the population and has reached 70% coverage in some parts of the country (NHS Executive, 1994 [2]). The introduction of a new category of fundholder ('community fundholder') will undoubtedly increase coverage still further. Fundholding is now a realistic option for most practices with more than one partner, and smaller practices (including single-handers) can become fundholders as part of a consortium. The government has confirmed that fundholding remains 'voluntary' (NHS Executive, 1994 [2]), although it remains to be seen whether this will continue. Commitment to fundholding in 1995 by the government appears to be at least as high as it was in 1990.

Benefits

There is substantial evidence that GP fundholding has brought about a range of service improvements, including moving consultant outpatient clinics to GP premises (Glennerster et al, 1992 and 1994; Handysides, 1994 [3]; Newton et al, 1993). There has clearly been a shift of power from hospital consultant to GP, reversing the move to consultant power established at the inception of the NHS (Laing and Cotton, 1994).

Glynn et al found a range of innovative budget ploys designed to improve services for practice patients (Glynn, Murphy and Perkins, 1992). Some of these improvements may have arisen because of 'first mover advantage', and there is some evidence that it may not be so easy for new fundholders in 1995 to achieve these benefits (Glennerster et al, 1994).

The Glynn study notes, however, that GP fundholders did not need to increase health promotion clinics after the 1990 contract because they were already providing them. It is likely that first wave practices were well organised and may have produced some of the apparent improvements in any case. Furthermore, a study of first wave fundholders in the South East makes the interesting observation that some of the benefits claimed (eg generic prescribing policies) for fundholding could also be found in non-fundholding practices (Corney, 1994). Notwithstanding this, the conclusion that power has shifted from consultant to GP is supported in this study. All of the fundholding practices working with the author have seen the benefits of this shift in power, with, for example, more 'responsive' consultants willing to hold outpatient clinics in surgeries. A further benefit achieved by fundholding practices appears to be improved management and information systems (Newton et al, 1993). The 'management allowance' given to fundholding practices has enabled them to appoint well qualified fund managers and purchase advanced computerised information systems.

Problems

Equity

One major problem uncovered by research published to date has been the apparent lack of equity in budget allocation between fundholding practices (Day and Klein, 1991; Appleby, 1994; Dixon et al (1994)). This problem appears to have arisen as a consequence of the complex information requirements of fundholding, with Regional Health Authorities relying on information provided by the practices themselves. There is, of course, an incentive to ensure that referrals are artificially high in the preparatory year of a practice, since later budgets will be based on referrals in this year.

Furthermore, it appears that fundholders have been funded more generously in relation to their hospital referral patterns than District Health Authorities, which may lead to tensions in the scheme being hidden (Day and Klein, 1991). Similarly, a recent study of secondary (hospital) care funding in North West Thames found that GP fundholders were funded more generously than non fundholders, although this may be due to need for care being greater in, and hospital prices higher for, fundholding practices. Perhaps the most significant criticism of fundholding has been from this perspective of 'equity'. However, as Appleby notes perceptively, it is the government's stated intention to improve services through competition, and this will inevitably create cyclical inequalities (Appleby, 1994). Glennerster et al refer to the potential problem of 'cream-skimming' in which fundholders offload high cost patients to other practices (Glennerster et al, 1992 and 1994, Glennerster, 1994). Non fundholding practices therefore stand to lose out on two fronts, the relative availability of hospital services and, potentially, 'dumping' of high cost patients onto them. (Pietroni, 1993).

Managing information costs

Fundholding practices have also been faced with problems in obtaining information needed for contract negotiation, including being faced with a wide range of prices. This is due to poor information being given by NHS Trusts (Glennerster et al, 1994; Glennerster, 1994; Appleby 1994). Furthermore, the large amount of time that fundholders have to spend on administration has been a particular problem noted in two studies of first wave fundholders (Corney, 1994; Newton et al, 1993).

The cost of managing fundholding has been estimated at £80,000 per fundholding practice, including some fixed costs at Health Authority level (Davies, 1995). Ham argues that the fragmentation of purchasing will lead to higher administrative costs (Ham, 1994). It is questionable whether such costs are sustainable in the long term (Glennerster, 1994).

It can also be argued that the small size of fundholding practices means that the prospect of a bulk buyer, the District Health Authority, getting 'real' improvements from providers as a result of economies of scale is better (Bowie and Harris, 1994).

The government agenda

Reassuring the public

Recent evidence suggests that savings from GP fundholding are declining in percentage terms, with some practices who underspent in the early years of fundholding now overspending (Anderson, 1994 [1]). One interpretation that could be placed on this is that the government is 'tightening up' on budgets that were at first very generous. Practices have been able to use underspendings for the benefit of the practice but, the smaller and more uncertain savings become, the more difficult this will be.

It has already been argued that the government intends the public to believe that it has funded the NHS adequately and that responsibility for rationing lies with the purchasing authority. The fundholding 'brochure' prepared by the Department of Health for public information states that:

> The amount of money they (fundholders) receive is carefully worked out to cover the needs of all the patients in the doctor's practice (Department of Health, 1992 [2])

This brochure could be interpreted as stating that all patient needs in a fundholding practice can be met, i.e. that all referrals needed in a year can be met and that the GP does not have to ration. A major difficulty in assessing such government claims is that there is no agreed measure of 'health need'. Clearly, rationing does exist, and more honest claim would surely be that fundholders could meet 'health need within limited resources'.

Recent developments

New services

The range of hospital and community services that can be purchased by GP fundholders increased substantially in 1993, including community nursing (Department of Health [Regulations], 1993). The financial limit on the provision of goods and services was increased to £6,000 from April 1994 (NHS Executive, 1994 [3)]. This trend towards a greater range of services will continue, particularly through the introduction of 'total fundholding'.

Total fundholding

As at March 1995, there are four 'total fundholding' projects in the UK, with twenty-five more coming on stream in April 1995 (Anderson, 1994 [2] and [3]). Total fundholding allows the practice to purchase all hospital and community services, including emergencies. The concept of 'total fundholding' undoubtedly gives the practices a degree of apparent financial power over providers (the Worth Valley project has an annual budget of £21 million), with of course corresponding financial responsibility if the budget is exceeded.

'Putting on the squeeze'

Drug budgets for fundholding practices from April 1995 onwards will be set on the basis of securing 'equity' between 'high spending' and 'low spending' practices (Fundholding, 1995 [1]. Staff reimbursement budgets are also being revised to transfer funds from 'high spending' to 'low spending' fundholding practices. The government is apparently trying to rectify the original faults in the budget setting process described earlier (Glennerster et al, 1994).

Planning and priorities guidance issued by the Department of Health in July 1994 will impact heavily on fundholders (NHS Executive, 1994 [1]). This guidance aims to constrain fundholders' referral patterns by increasing day case surgery and reducing 'ineffective' treatments. It sets as a priority a switch from hospital to primary care, since the latter is seen as a cheaper way of providing health care. Presumably, since GP fundholders (and indeed all GP's) are charged with providing primary care, workload requiring direct GP involvement will increase. GP fundholders will therefore suffer a reduction in their hospital referral budget, but will receive a smaller increase in resources devoted to their own services.

Consortia and multifunds

Another recent development has been the introduction of consortia and multifunds. These allow practices to pool management of a fund, thereby enabling more practices to become fundholders. One of the multi-funds (Birmingham) has 139 GP members and covers 60 practices (Davies, 1994).

Three of the practices currently working with the author are in fundholding consortia. The experience of these practices is that they have perceived themselves as being able to exercise more influence over providers than before, and that the consortia managers have been able to secure good 'deals' for them.

Two of the other practices are in non-fundholding consortia, but, interestingly, they perceive that they have also been able to secure influence over the services provided by NHS Trusts. The non-fundholding consortia work in partnership with the DHA to purchase services, but without the formality of fundholding budgets. Two published reports on 'alternatives to fundholding' provide similar conclusions (Graffy and Williams, 1994; Black, Burchall and Trimble, 1994).

'Fundholding for all'

Arguably the most significant development in fundholding is the expansion of the scheme announced in October 1994 (NHS Executive, 1994 [2]) This scheme explicitly aims for ‘a major expansion of GP fundholding’.

Three new types of GP fundholder are introduced: 'community', 'standard' and 'total'). The 'community' fundholders will not have budgets for acute hospital services, but will have most of the other normal fundholding budgets, including drugs. It is difficult to see where the benefits will come for such practices, since most of the recorded 'benefits' of fundholding derive from the hospital referral budgets. The potential disadvantages to practices of having their drug expenditure capped do not, therefore, appear to be matched by corresponding benefits.

In addition, a new draft accountability guide for fundholders has recently been issued for consultation (NHS Executive, 1995). This guide refers to four levels of accountability:

(1) management accountability (e.g. practice planning, reporting problems to Health Authorities, reviewing performance)

(2) accountability to patients and the wider public (sending copy plans to DHA, introducing a practice complaints system)

(3) financial accountability (providing accounts for audit, providing monthly information for monitoring by the local Health Authority, securing Health Authorities' agreement to using savings, contributing to efficiency savings)

(4) clinical and professional accountability (taking part in audit)

The 'constraining and controlling' nature of these proposals is striking, particularly the new role of Health Authorities/Health Commissions. The terminology used emphasises the objective of increased financial accountability (including 'efficiency savings', arguably cuts dressed up in acceptable language), although there is no reference to 'direction' or 'line management'. 'Fundholding' magazine expresses the fear of fundholders succinctly:

> The DoH's draft accountability framework has sent a shiver of unease down the spines of many GP's.(Fundholding, 1995 [2])

Commissioning

District Health Authorities and Family Health Service Authorities will be merged into Health Commissions from April 1996 (NHS Executive, 1994 [2]). Many Health Commissions have already been formed, with the old authorities remaining in shadow form until 1996. The Commissions will form the focus for operating the new accountability framework, although there may be some tension in this relationship since they are in effect purchasers 'competing' with GP fundholders.

Reflections

Hopwood suggested roles that accounting might play in processes of organisational change, one of these roles being the 'creation of a domain of economic action' (Hopwood, 1989). The allocation of budgets to GP's in their capacity as fundholders and the associated technology of accounting has inflicted the domain of the 'economic' on practices where the domain of the 'social' and the 'ethical' had typically predominated. The problem of 'equity' stands out as a major issue, with accounting implicated in the active creation of inequity.

Hierarchical financial accountability has been imposed on GP's, with consequent divisions and tensions being created between fundholding and non-fundholding practices, practices and Health Authorities and, in some cases, between GP's and consultants (see Roberts, 1991; also Ezzamel and Willmott, 1993).

The transfer of power from hospital consultants to GP's could be seen as a benefit for GP's, although the long term benefits to patients of creating tension and uncertainty are questionable.

'Alternatives to fundholding', in which GP's develop their own solutions on their own terms to perceived power imbalances with the hospital sector may be a more acceptable way forward (see also the possibility of a 'home-grown solution' in Dent, 1991). It has been seen that other 'benefits' claimed for fundholding also exist in non-fundholding practices.

It could be argued that clinical rationing decisions should be taken by GP's, since they are in a position to take effective decisions within resource constraints. An alternative perspective is that the patient's 'advocate' has become the 'rationer' who decides whether the patient shall or shall not be treated. The argument that government information to patients has presented a somewhat distorted view of resource decisions is a powerful one, and again tensions, this time between patients and doctors, may be created.

Recent changes in arrangements for fundholding appear to be designed to entice more practices into the 'web' of accountability (see Humphrey , Miller and Scapens, 1993). Practices appear to feel 'forced' to become fundholders, either because of perceived inequities for their patients or as a result of competition between practices. There is, however, a fundamental conflict between the government's expressed aims of increasing fundholding and reducing administrative costs, since fundholding is very expensive to administer. Furthermore, the very existence of fundholding makes macro-planning more difficult to coordinate, since many providers are assessing health needs for a given population (Gillam, 1992). Arguably, fundholding has been a very effective means of capping drug expenditure and increasing control over GP's whose benefits for GP's are becoming less apparent as the scheme develops. It has been argued that the reforms are 'evolutionary' rather than 'revolutionary', and this is supported by recent developments (Appleby, 1992, page 6).

Interestingly, it appears that some GP fundholders actually believe that real 'deals' are there to be made:

> The deals are there to be made if the districts (District Health Authorities) want them (Anderson, 1994 [4]).

Is it possible for 'deals' to be made in a 'quasi-market'? It is argued that this is an example of 'illusory autonomy', where fundholders have been so absorbed by the apparatus of fundholding that they have objectified the concepts of the market and cannot see that the potential for 'deals' is disappearing rapidly. Alternatively, the 'control' perspective of professionalism is being used by the government to reduce the power of professionals and give control back to the consumer.

FHSA management: Illusions of freedom?

Terms of reference

As noted earlier, Family Health Service Authorities replaced the old Family Practitioner Committees (FPC's) in 1990. The FHSA's were required to improve the quality of provision and delivery of family practitioner (medical, dental, pharmaceutical) services in their localities, in addition to the old FPC duties (Secretary of State for Health et al, 1989 [2]). The FPC's had been administrative offices responsible for paying family practitioners; service management responsibilities were not significant.

The degree of 'power' that the FHSA actually has to perform these duties is questionable. As Huntingdon points out, only 10% of the GMS (GP payments) budget is 'discretionary', this being in respect of reimbursements for staff and premises costs (Huntingdon, 1993). A recent Audit Commission Report ('Practices Make Perfect: The Role of the FHSA') puts the problem as follows:

> The powers of FHSA's are limited. They must rely on persuasion backed by modest incentives from the cash-limited part of their budget. (Audit Commission, 1993)

Laughlin et al found little evidence of FHSA's taking a directive role, although they noted fears by GP's that this would change (Laughlin, Broadbent and Willig-Atherton, 1994). It will be argued in this paper that these fears may be realised, with FHSA's claiming to be seeking 'empowerment for GP's', but with the ultimate objective of 'control'. The motivating force for such behaviour is, as argued earlier, government's wish to control expenditure by GP's.

Evidence

Use of 'limited' powers The recent Audit Commission study of FHSA's found that the structures for holding GP practices to account had been weak, with a wide variation in standards between practices (Audit Commission, 1993). It is interesting that this report recommends strongly that 'practice agreements' should be used to set objectives for practices and to monitor performance.

One area in which the limited powers of FHSA's have been used is that of 'cost rent' and practice staff reimbursements. Huntingdon found that FHSA's have been using their ability to withhold these reimbursements to bargain for changes in service or improvements in quality (Huntingdon, 1993).

As with fundholding, FHSA's have also been using levels of reimbursement to reduce perceived 'inequalities' between practices. In two of the practices currently working with the author the FHSA policy of 'freezing' inflation increases in staff reimbursement for 'high' spending practices has created considerable tensions within the practices. It has meant, for example, that receptionists in one practice have not had a pay increase for three years. Arguably, of course, the GP's have two simple remedies, reduce staff hours or pay the increase out of practice profits. The difficulty with the first alternative is that it will reduce clinic hours in practices that have historically offered long hours, with consequent implications for the perceived quality of service. The second alternative creates additional tensions within the practice. In this way, what appears to a great benefit for practices, a substantial contribution to their overheads, has become a 'two-edged sword'.

It is a mistake to search for 'directive' behaviour in circumstances where the power required to exercise such behaviour does not exist. Other types of 'management' behaviour have been suggested, including 'management by walking about' (see Peters and Austin, 1986 pages 8 to 33; Glendinning, Chew and Wilkin, 1994; Huntingdon, 1993). 'Management by walking about' has been experienced by all the practices currently working with the author. Senior FHSA staff visit practices regularly to 'keep in touch' and, potentially, to demonstrate 'leadership'.

Role of the FHSA in managing the 1990 contract

The FHSA is responsible for monitoring compliance by GP's with the 1990 contract. (Secretary of State for Health et al, 1989 [2]). The reactions of GP's to the contract have already been discussed, but it is interesting to note that Glendinning et al found a similar reaction to aspects of the contract among some FHSA staff (Glendinning, Chew and Wilkin, 1994). The latter survey looked specifically at assessments for the over 75s, and found considerable variation in standards of evaluation of GP practices between FHSA's. 'Low profile' approaches to monitoring the requirements of the contract in this case may have been due to the controversial nature and loose definition of the requirement. Similarly, one of the practices working with the author has not yet produced a practice leaflet, as required by the contract. This has not yet produced a directive response from the FHSA. FHSA's covering the practices working with the author have concentrated their efforts on monitoring contracted levels of service through, for example, analyses of night visit claims. Apparently 'excessive' levels of claims have been investigated, leading in one case to legal action for fraudulent claims. The FHSA's appear to be content to allow the financial incentives in the contract (e.g. minor surgery, target payments) to drive the GP's towards government targets. FHSA's have not, it appears, been directive in managing the 1990 contract because there are other concerns of more importance.

Indicative drug amounts

The FHSA is also responsible for monitoring 'Indicative Drug Amounts', quasi-budgets for drugs prescribed by GP's. The FHSA medical advisor is responsible for this function, but has largely confined this role to interpreting prescribing information and cost data ('PACT' data) and encouraging use of 'protocols' (ie standardised treatment regimes) (Panton, 1993). This 'softly softly' approach should not, however, be misinterpreted. As argued above, drug budgets are likely to become 'real' in the near future for most practices, through the mechanism of fundholding.

Planning to constrain

It is through the mechanism of practice planning that the FHSA's covering the practices working with the author have been influential. One interpretation of planning is that it is a calculative, constraining activity which aims to direct the disparate parts of an organisation towards the goals and objectives of the centre, in other words:

> _ _budgets and plans can be built around what is to be (Burchell, Clubb, Hopwood and Hughes, 1980)

In effect the planning activity can be used to rationalise predetermined action, provided that practices can be persuaded to plan within FHSA guidelines. This is achieved by ensuring that those practices that plan to the 'rules' are allocated a large share of any new resources. One Health Commission puts it thus:

> The plan is also a vehicle for letting the Health Commission know about the practice and its needs; for making bids for development _ _ _ (The Health Commission For X, 1994).

The same Health Commission describes the purpose of the practice (health) plan for fundholders as a basis for reviewing performance:

> _ _ for the practice to set out *what it is going to achieve and how* (The Health Commission For X, 1994)

The requirement to plan has grown out of the annual reporting exercise required by the 1990 contract. The annual report was a historical document whose perceived purpose was to monitor practice activity (Record et al, 1994). This can be compared to the prospective nature of the annual practice plan. Production of a plan is only mandatory for fundholders, but has effectively become compulsory for non-fundholders. The FHSA has limited sanctions to ensure such compliance, but can make life difficult for a recalcitrant practice (Huntingdon, 1993; Audit Commission, 1993).

Partnership?

There are numerous examples of GP's working in genuine partnership with FHSA's. It has been suggested that involving non-fundholders in purchasing has given them similar benefits to fundholding (Morley, 1993; Starey, Bosanquet and Griffiths, 1993). Johnson describes how the Manchester medical audit group has worked closely with the FHSA (Johnson, 1994). A recent survey by the Royal College of General Practitioners found many instances of positive help and advice from FHSA's and some instances of 'joint planning' (McBride, 1994).

Recent government proposals, however, aim for 'a *stronger* partnership between Health Authorities and *all* GP's' (Department of Health, 1994 (2)). The desire for a stronger partnership is expressed alongside the above strengthened accountability arrangements for GP's. It is difficult to reconcile these two objectives, since, as argued above, the main thrust of government proposals in recent years has been to strengthen *control* rather than partnership.

Recent developments

It was argued earlier that FHSA's have been using practice plans and practice agreements to monitor the performance of practices. This theme has been picked up in the recent draft accountability guide for GP fundholders (NHS Executive, 1995), which is likely to apply to all GP's (NHS Executive, 1994 [2]). The FHSA (Health Commission from 1996) will be expected to monitor the performance of practices, albeit with the only clear 'sanction' for poor performance being exclusion from fundholding. This sanction is, however, powerful, since it could lead to reductions in list size (and hence profit) for a practice in an area dominated by fundholding practices.

The development of Health Commissions will impact on fundholding and non-fundholding practices alike. One powerful organisation will oversee the purchasing of all health care services, and 'control' over practices is likely to be a high priority.

The strategic plan for Health Commission 'X' refers to developing practice based contracts, identifying direct and overhead costs for each practice and developing outcome measures for practices (The Health Commission For X, 1993). All of these aims have a clear control objective.

NHS Trusts are aiming for increasing amounts of day surgery and reduced lengths of stay. These have had a significant impact on practices because responsibility for care has been passed back to the GP. It has been proposed that trusts have been forced into such policies as a direct result of the introduction of the internal market, with GP workload increasing as a consequence (Noakes, 1992).

Reflections

Coercive power derives from relationships of dependence (Fox 1985, page 55). FHSA's (and Health Commissions) have limited overt powers to direct GP's. They do, however, have the power to withhold resources from GP's, particularly if they wish to develop their practices. This power has been used to coerce practices to, for example, plan in accordance with government priorities even though they may disagree with those priorities (see Laughlin, Broadbent and Willig-Atherton, 1994).

Control through consent depends upon pursuit of common objectives (Fox 1985, page 67). It has been argued that GP's and FHSA's have the same objectives of better quality care (Lawrence, 1992). Whilst it may be true that there is an overriding objective of patient care, there are conflicting objectives. GP's, for example, have fought against government proposals to reduce payments for providing night cover because their profits will fall. From the government's perspective, the 1990 contract resulted in claims for night visits going up (Baker, Klein and Carter, 1994), and proposals to cap expenditure are therefore justified. The outcome of such conflicts will be resolved in favour of the party who has the balance of power, who, on the basis of past experience, will be the government.

As Gould has observed:

> GP's have found themselves directed and constrained in their activities to at least the same degree as a salaried employee is controlled, but without the advantage of having the boss responsible for the chore of providing and organising the tools of the trade and _ _ _ funding out of hours and holiday cover. (Gould, 1991)

Consumerisum: Unleashing the consumer?

As noted earlier, a 'Patients' Charter' was issued in 1992. The Charter is available to all patients of the NHS, and a section of the Charter is devoted to GP services. The word 'right' is shown in bold type, and is used six times in the GP services section. There are no 'duties' expected of the patient, although it is interesting to note the tone of the vague reference to 'helping the NHS by only calling out your GP at night if it cannot wait until the next day'. There is also a reference to 'encouraging' GP practices to develop their own charters. Handysides, in a review of morale among GP's, puts it thus:

> General practitioners I talked to in Sheffield expressed frustration at the rising expectations of patients encouraged by the patients' charter. _ _ the general practitioners face increasingly strident and inappropriate demands for their services (Handysides, 1994 [2])

All of the GP's working with the author have expressed the view that the government has encouraged patients to make heavier use of services. These additional burdens are experienced by all practice staff. Surgeries are longer and night calls more frequent (see Day and Klein, 1994), which has increased the burden on GP's. The receptionists have noticed a more demanding attitude by patients and complain particularly about rude patients who become more deferential when meeting the GP (see Laughlin, Broadbent and Willig-Atherton, 1994 with regard to gender implications).

The 1990 contract increased the importance of list size on practice profits, as noted earlier. This in itself represents 'consumerism', since financial reward now appears to depend upon keeping patients on the list. If there are competing practices in the same town this has become a serious consideration. It is noticeable that the GP's working with the author are all heavily focused on list size and review increases or decreases in some depth, frequently on a monthly basis. The requirement to produce practice leaflets contained in the 1990 contract is a further 'consumerist' development, and a study of the content and usage of these leaflets found that they have been well received by patients (Albert and Chadwick, 1992). Furthermore, assessments of the over 75s, viewed as an unnecessary inclusion in the contract by GP's (Morrell, 1991), are liked by patients (Tremellen, 1992).

It can be argued that the government is using 'consumerism' to force GP's to be more responsive to patient demands. A 'control' perspective on professionalism is assumed by this argument, and doctors must therefore be 'forced' to take account of the views of their patients.

With regard to 'markets', the language of the 'market' requires that consumer decisions dictate the allocation of resources. It has been argued that the 'internal market' of the NHS is misnamed because consumers have no means of influencing the decisions of their surrogate purchasers (Brennan, 1994). This market 'imperfection' can only be overcome fully by allowing patients to take their own purchasing decisions, which would be impossible because of insufficient medical knowledge (the 'bounded rationality' described by Bartlett, 1991). An alternative strategy is to force the views of patients on their surrogate purchasers, the GP's, and to 'persuade' all GP's to become fundholders. It can be argued that this strategy has been adopted by the government.

Change?

'Accountability' changes

GP's have been subjected to a tidal wave of externally imposed accountability changes. The government is clearly convinced that increased accountability will change behaviour. Huntingdon puts it thus:

> under a barrage of 'attention' from a determined authority, most practices will change (Huntingdon, 1993)

This deterministic perspective underpinned the 1990 contract (see Laughlin et al, 1992 and 1994). There is substantial evidence that the financial incentives in the contract have influenced, for example, night visits (Baker, Klein and Carter, 1994; Salisbury, 1993). A study by Bosanquet and Leese found that GP's are influenced by economic incentives, although this study was carried out before the 1990 contract (Bosanquet and Leese, 1989). Arguments for the potential failure of this deterministic model have been discussed earlier (Humphrey, Miller and Scapens, 1993; Gray and Jenkins, 1993). Wilson demonstrates how models of planned change assume that managers alone can effect change, which in turn depends upon unquestioning acceptance of managerial control within an organisation (Wilson, 1992).

Laughlin, Broadbent and Willig-Atherton consider that GP practices have not yet undergone 'second-order' change (Laughlin, Broadbent and Willig-Atherton, 1994). This conclusion is based on Levy's model of change and observations of the reactions of practices to the 1990 contract (Levy, 1986). In order to assess whether 'second-order' change has occurred, the 'culture' and 'values' of the practice must be seen to change. It is, of course, very difficult to find conclusive evidence of 'cultural' change, posing the fundamental problems of defining culture and identifying its 'ownership'.

There seems to be an implicit assumption in the Laughlin study that absence of additional administrative burdens on GP's as a result of the new contract means that they have been relatively unaffected by it. They are seen to have 'delegated' the additional burden to practice managers and nurses, and carried on as before (findings supported elsewhere, see Pringle, 1992). So far as the 1990 contract is concerned, this may well be the case, but it has been argued above that other changes are more significant. Additionally, the fact that the additional work falls on practice managers does not necessarily mean that the values of GP's haven't changed.

All of the GP's currently working with the author have confirmed that they will 'play the FHSA game ' to secure additional resources for their practice. It appears that FHSA's are using a mixture of 'collaboration' and 'coercion' in an attempt to secure 'transformational' change (Dunphy and Stace, 1988; Fox, 1985). The extent to which long term change has been secured through strengthened accountability is, however, doubtful. The practices currently working with the author have certainly changed 'structurally' and 'behaviourally', but there is little evidence so far that they have changed 'culturally' (Wilson, 1992).

'Market' changes

It is proposed here that the 'market' changes imposed on practices will inevitably have a fundamental effect on the way that practices operate. The issue of 'culture' and 'values' is not central to this argument, since it is fundamental *relationships* that have been changed:

(1) GP and patient, with GP's effectively taking being seen by the patient to take responsibility for rationing of hospital resources

(2) GP and consultant, because of the economic power given to GP's

(3) GP and GP, because of the 'equity' problem created by fundholding

Having brought GP's on board to fundholding, albeit reluctantly in many cases, it appears that the government is changing the rules of the game to entice more practices. Fundholding practices are then trapped in a web of accountability rules, particularly in their role as budget holders for expenditure previously managed by others. Furthermore, the practices are then subject to rule changes that may penalise them, including so-called 'efficiency' savings and reductions in budgets held by so-called 'high-spending' practices. It is argued that, if fundholding is retained for the long term, GP practices will inevitably change. The 'culture' of a practice includes the philosophy of patient care adopted by the GP's. Encirclement of a GP's freedom to prescribe through financial calculus reduces this philosophy to an unrealistic statement of the 'ideal'. 'Colonization' change, according to Laughlin, will occur when medical judgements are made on cost *and* medical grounds (Laughlin, 1991). It is argued that this type of change has indeed occurred.

'Consumerism' changes

Patients have been encouraged, through the Patients' Charter and other government pronouncements, to make heavier use of GP services. Increasing demands either reduce the time devoted to other patients or increase the working hours of GP's and other staff. Consequently, as discussed earlier, all the practices working with the author have experienced additional burdens. It has been argued that this has resulted in increased 'stress' levels for GP's (see Howie et al, 1992). It is likely that these developments will result in changes in the philosophy of care within practices and will change fundamentally the relationships between GP, practice staff and patient. Such changes are already being seen in the practices working with the author.

'Seeing the wood for the trees'

It is extremely difficult to 'disentangle' the impact of recent changes in society, which arguably impact on GP's more than other people. GP's are exposed on a daily basis to the effects of unemployment, divorce, poverty and other social problems. Jefferys and Sachs proposed that GP's were very vulnerable to general changes in social mores because of their *'visibility'* to the population:

> GP's are _ _ _ more likely to hold a salient position in the lives of the population than, say, an _ _ _ accountant (Jefferys and Sachs, 1983, page 23).

Furthermore, GP's have been drawn increasingly into the role of effective primary health care team manager. Theoretical analysis of the impact of external changes in such circumstances is, therefore, far from easy. Any conclusions from such analysis must be treated with great caution.

Conclusion

The government has imposed accountability and market changes on GP practices with three clear aims. Firstly, there is a wish to increase managerial control over the use of resources by GP's and improve 'efficiency' and 'efficiency' as a consequence. Secondly, there is a belief that 'markets' will allocate resources more effectively and reduce costs. Thirdly, the government intends that the ultimate consumers of health resources (patients) view rationing as a 'professional' decision to be made by their GP.

The paper has used the 'models' of professionalism proposed by Harrison and Pollitt (Harrison and Pollitt, 1994) to analyse the nature of and recent developments in GP fundholding and FHSA management. It can be argued that fundholding is an example of the 'illusory' model, where GP's have become trapped in a web of apparent autonomy and power that is in reality compromising the freedoms that they have enjoyed for so long. 'Managerialism' on the part of FHSA's has been slow to develop, but has been gathering pace in the past year. It has been argued that the use of 'coercive' power will become more apparent with the advent of Health Commissions and new proposed accountability frameworks. Finally, 'consumerism' has been used to 'force' GP's to take account of patients' views and to overcome the market 'imperfections' so apparent in a 'quasi-market'.

The changes can be viewed from an alternative perspective, since there are limited resources to be devoted to health care. This perspective would see that it is necessary to increase control in circumstances where GP's have all the advantages of self-employment with none of the risks. Additionally, it may be 'right' to make GP's more accountable to their patients. Nevertheless, it is clear that GP's are being drawn into externally imposed changes that will change the pattern of relationships between their practices and the outside world in a fundamental way. The extent to which the culture of practices will change as a consequence is a matter for further research effort, but it is proposed here that such change is inevitable, if it has not already occurred.

References

Albert, T. and Chadwick, S. (1992), 'How Readable are Practice Leaflets?', *British Medical Journal,* Vol. 305, pp 1266-1268.

Anderson, P.(1994) (1), 'Savings: The Reality', *Fundholding,* 7 June 1994, pp 14-16.

Anderson, P.(1994) (2), 'Total Fund Projects Make Their Mark', *Fundholding,* 7 December 1994, pp 22-23.

Anderson, P.(1994) (3), 'Total Control', *Fundholding,* 7 May 1994, pp 14-18.

Anderson, P.(1994) (4), 'Are DHA's the Real Two-tier Villains?', *Fundholding,* 21 April 1994, pp 14-16.

Appleby, J. (1992), *'Financing Health Care in the 1990's',* Open University Press, Buckingham.

Appleby, J. (1994), 'The Reformed National Health Service: A Commentary', *Social Policy and Administration,* Vol. 28, No. 4, pp 345-358.

Armstrong, D. (1989), *'An Outline of Sociology As Applied to Medicine'* Butterworth Heinemann, Oxford.

Audit Commission (1993), *'Practices Make Perfect: The Role of the Family Health Services Authority',*Department of Health, London.

Bain, J. (1991), 'General Practices and the New Contract. I-Reactions and Impact', *British Medical Journal,* Vol. 302, pp 1183-1186.

Baker, D., Klein, R. and Carter R. (1994), 'Impact of the 1990 Contract for General Practitioners on Night Visiting', *British Journal of General Practice,* February 1994, pp 68-71.

Bartlett, W. (1991), 'Quasi-Markets and Contracts: A Perspective on NHS Reform', *Public Money and Management,* Autumn 1991 pp 53-61.

Bevan, G. (1989), 'Reforming UK Health Care: Internal Markets or Emergent Planning', *Fiscal Studies,* Vol. 19, No. 1, pp 53-71.

Black, D.C., Burchall, A.D. and Trimble, I.M. (1994), 'Non-Fundholding in Nottingham: A Vision of the Future', *British Medical Journal,* Vol. 309, pp 930- 932.

Bosanquet, N. and Leese B. (1989), *'Family Doctors and Economic Incentives',* Aldershot, Dartmouth/Gower.

Bowie, C. and Harris, T. (1994), 'The Fundholding Fandango', *British Journal of General Practice,* January 1994, pp 38-40.

Brennan, I. (1994), 'Why the NHS 'Internal Market' is Misnamed', *Accountancy Age,* 30 June 1994, page 12.

Burchell, S., Clubb, C., Hopwood, A. and Hughes, J. (1980), 'The Roles of Accounting in Organizations and Society', *Accounting, Organizations and Society,* Vol. 5, No. 1, pp 5-27.

Corney, R. (1994), 'Experiences of First Wave General Practice Fundholders in South East Thames Regional Health Authority', *British Journal of GeneralPractice,* January 1994, pp 34-37.

Davies, J.(1994), 'How Well are Multifunds Working for Their GP's?', *Fundholding,* 7 November 1994, pp 14-15 and 27.

Davies, J.(1995), 'How Much Does the Scheme Cost?', *Fundholding,* 18 January 1995, pp 22-24.

Day, P. and Klein, R. (1991), 'Variations in Budgets of Fundholding Practices', *British Medical Journal,* Vol. 303, pp 168-170.

Dent, J.F. (1991), 'Accounting and Organizational Cultures: A Field Study of the Emergence of a New Organizational Reality', *Accounting, Organizations and Society,* Vol. 16, No. 8, pp 705-732.

Department of Health (1992 and 1995), *'The Patients' Charter',* Department of Health, Leeds.

Department of Health (1992) (2), *'General Practice Funding: What It Means and What it Means to You',* Department of Health, Leeds.

Dixon, J., Dinwoodie, M., Hodson, D., Dodd, S., Poltorak, T., Garrett, C., Rice, P., Doncaster, I. and Williams, M. (1994), 'Distribution of NHS Funds Between Fundholding and Non-Fundholding Practices', *British Medical Journal,* Vol. 309, pp 30-34.

Dunphy, D.C. and Stace, D.A. (1988), 'Transformational and Coercive Strategies for Planned Organisational Change', *Organisation Studies,* Vol. 9, No. 3, pp 17-34.

Ezzamel, M. and Willmott, H. (1993), 'Corporate Governance and Financial Accountability', *Accountability, Auditing and Accountability Journal,* Vol. 6, No. 3, pp 109-132.

Fox, A. (1985), *'Man Mismanagement',* Hutchinson, London.

Freidson, E. (1970), *'Profession of Medicine: A Study in the Sociology of Applied Knowledge'*, Dodd Mead, New York.

Fundholding Article (1995) (1), 'GP's Fear Rise in Overspending', *Fundholding*, 15 February 1995, p 5.

Fundholding Editorial (1995) (2), 'Manage Commissions Before They Hem You In', *Fundholding*, 4 January 1995, p 13.

Fundholding Article (1994), 'TV GP's drop Their Opposition and Become Fundholders', *Fundholding*, 21 April 1994, p 6.

Gillam, S.J. (1992), 'Assessing the Health Care Needs of Populations-The General Practitioner's Contribution', *British Journal of General Practice*, October 1992, pp 404-405.

Glendinning, C., Chew, C. and Wilkin, D. (1994), 'Professional Power and Managerial Control: The Case of GP Assessments of the Over-75's', *Social Policy and Administration*, Vol. 28, No. 4, pp 317-332.

Glennerster, H. (1994), 'New Challenges for Management Accounting: Issues in Health and Social Services', *Financial Accountability and Management*, Vol. 10, No. 2, pp 131-141.

Glennerster, H., Matsaganis, M., Owens, P. and Hancock, S. (1994), *'GP Fundholding: Wild Card or Winning Hand'*, in Robinson, R. and Le Grand J., *'Evaluating the NHS Reforms, Policy Journals'*, London.

Glennerster, H., Matsaganis, M. and Owens, P. (1992), *'A Foothold For Fundholding'*, King's Fund Institute, London.

Glynn, J.J., Murphy M.P. and Perkins, D.A. (1992), 'GP Practice Budgets: An Evaluation of the Financial Risks and Rewards', *Financial Accountability and Management*, Vol. 8, No. 2, pp 149-161.

Goode, W.J. (1960), 'Encroachment, Charlatanism and the Emerging Profession: Psychiatry, Sociology and Medicine', *American Journal of Sociology*, Vol. 79, pp 45-67.

Gould, D. (1991), *'Examining Doctors: Medicine in the 1990's'*, Faber and Faber, London.

Graffy, J.P. and Williams, J. (1994), 'Purchasing For All; An Alternative to Fundholding', *British Medical Journal*, Vol. 308, pp 394-397.

Gray, A. and Jenkins, W. (1993), 'Codes of Accountability in the New Public Sector', *Accountability, Auditing and Accountability Journal*, Vol. 6, No. 3, pp 52-67.

Ham, C. (1994), 'Reforming Health Services: Learning from the UK Experience', *Social Policy and Administration*, Vol. 28, No. 4, pp 293-298.

Handysides, S. (1994) (1), 'Could the Right Contract Improve Morale?', *British Medical Journal*, Vol. 308, pp 455-458.

Handysides, S. (1994) (2), 'Morale in General Practice: Is Change the Problem or the Solution?', *British Medical Journal*, Vol. 308, pp 32-34.

Handysides, S. (1994) (3), 'New Roles for General Practitioners', *British Medical Journal,* Vol. 308, pp 513-516.

Harrison, S. and Pollitt, C. (1994), *'Controlling Health Professionals',* Open University Press, Buckingham.

Hopwood, A.G. (1989), 'Accounting and Organisation Change', *Accounting, Auditing and Accountability Journal,* Vol. 3, No. 1, pp 7-17.

Howie, J.G.R., Hopton, J.L., Heaney D.J. and Porter A.M.D. (1992), 'Attitudes to Medical Care,the Organization of Work and Stress among General Practitioners', *British Journal of General Practice,* May 1992, pp 181-185.

Humphrey, C., Miller, P. and Scapens, R.W. (1993), 'Accountability and Accountable Management in the UK Public Sector', *Accountability, Auditing and Accountability Journal,* Vol. 6, No. 3, pp 7-29.

Huntington, J. (1993), 'From FPC to FHSA to .....Health Commission?', *British Medical Journal,* Vol. 306, pp 33-36.

Independent Law Report (1995), 'Withholding of Treatment for Cancer Upheld', *The Independent,* 14 March 1995, p 11.

Irvine, D.R. (1993), 'Educating General Practitioners', *British Medical Journal,* Vol. 307, pp 696-697.

Jefferys, M. and Sachs, H. (1983), *'Rethinking General Practice',* Tavistock Publications, London.

Johnson, R. (1994), 'Where Have All the Pennies Gone? The Work of the Manchester Medical Audit Group', *British Medical Journal,* Vol. 309, pp 98-102.

Johnson, T.J. (1972), *'Professions and Power',* Macmillan, London.

Laing, A. and Cotton, S. (1994), *'Towards a Model of Health Care Purchasing: The Purchasing Behaviour of General Practice Fundholders',* University of Aberdeen.

Lapsley, I. and Pettigrew, A. (1994), 'Meeting the Challenge: Accounting for Change', *Financial Accountability and Management,* Vol. 10, No. 2, pp 79-92.

Lapsley, I. (1991), 'Accounting Research in the National Health Service', *Financial Accountability and Management,* Vol. 7, No. 1, pp 1-14.

Laughlin, R., Broadbent J. and Willig-Atherton, H. (1994), 'Recent Financial and Administrative Changes in GP Practices in the UK: Initial Experiences and Effects', *Accounting, Auditing and Accountability Journal,* Vol. 7, No. 3, pp 96-124.

Laughlin, R. (1991), 'Can the Information Systems for the NHS Internal Market Work?', *Public Money and Management,* Autumn 1991 pp 37-41.

Laughlin, R., Broadbent J. and Shearn, D. (1992), 'Recent Financial and Accountability Changes in General Practice: An Unhealthy Intrusion into

Medical Autonomy?', *Financial Accountability and Management,* Vol. 8, No. 2, pp 129-148.

Lawrence, M. (1992), 'Caring for the Future', *British Medical Journal,* Vol. 305, pp 400-402.

Levy, A. (1986), 'Second-Order Planned Change: Definition and Conceptualisation', *Organisation Dynamics,* Vol. 15, No. 1, pp 5-23.

Marsh, G.N. (1992), 'Flourishing or Floundering in the 1990's', *British Journal of General Practice,* July 1992, pp 266-267.

Mcbride, M. (1994), 'GPs and Managers', *Health Service Journal,* 13 October 1994, pp 24-26.

Mihill C (1995), 'Guideline Plea for Rationing of Treatment', *The Guardian,* 11 March 1995, p 5.

Milford, P. (1993), *'General Medical Practitioners: Measures of Financial Performance and Perceptions of Success',* Paper Presented to British Accounting Association Conference 1993.

Morley, V. (1993), 'Empowering GP's as Purchasers', *British Medical Journal,* Vol. 306, pp 112-114.

Morrell, D. (1991), 'Role of Research in Development of Organisation and Structure of General Practice', *British Medical Journal,* Vol. 302, pp 1313-1316.

Newton, J., Fraser, M., Robinson, J. and Wainwright, D. (1993), 'Fundholding in Northern Region: The First Year', *British Medical Journal,* Vol. 306, pp 375-378.

NHS Executive (1994) (1), *'Priorities and Planning Guidance for the NHS: 1995/96',*Department of Health, Leeds.

NHS Executive (1994) (2), *'Developing NHS Purchasing and GP Fundholding',* Department of Health, Leeds.

NHS Executive (1994) (3), *'GP Fundholding: List of Goods and Services',* Department of Health, Leeds.

NHS Executive (1995), *'Draft Accountability Framework for GP Fundholding',* Department of Health, Leeds.

Noakes, J. (1992), 'The Case for a Primary Health Care Authority', *British Journal of General Practice,* September 1992, pp 355-357.

Panton, R. (1993), 'FHSA's and Prescribing', *British Medical Journal,* Vol. 306, pp 310-314.

Paton, C. (1992), *'Competition and Planning in the NHS',* Chapman and Hall, London.

Paton, C. (1993), 'Devolution and Centralism in the National Health Service', *Social Policy and Administration,* Vol. 27, No. 2, pp 83-108.

Peters, T. and Austin, N. (1986), *'A Passion For Excellence',* Fontana, London.

Pietroni, R. (1993), *'General Practitioners and the Market',* in Tilley, I., *'Managing the Internal Market'*, Paul Chapman, London.

Pollitt, C.J. (1993), *'Managerialism and the Public Services: Cuts or Cultural Change?'*, Blackwell, Oxford.

Pringle, M. (1992), 'The Developing Primary Care Partnership', *British Medical Journal,* Vol. 305, pp 624-626.

Record, M.C., Spencer J.A., Jones R.H. and Jones, K.P. (1994), 'General Practitioners' Views About the Practice Annual Report', *British Medical Journal,* Vol. 309, pp 849-852.

Roberts, J. (1991), 'The Possibilities of Accountability', *Accounting, Organizations and Society,* Vol. 16, No. 4, pp 355-368.

Salisbury, C. (1993), 'Visiting Through the Night', *British Medical Journal,* Vol. 306, pp 762-764.

Secretary of State for Health, Wales, Northern Ireland and Scotland (1989) (1), *'General Practice in the National Health Service. A New Contract',* London, HMSO.

Secretary of State for Health, Wales, Northern Ireland and Scotland (1989) (2), *'Working for Patients',* London, HMSO.

Smith, J. (1992), 'Charter Moves into the Surgery', *British Medical Journal,* Vol. 305, page 1455.

Stacey, M. (1988), *'The Sociology of Health and Healing',* Routledge, London.

Starey, N., Bosanquet, N. and Griffiths, J. (1993), 'General Practitioners in Partnership With Management: An Organisational Model for Debate', *British Medical Journal,* Vol. 306, pp 308-310.

Tremellen, J. (1992), 'Assessment of Patients Aged Over 75 in General Practice', *British Medical Journal,* Vol. 305, pp 621 -624.

Wilson, D.C. (1992), *'A Strategy of Change',* Routledge, London.

5 Control triggers: A control concept come of age

Irvin T. Nelson and Richard L. Ratliff

Introduction

This paper introduces a potent internal control concept. Called 'control triggers,' these controls initiate the right activity at the right time. They play an important role in the control systems of any organization, but especially in high performance systems. Curiously unrecognized before, a brief study of some history may help explain the oversight.

The last half century has seen a growing concern among accountants, auditors, and managers with respect to internal control. As part of the process of attestation of financial statements and in contrast to the first half of the 20th Century, external auditors today rely heavily on their examination and evaluation of internal controls. Established in 1985 in response to increasing concern about fraudulent financial reporting, the Treadway Commission recommended a broad range of internal control applications, encompassing virtually all of management policies and procedures. Management's growing concern over internal control has even spawned an entire profession, maturing only in the last 20 to 30 years: internal auditing's primary focus is on the design and practice of good internal control.

As might be expected, given the several objectives of the interested parties, diverse perspectives and attitudes have arisen regarding internal control. Operations managers, financial managers, accountants, internal auditors, and external auditors have had different, and even opposing, notions of what internal control is and should be. In 1992, a report was issued by a committee sponsored by the major professional organizations interested in internal control: the American Institute of CPAs (AICPA), the Institute of Internal Auditors (IIA), the Financial Executives Institute (FEI), the Institute of Management Accountants (IMA), and the American Accounting Association (AAA). *Internal Control--Integrated Framework,* the report of the Committee on Sponsoring Organizations of the Treadway Commission, or 'COSO', as it was called, attempted to integrate, unify, and harmonize these notions. The report represents the most recent and broadest-based effort to establish generally accepted practice, or the 'doctrine', of internal control (Coopers & Lybrand).

Throughout this growth of interest and activity, the core of internal control has remained embedded in the theory of bureaucracy. In rewriting management theory, the quality revolution's dismantling of bureaucracy now exposes some weaknesses in traditional approaches to internal control. Fundamentals of the new management practices, such as customer-focus, empowerment of employees, just-in-time production, poka yoke systems, and partnering frequently seem inconsistent with traditionally recommended internal control practices. There is a need to rethink much of what we have accepted as good internal control.

This paper recommends control triggers as one control concept as a step toward that objective. The main points of this paper are (1) that control triggers compose an important internal control concept, (2) that they previously have gone unrecognized as such, (3) that control triggers are important to the control and application of operations, and (4) that they are critical to the application of what may be described as world-class management practices.

The basic argument

The following section provides a proof of the argument in this article through the use of simple rules of deduction:

Premise 1

> The most fundamental control objective is to assure that the right thing happens at the right time.

Organizations are created to achieve various goals and objectives. In order to achieve those purposes, organizations do specific things--e.g., produce and sell products and services. In the process of doing those things for which the organizations were created, they do a variety of other things--e.g., hire people, build production lines, buy inventory, collect money, pay bills, and so forth. In addition to things being done by organizations, things happen in organizations--e.g., people learn, production processes change, etc.

Good control assures the right things are done and the right things happen in order to achieve an organization's purposes, generally expressed in the form of objectives and goals. This point is fundamental to successful operations. "The overall control system...is...used by an organization to achieve its objectives and goals." [IIA, 300.06.4] Because timing is critical, good control also assures that these right things are done at the right times.

Premise 2

> A related fundamental control objective is to avoid anything else.

Although logically redundant, this second premise bears a psychological dimension different from Premise 1. The IIA standards define three categories of controls: preventive (i.e., to 'deter undesirable events'), detective (i.e., 'to detect and correct undesirable events which have occurred'), and directive ('to cause or encourage a desirable event to occur') (IIA, 300.06.1). While directive controls relate specifically to Premise 1, preventive and detective controls deal with avoiding anything *other than* the right thing at the right time.

Remember that the overall purpose of controls is achievement-motivated--to achieve objectives and goals. Notice, however, that two of the three types of controls are avoidance-motivated--to prevent and to detect undesirable events.

Premise 3

> The methods of such assurances may be described as 'control methods,' or simply as 'controls.'

'A control is any action taken by management to enhance the likelihood that established objectives and goals will be achieved.' (IIA, SPPIA, 300.06) Examples of general control methods include the following listed by the IIA (IIA, 300.03.2):

- Authorizing performance.
- Monitoring performance.
- Comparing actual with planned performance.
- Documenting activities.

The AICPA has specified five general control methods [AICPA, AU 319.11]:

- Authorization of transactions and activities.
- Segregation of duties that reduce the opportunities to allow any person to be in a position to both perpetrate and conceal errors or irregularities in the normal course of his duties.
- Documents and records to help ensure the proper recording of transactions and events.
- Adequate safeguards over access to and use of assets and records.
- Independent checks on performance.

General control methods uniquely defining bureaucratic organizations include:

- Functionally structured organization.
- Specialized division of labor.
- Limited span of control.
- Scalar relationships (i.e., chain of command) and unity of command (i.e., one boss per person).

With the advent of modern management methods and production techniques, new types of management practices have evolved. Because such practices are intended to influence the results of business operations, they may also be thought of as control methods.

Examples include:

- Statistical process control systems.
- Quick change-over systems.
- Just-in-time systems.
- Cross-functional teams.
- Value analysis.
- Partnering.

All of these various methods are intended to assure the right things happen at the right times, and to avoid anything else.

Premise 4

> A necessary element of such assurances is the initiation of the right actions at the right times to produce a desired outcome[1].

Causes are a necessary condition of effects. Accepting the principle of cause and effect, and given that action is the effect, then something must cause the action. Thus, in an attmpt to influence the outcome of their processes, managers and workers cues designed to initiate the right actions, leading to desirable outcomes. In the absence of such signals, there can be no initiation, resulting in no action, resulting in turn in no favorable outcomes.

Premise 5

> By definition, methods of controlled initiation may be called 'control triggers.'

Control triggers are the things which signal, initiate, and cause a specific, correct action to happen at the right time. No action can be assured to happen at the right time without an appropriate trigger. Thus, no process can be controlled without a series of triggers systematically embedded throughout the system.

Six possibilities exist with respect to the initiation of an action:

- The right action can be initiated at the right time.
- The right action can be initiated at a wrong time.
- The right action can fail to be initiated.
- A wrong action can be initiated at the right time.
- A wrong action can be initiated at a wrong time.
- Wrong action can fail to be initiated.

The point of controlled initiation is to limit the outcomes to the first and last possibilities only: to initiate precisely the right action at exactly the right time, and avoid anything else. Any other possibility suggests a lack of control. Simply as a matter of definition, methods of controlled initiation may be called 'control triggers.' The point of a 'trigger' is to initiate some action. The adjective 'control' suggests the initiation of the right action, i.e., management's desired action, at the right time.

Obviously, some triggers are more effective than others. The better the quality of the trigger, the better the control. Faulty triggers may misfire, fire at the wrong time, or motivate some wrong action. Missing triggers fail to initiate action. Reliable triggers fire at exactly the right time, every time, and motivate precisely the right action.

Triggers may be either 'built-in' (systemic) or 'tacked on' (attached) to a process. They may be inexpensive or costly. They may be simple or complex. They may be formal or informal. Yet, for the right actions to consistently occur at the right times, control triggers must be present.

Conclusion

> Therefore, control triggers constitute a necessary control method to initiate actions producing desired outcomes.

Under the rules of deductive logic, a conclusion must be true when the supporting premises are true. If the above premises are accepted as true, control triggers must be accepted as a control method necessary for all processes.

Perhaps as compelling as a formal proof is the simple intuitive appeal of the argument. The need for systematic means to initiate the right actions at the right times as methods of control would seem to be quite logical and instinctively appealing.

Because there are numerous possible control trigger methods, all of which may be differentiated from the others in some particulars, yet all of which bear the same essential characteristics of control triggers, they may be said to compose a category of control methods and a general control concept.

Observations about the basic argument

At least three observations may be made about the above argument:

Observation 1: Control Triggers have not generally been recognized as a control concept.

A search of authoritative auditing, accounting, and management literature, and interviews with recognized authorities in control theory and practice, failed to identify a reference to activity initiation as a control concept--by the name of 'triggers' or by any other reference.

The concept of 'triggers' as a class of control devices or methods is also not addressed in main stream engineering control theory. The engineering concept of 'actuators' seems to be closely related, but not synonymous. '...[M]achine output...[is] initiated by prime movers...[called] actuators....' [Lentz, p. 64.] The discussion of actuators, however, suggests that while they may motivate some machine action, they do not of themselves 'trigger' a specific action at a specific moment.

Consider, for example, a forced air gas furnace system (Eveleigh, pp. 3-4):

> An electronic thermostat, or temperature sensor, is placed in a central location....When the room temperature drops below a preset reference level, a relay is actuated to turn on the furnace fire. When the temperature in the furnace air duct system reaches a reference level, a blower fan is activated by another relay to force the warm air throughout the building. When the room temperature reaches a maximum limit...the furnace is turned off. The blower runs until the residual heat in the system has been dissipated and then also turns off automatically....The *actuators* in our gas heater system are the *furnace fire* and the *blower*. (emphasis added)

Note the difference between the 'actuator' and the 'trigger' in the above example. While the furnace fire (actuator) motivates the initiation of the blower fan by increasing the heat, the 'trigger' to actually turn on the fan is the thermostatic switch which trips the fan relay. Again, while the blower (actuator), by moving the heat through the system, motivates the turning-off of the furnace fire, the 'trigger' to turn off the furnace fire is another thermostatic switch. Without these switches as control triggers, the specific actions critical to the success of the system would fail.

Observation 2: Control Triggers are important to all organizational processes both in traditional bureaucracies and in today's new management environments.

Regardless of the organizational context, actions of many types are taken. All actions are specifically initiated in some way--i.e., they must all somehow be 'triggered' or they would not be undertaken.

The importance of the role of control triggers becomes clearer when we understand that some actions are improperly initiated, or are initiated at the wrong times. In other instances, actions may fail to be initiated due to missing triggers or trigger malfunction. In such instances, the related operating systems are ineffective, inefficient, and/or dysfunctional. In other words, they lack internal control.

Observation 3: Control Triggers are particularly critical to world-class performance.

Much has been written in recent years about time performance becoming the chief distinguishing feature among today's new generation of successful companies. World-class management success is specifically dependent upon the speed and accuracy of actions taken in response to changing conditions. Thus, in an environment of time-based competition, the importance of precise, dependable control triggers is greatly magnified.

For example, control triggers are in fact the central feature of kanban systems. A kanban signal--in whatever form that signal may take--that indicates a need for a resupply of work from the previous work station, triggers a specific action (the resupply of work) at a specific time (the moment of signal). Thus, the signal, or trigger, is in fact the heart of the kanban system. As a second obvious example, the success of statistical process control rests squarely upon triggers which control feedback and adjust the production process.

Illustrations of control triggers

A portion of a typical flow chart of a purchasing function can help illustrate 'control triggers.' Figure 1 shows the purchasing process from the preparation of a purchase requisition in the stores department to the filing of one copy of the purchase requisition with a copy of its related purchase order delivered from the purchasing department. Figure 1 has four columns: the first shows the flow chart itself; the second states the control objective at each trigger point (what action is to be initiated); the third identifies a typical control trigger to fill that need; and the fourth column states the control risk related to trigger failure.

The control objective of the first trigger point on the flow chart is to initiate the preparation of the requisition. An example of a simple trigger at this point is a verbal request by the stores supervisor. In a more sophisticated JIT environment, the trigger signal might be initiated by the MRP computer system which senses a need for the item to be requisitioned. In either case, without a proper trigger, the control risks include failure to order the needed item, ordering the wrong item, and/or ordering the correct item at the wrong time.

The control objective of the second trigger point is to initiate the delivery of the completed requisition to the purchasing department. Again, the control risk here is the failure to order, or perhaps a delay in the order due to delayed delivery of the requisition. In this case, specific times may trigger such delivery, at say, 11 a.m. and 4 p.m. daily. In sophisticated, paperless systems, the delivery of a requisition may be automatic, triggered by a simple keystroke on the computer keyboard.

The control objective at the third trigger point is to initiate filing of the second and third copies of the purchase requisition. The control risk is the loss or misplacement of these documents. A typical control trigger in simple systems such as the one depicted here would be placement of the copies in a file clerk's in-basket. The presence of the documents in the basket triggers the filing action by the clerk. Again, in computerized systems, such filing (on disk) may be triggered immediately and automatically by a keystroke.

The control objective at the fourth trigger point on the flow chart is to match and compare the purchase order completed by the purchasing department with the requisition. The related control risk is a failure to check the order for errors, and thus to risk erroneous orders and subsequent inefficiencies in the purchasing operations. The arrival of the copy of the purchase order could act as the trigger for the stores clerk to make the comparison.

The control objective of the fifth trigger point is to file the paired documents in a timely manner. The control risk here is lost support documentation for the purchase. A simple control trigger to initiate filing might be the stapling of the two documents together.

Again, were this system automated, it would certainly be a simple matter to illustrate systemic computerized control triggers satisfying the same initiating functions in the process. The point of the example is to illustrate the major role that these very simple triggers play in a control process. Without them, an accurate purchase would not occur in a timely manner, and the supporting documentation would be faulty, at best. Such triggers are present in every system, yet they are largely taken for granted. Because their importance to internal control has not been formally recognized, too often, little thought is given to their design and little effort is made to measure their effectiveness.

Implications

Control triggers have significant implications related to the reliability, efficiency, and effectiveness of operations.

Reliability of operations

Reliability may be defined as 'doing the right thing every time.' Any time something is supposed to happen and it does not, the system is said to be unreliable. An operation can be no more reliable than its control triggers. An otherwise perfectly reliable accounts payable system will be totally unreliable without a control mechanism to trigger the writing of checks. And should that control trigger not be completely reliable in initiating the writing of the check to the right party at the right time, then the entire system is only partially reliable.

Efficiency of operations

Efficiency may be defined as 'doing the right thing the right way.' Reliable control triggers help do things the right way. On the other hand, unreliable and untimely triggers cause inefficient operations, because they create a need for more burdensome detective and corrective controls. Unfortunately, by the time detection and correction become necessary, errors have already occurred. The detection and correction of errors are expensive in terms of both time and money, not to mention the cost of the errors, themselves.

Conversely, good triggers may reduce the overall cost of operations by eliminating the need for other, and frequently more expensive, controls. Some feedback controls, such as some inspections and some checks on performance, become unnecessary if systemic triggers are designed and built into a process. For example, suppose that in order to avoid missed billings, a billing department employs a part-time clerk to check the monthly billings before mailing. A perfectly reliable, computer-generated control trigger which motivates the creation of accurate bills for every account requiring them, immediately whenever they are required, would eliminate the need for the clerk. The computerized trigger may be both less expensive and less time-consuming than the manual detection control.

Effectiveness of operations

Effectiveness may be defined as 'hitting the right mark.' A reliable system of control triggers, that assure the right action at the right time, obviously makes an organization more effective in achieving its goals. Conversely, missing or faulty triggers that fail to initiate needed actions or which initiate some wrong action, thwart the organization's progress toward its objectives, because they fail to make good things happen and they may even make bad things happen.

One horrendous example occurred when a commercial air company bought a new aircraft and put it into operation, but because of a missing trigger to record the purchase, the company treasurer was not alerted to the sizable related liability until a bill was received some months later. No money had been budgeted to pay for the plane, and because of a fierce competitive environment, the company did not have the financial reserves to pay the bill. As a result of this internal control failure, along with an accumulation of other similar, although individually less severe, control problems with the financial management system, the company was forced out of business. While the plane operations functioned very well, the financial management system was ineffective. Because of faulty or missing control triggers, the system failed to 'hit the right mark.'

Limitations and unanswered questions

While control triggers are necessary to the successful operation of a system, they are not sufficient for success. Initiating an activity does not necessarily assure its successful completion. Therefore, control triggers constitute only one element of an effective control system.

Acknowledgment of triggers as a control concept which has always existed but has not been formally recognized as such raises a disturbing question: What other control concepts have gone unrecognized? Perhaps an answer lies in the further dismantling of bureaucracies. If traditional control systems have arisen from the control needs of bureaucratic structures, then it is reasonable to expect that new control principles and methods will surface to meet the needs of a new generation of management systems and organizational structures. Nevertheless, it is apparent from the above discussion that control triggers are important even to bureaucracies. One cannot help but wonder why they have not been recognized as such.

Summary and conclusion

In summary, control triggers constitute a category of control methods intended to initiate desired actions in an organization at the right times. As a control concept, triggers have not been recognized in the main stream literature on control theory in accounting, business, or engineering. Control triggers are important to the success of any enterprise, but are especially important to world-class operations. Implications of control triggers affect the reliability, efficiency and effectiveness of an organization's operations. As important as they are, however, the initiation of actions does not assure their successful completion. Other controls are also necessary for a complete control system.

Note

1. In this case, the 'outcome' is the right thing happening at the right time, and nothing else, as expressed in Premises 1 and 2.

References

American Institute of Certified Public Accountants, *Codification of Statements on Auditing Standards*, 1994.

Coopers & Lybrand, *Internal Control--Integrated Framework*, Committee of Sponsoring Organizations of the Treadway Commission, National Committee on Fraudulent Financial Reporting, 1992.

Institute of Internal Auditors, Inc., *Codification of Standards for the Professional Practice of Internal Auditing*, 1993.

Kendrick W. Lentz, Jr., *Design of Automated Machinery*, Van Norstrand Reinhold Company, 1985.

Virgil W. Eveleigh, *Introduction to Control Systems Design*, McGraw Hill Book Company, 1972.

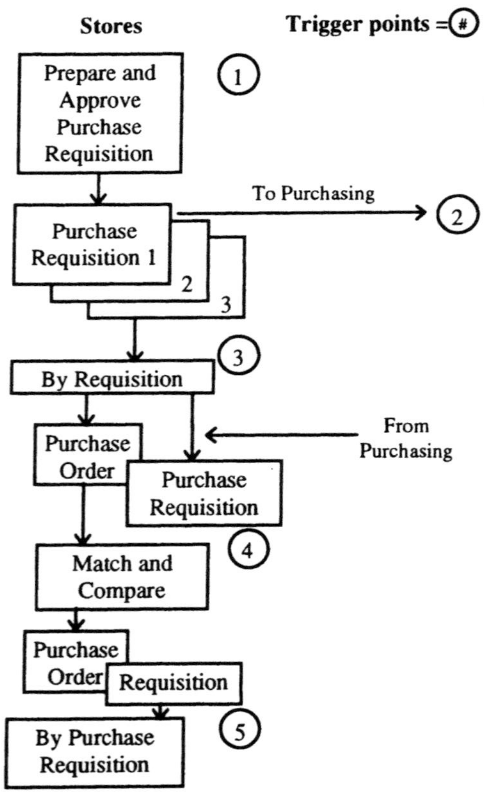

Trigger Objectives	Trigger Methods	Control Risks
Specific initiation of preparation	Requested by Store Supervisor. Computerised signal.	Failure to order, or wrong order. Results in shortage or excess of material
Initiation of delivery	Time Trigger - eg 11am and 4pm. Computer keystrokes.	Failure to convey requisition results in failure to order. Delayed conveyance results in delayed order.
Initiation of filing	Basket input Computer keystrokes.	Failure to file promptly results in increased risk of lost documents
Initiation of matching and comparison	Arrival of P.O.	Failure to match and compare increases risk of mismatch between requisitioned and ordered goods.
Initiation of filing	Completion of matching process and stapling	Failure to file increases risk of lost documents.

Figure 1. Flowchart of Control Triggers

Part Three
CURRENT ISSUES IN FINANCIAL REPORTING

6 The effects of using confirmatory processes on auditors' decision-making: A review and identification of research areas

Magda H. Abou-Seada

Introduction

Motivated in part by research findings in psychology, the auditing literature has recently begun to focus on auditors' use of confirmatory processes in evidence search and evaluation. Confirmatory processes mean that auditors prefer to search for evidence confirming their initial hypotheses (beliefs) and also evaluate this evidence in a way that confirms their hypotheses. If the auditor depends on using confirmatory processes, his efficiency in searching for evidence and his effectiveness in evaluating this evidence will depend on the plausibility of the initial hypotheses (Church, 1990).

Hogarth (1980) suggests that the process of decision-making can be divided into three stages; evidence (information) search, evidence processing, and output. The first stage, evidence search, is of great importance and is considered the basis for audit decision-making because auditing is simply a sequential process in which an auditor gathers and evaluates pieces of evidence relative to audit assertions. However, this stage has not received much attention from audit researchers. In addition to the importance of evidence search to the audit process, many judgements made by the auditor are subjective and amongst these judgements are evidential planning judgements, so it is the purpose of studying the process of evidence search and evaluation to make this process more structured, thus turning toward more objectivity in auditors' decisions.

Evidence which auditors gather could be confirming evidence, disconfirming evidence, or a mix of confirming and disconfirming evidence (Church, 1990). If the auditor formulates a correct (plausible) hypothesis and searches only for confirming evidence, his performance will be more efficient than if he searches for both confirming and disconfirming evidence, and more effective than if he - due to professional skepticism - searches for disconfirming evidence only. Thus, if the auditor formulates a correct hypothesis, the use of confirmatory processes is strongly advised. However, this is not the case if the auditor formulates an implausible hypothesis, and this is why hypotheses formulation is of great importance to using confirmatory processes.

It is important to note that some researchers refer to confirming and disconfirming evidence as positive and negative evidence respectively. This should be differentiated from the definition of positive and negative evidence as evidence indicating favourable or unfavourable characteristics of a client. The latter definition is consistent with that employed by Anderson & Maletta (1994), and Smith & Kida (1991).

Ashton et al. (1988) highlighted the importance of the need for future research on auditors' use of confirmatory processes and its effect on their decision making. As the use of confirmatory processes is an evolving issue in auditing, some problems are associated with the use of these processes. These problems are related mainly to factors affecting auditors' search for evidence, and the process of auditors' hypotheses updating (belief revision). This paper represents a review of the auditing literature on factors affecting auditors' search for evidence. Four exploratory interviews were carried out to determine factors affecting auditors' strategies in searching for evidence. The most important result of these interviews is that auditors do not form hypotheses before searching for evidence. This issue has not been investigated by prior auditing studies. The rest of the paper is organised in three sections. The following section presents the literature review. The second section reports the results of the exploratory interviews. The last section is a discussion and identification of areas for future research.

Literature review

By reviewing the auditing literature, it has been found that factors affecting auditors' search for evidence can be classified into seven factors. These factors are hypotheses formulation, confirmation bias, diagnostic content of evidence, expertise, motivational factors, cognitive factors, and professional skepticism. The first four factors have received much attention than the last three. Thus, the following literature review will focus on the first four factors followed by a brief discussion of the last three factors.

Hypotheses formulation

Research in auditing decision-making has emphasised the importance of hypotheses formulation because of its effect on information search and evaluation (Libby, 1985; Bedard & Biggs, 1991; & Einhorn, 1976). As auditing is an ill-structured task, it requires the auditor to generate and test hypotheses to help structure the task (Einhorn, 1976). Hypotheses help auditors focus information search and evaluation, thus making the auditing process more tractable (Peters, 1990). The importance of hypotheses formulation is also demonstrated by the

American professional standards for analytical procedures that call for auditors to hypothesise likely causes of unexpected patterns in financial statement balances and to develop plans to investigate (SAS 56). Therefore, audit efficiency and effectiveness depend on competency in recognising patterns in financial data and in hypothesising likely causes of these patterns to serve as a guide for further testing (Bedard & Biggs, 1991).

The effect of auditors' hypotheses on their search for evidence can be either due to the source of hypotheses or due to the hypotheses frame. According to the source of hypotheses, hypotheses could be generated or inherited. Generated hypotheses refer to hypotheses formulated by the auditor himself. Inherited hypotheses, on the other hand, refer to hypotheses provided to the auditor who may inherit hypotheses that are:

(a) suggested by client personnel,
(b) suggested by his superiors,
(c) suggested by other member of the audit team, or
(d) obtained from decision aids such as expert systems or decision support systems.

Self-generated hypotheses depends on creativity or what is called the critical imagination and the ability to vary the range over which hypotheses are generated (Popper, 1977). Eltsein et al. (1978) confirm the need for this ability to generate a diverse set of hypotheses. This ability consistently leads to a correct diagnosis being made.

In a study by Kida (1984), he reported that a number of psychological studies concluded that the source of hypotheses has no effect on evidence search. The overwhelming conclusion was that individuals preferentially collected evidence that tended to confirm, rather than disconfirm, their hypotheses. In addition, it appeared not to matter where their hypotheses originated, how likely it was that the hypothesis would prove accurate or inaccurate, or whether substantial incentives for accurate hypotheses testing were offered.

However, Kida's findings do not seem to apply in auditing settings. The source of hypotheses could affect auditor's commitment to his hypotheses, and thus affects his search for evidence. A few studies in the auditing literature addressed this issue. Bedard and Biggs (1991) conducted a laboratory study in which 21 auditors were asked to think aloud while performing an analytical procedures task. One of the results of their study indicated that a number of subjects had difficulty in evaluating hypotheses. One of the auditors who at one point proposed the correct hypothesis, was unable to disconfirm an early hypothesis. This auditor and seven others did not disconfirm their self-generated hypotheses, even though disconfirming cues had already been acquired. This result indicates that auditors are fully committed to generated hypotheses to the extent that they are not able to disconfirm them, even if these generated hypotheses were wrong. However, this result cannot be generalised because there are some limitations on Bedard & Biggs' study. First, their study contains less information than the real audit environment. Second, consultation with other members of the audit team was not available, which is not the real situation. Third, they conducted their study using verbal protocol procedures that may not provide a complete trace of all thoughts during a decision process.

Kaplan et al. (1992) suggest that the use of decision aids in the audit process provides the auditor with hypotheses that could plausibly explain ratio fluctuations discovered in an analytical review. The trend for firms to adopt such decision aids overcomes potential difficulties auditors might have in retrieving hypotheses from memory. However, the problem with decision aids is that the auditors will still have to assess the plausibility of the hypotheses provided by these aids.

According to hypotheses frame, auditors' hypotheses concerning the fairness of a client's financial statements can take one of two broad frames:

(a) That a material error exists in the financial statements, and this is called the error frame.
(b) That no material error exists and any changes in the financial statements are attributed to environmental factors, and this is called the environmental frame.

McMillan & White (1993) investigated the effect of hypotheses frame on auditors' search for evidence. They concluded that auditors who favoured the error frame acted in a confirmatory manner, while auditors who favoured the environmental frame acted in a disconfirmatory manner due to professional skepticism. Their findings seem to be true when investigating the effect of hypotheses frame isolated from other factors. However, this may not be the case if hypotheses frame is combined with other factors especially auditors' commitment to their hypotheses. Kida (1984) stated that if confirmatory strategies are employed by auditors, the final decisions will depend on the initial framing of the hypothesis. He added that to overcome search biases, the decision task could be presented so as to force consideration of alternative hypotheses. For example, a simple listing of data relevant for testing competing hypotheses may be employed, or the hypothesis to be tested could initially be framed to avoid making the most costly error. Kida (1984) conducted a study, in which 77 partners and managers participated, to test whether auditors attend to more confirmatory evidence, disconfirmatory evidence, or equal amounts of both when testing a hypothesis. Auditors were given alternative hypotheses depending on their experimental group. Results indicate that the hypotheses framing had some impact on the type of information auditors searched for, providing limited support for confirmatory strategies. However, this result cannot be generalised because subjects of the study were provided with the hypotheses to be tested, thus excluding the effect of the source of hypothesis.

Confirmation bias

Prior research in psychology showed that people are usually confirmatory biased. Stated differently, people usually seek information which is consistent with their beliefs. However, research in auditing found just the opposite. In a research by Butt & Campbell (1989), the results suggested that unless specifically requested to do so, auditors do not generally seek confirming evidence.

Knechel & Messier (1990) presented the results of an experiment that examined five hypotheses related to the information search and evidence evaluation that takes place as part of an auditor's sequential decision process. One of their hypotheses related to confirmation bias. The results of their study indicated that negative evidence, in general, led to greater judgement revisions than positive evidence, and the most reliable negative evidence led to the greatest revisions. However, they stated two limitations to their study. First, it was assumed that auditors evaluate each piece of evidence sequentially which may not be true. Second, because the evidence provided to the subjects was of a subjective nature, not all auditors may have perceived it to be positive or negative.

Research findings by Ashton & Ashton (1988) and Tubbs et al. (1990) also suggest that auditors will readily revise their beliefs in response to new evidence and that they are particularly sensitive to disconfirming evidence.

Ashton & Ashton's study (1990) supported the previous findings. They conducted four experiments in two auditing and two nonauditing tasks and concluded that the auditors were more responsive to negative (disconfirming) evidence than to positive (confirming) evidence. They also conducted two additional experiments, in the same nonauditing tasks, which show that another group of professional subjects (business executives) are confirmatory biased.

Diagnostic content of evidence

McMillan & White (1993) pointed out that diagnostic content of evidence might be an important factor that affects auditors' search for evidence. They defined diagnostic content of evidence as evidence that allows auditors to distinguish between alternatives. However, the none of the previous auditing studies addressed directly the effect of the diagnostic content on auditors' search for evidence.

Hackenbrack (1992) investigated the role that nondiagnostic evidence, which he considers a priori irrelevant, can have in audit judgement. He conducted a laboratory experiment in which audit seniors assessed how much company's exposure to fraudulent reporting changed during a year, given a mixture of diagnostic and nondiagnostic evidence. He considered three types of nondiagnostic evidence: favourable and unfavourable (collectively called nonneutral) and neutral. In the fraud-risk setting, favourable nondiagnostic evidence describes client features an auditor would find encouraging, such as the client's willingness to prepare schedules requested by the auditor. Unfavourable nondiagnostic evidence describes negative client features, such as the recording of a recurring transaction effectively but not efficiently. Neutral nondiagnostic evidence includes routine, unexceptional items like a generic organisational chart. The findings of Hackenbrack suggest that auditors given a mix of diagnostic and nondiagnostic evidence made decisions that were less extreme (more regressive) than those made using only diagnostic evidence. He stated that the magnitude of the observed effect was in some cases directly related to the capacity of the nondiagnostic evidence to hold the auditor's attention. Although this study does not directly investigate the effect of diagnostic content on auditors' search for evidence, but at least it draws attention to the importance of nondiagnostic evidence.

In a study by Ayers & Kaplan (1993), their main finding was that auditors are prone to use confirming strategies when making information choices in an analytical procedure task. This finding contradicts with findings of other auditing studies which proved that auditors are disconfirming biased. Ayers and Kaplan attributed their finding to that auditors may merely have believed that the confirming cues were more diagnostic. However, this is not the fact, because diagnostic content may be allotted to both confirming and disconfirming evidence.

Trope & Bassok (1982) investigated the effect of confirmatory and diagnosing strategies in social information gathering. Their results showed diagnosticity to be the major determinant of the information-gathering preferences.

Skov & Sherman (1986) also pointed out that research in information-gathering strategies suggests that people can employ one of three strategies of information seeking. The first strategy is a confirmatory one under which evidence is being sought to the extent that it is more likely under the hypothesis being tested than under the alternative. The second strategy is also a confirmatory strategy under which people will tend to gather information that will have the effect of making the hypothesis under test appear to be true. The third strategy is a diagnosing strategy under which people prefer evidence that is most differentially probable under the hypothesis and the alternative. The findings of Skov and Sherman supported the predominance of the diagnosing strategy and a less significant tendency to follow the confirming strategies.

The previous findings support the importance for further research as to the effect of diagnostic content on auditors' search for evidence.

Expertise

The role of professional experience in auditing decisions is significant for a number of reasons. Many judgements made by the auditor are subjective. Also, the cognitive psychology literature suggests that the quality of decisions improve with experience (Colbert, 1989). Auditors with different amounts of professional experience or with specialised experience in various industries may have different audit strategies (Krogstad, Ettenson, & Shanteau, 1984). The use of different audit strategies by professionals with various levels of experience is not, in and of itself, cause for concern since different approaches can lead different auditors to similar conclusions. However, problems may arise if differing judgements lead some auditors to either underaudit (of primary concern because audit risk may rise above acceptable levels) or overaudit (of secondary concern because the audit is presumably effective although it may be inefficient) (Colbert, 1989).

Although expertise is a very important factors, a few studies examined its effect on auditors' search for evidence. Bedard & Biggs (1991) investigated the effect of expertise on hypotheses generation. They conducted a laboratory study in which 21 auditors were asked to think aloud while performing an analytical procedures task. One of their results indicated that hypotheses generation was the stage at which process errors most frequently occurred, and the least experienced auditors had the most difficulty at that stage. Among the problems the least experienced auditors faced in generating the correct hypothesis were addressing only part of a recognised pattern, and fixating on a certain error type. However, just because an auditor has many years of experience does not mean that the auditor will generate correct hypotheses in every situation, or even in a majority of the situations encountered. On the other hand, expertise may also have some unwanted effects. Experienced auditors seldom receive outcome feedback, and so bad habits may go uncorrected (Davis and Solomon, 1989). This may be due to the experienced auditors' overconfidence of themselves, and thus they may fall into the trap of generating and testing an incorrect hypothesis.

In a study by Bouwman (1984), he analysed protocols of five students and three certified public accountants. His findings suggested that experts rely more heavily on rules of thumb and examine more years of data than the novices. Experts were also found to develop a 'feeling' or 'picture' of the firm. Experts did this by summarising groups of related findings, formulating hypotheses, and using a list of typical problems. Novices employed a passive, sequential strategy to examine the information.

In an auditing study, Biggs & Mock (1983) compared the audit scope decisions relating to accounts receivable confirmation of two inexperienced and two experienced audit seniors. Each auditor was required to think aloud while making sample-size decisions. They concluded that experienced auditors tended to approach the problem by relying on stored information from prior experience, which was brought to bear on developing an overall picture of the firm. The less experienced auditors tended to handle the problem in an ad hoc serial processing fashion because it appears that they were unable to organise the wide range of information that was given. They were forced to chunk the information into smaller portions. In an empirical study by Kaplan & Reckers (1989), auditors were given the results of analytical tests and asked to assess the likelihood that observed abnormalities were due to accounting error or irregularity as distinct from environmental change. They were also asked to indicate the information they would seek in response to the test results. The results indicated that for relatively inexperienced auditors, their initial hypothesis will positively correlate with the type of information they will subsequently seek. In other words, inexperienced auditors will follow a hypothesis confirming strategy. For relatively experienced auditors, the results showed that their initial hypothesis will not correlate with the type of information sought but rather they will follow a balanced information search strategy. These findings provide evidence that audit experience acts to moderate the information seeking judgements of auditors and that more experience is associated with more conservative information seeking judgements. These results were reached using a rank measure of information seeking. However, a second measure of information seeking based on unranked questions did not support these results.

Motivational factors, cognitive factors and professional skepticism

The effect of motivational factors, cognitive factors, and professional skepticism on auditors' search for evidence has not received much attention from the auditing researchers. A very few studies pointed out to the importance of concerning these factors while investigating the process of evidence search and evaluation.

Church (1990) pointed out to the importance of both motivational and cognitive factors. He suggests that there are two sets of motivational factors that may have an effect on auditors' strategies in searching for evidence. These two sets are cognitive consistency and seeking the approval of others. Cognitive consistency refers to maintaining a consistent set of cognitions. Inconsistent cognitions will arise from disconfirming evidence, and this is why auditors who are strongly committed to their hypotheses may ignore disconfirming evidence. This may result in serious effects if an initial hypothesis is implausible.

Auditors may also be motivated to seek the approval of others specially their superiors and their clients (Staw & Ross, 1987; & Simon & Francis, 1988). This could lead auditors to follow a confirmatory strategy when searching for evidence even if their hypotheses were implausible. This is what lead Church (1990) to suggest the importance of investigating the effect of this motivational factor on auditors' search for evidence. Motivational factors are expressed in terms of auditors' commitment to their hypotheses which may lead auditors to follow the confirmatory strategy during evidence search and evaluation.

Cognitive factors, on the other hand, are related mainly to hypotheses formulation and evidence explanations (Evans, 1987). Church (1990) suggests that there are three sets of cognitive factors; knowledge structures, recency and frequency, and remembering confirming and disconfirming evidence. The organisation of auditors' knowledge structures in a way that enables more efficient use of memory capacity could result in a more effective auditing performance (Salthouse, 1991). The organisation of knowledge structures is not well understood, however, prior studies showed that experts are able to store knowledge in ways that allow them to perform tasks efficiently (Church, 1990).

Libby (1985) demonstrated the importance of frequency judgements. He found that auditors rely on their judgements of frequency of occurrence of financial statement errors when generating hypotheses in an analytical review task. Church (1990) suggests that the likelihood that an item is accessed from the memory is directly affected by the recency and frequency with which it has been accessed previously. This could affect auditors' abilities to access alternative hypotheses and explanations for evidence.

Auditors' memories have a significant effect on their decision-making (Johnson, 1994). Social research findings (Srull, 1981; & Hastie, 1980) demonstrated that individuals in general can remember disconfirming information better than confirming information. The effect of auditors' memories of confirming and disconfirming evidence on their search strategies is an issue that has not yet been addressed by auditing studies

McMillan & White (1993) investigated the effect of professional skepticism on auditors' search for evidence. The results of their study pointed out that many may consider error-bias behaviour favourable because it indicates a responsiveness to professional skepticism and a demonstration of conservatism. However, they suggested that the actual strength and role of this decision bias needs further investigation because of its potential effects on the efficiency and effectiveness of audit decision making. This is obvious because an approach that is too conservative may lead to the performance of unnecessary audit procedures and thereby reduces audit efficiency. Although professional skepticism represents an important factor that might affect auditors' search for evidence, because it is mainly related with the education and training of auditors, it has not received much attention in auditing studies.

Results of some exploratory interviews

Four exploratory interviews were carried out to determine factors affecting auditors' use of confirmatory processes during evidence search and evaluation. Interviewees were auditors with different level of experience.

One important issue that directed the interviews was whether auditors formulate hypotheses before their search for evidence. Three of the interviewees said that they do not form any hypotheses or beliefs and they search for evidence with an open mind. One of these three said that he might have an idea in mind but it is neither a hypothesis nor a belief, and he does not feel at all committed to this idea. Depending on this, the interviewee said that he can not classify evidence to confirming and disconfirming because he does not have a hypothesis to confirm or disconfirm. Another interviewee of the three who do not form hypotheses said that she might form a direction but not a hypothesis or a belief, and, again, she does not feel at all committed to this direction. The third interviewee said that less experienced auditors, like juniors, could not form any hypotheses or beliefs because all what they have to do is 'filling forms', or in other words, their tasks are more structured and less creative. He suggested that carrying out the interviews with audit partners or managers could be better because it is the partner or the manager who could form a hypothesis or belief.

The fourth interviewee said that he forms a hypotheses but depending on the size of the client. With small-size clients, he does not form any hypotheses, but with large-size clients he forms a hypotheses. This is because with small-size clients the auditor is the one who usually prepares the financial statements and then he reviews them.

Whether auditors form hypotheses or not is an important issue which still needs further investigation. Most of the prior auditing studies on auditors' search for evidence did not investigate this issue. They assumed that all auditors formulate hypotheses, and the studies were carried on this assumption. The importance of hypotheses formulation has been demonstrated by the American standards for analytical procedures that call for auditors to hypothesise likely causes of unexpected patterns in financial statements and to develop plans to investigate (SAS 56). The British standards do not refer to the importance of hypotheses formulation (Chandler, 1994). It is therefore of great importance before studying auditors' use of confirmatory processes in evidence search and evaluation to study the process of hypotheses formulation to find out whether auditors form hypotheses before searching for evidence or not, and if they do not is it important to do so, and whether this will affect auditors' decision-making or not.

It was difficult to carry out the interviews with subjects who do not form hypotheses, but some results were reached. According to the source of hypotheses, the only interviewee who agreed upon forming a hypothesis with large-size clients, said that the main source of his hypothesis would be the firm's policy. This adds another source of inherited hypotheses to the list suggested by previous studies, which includes client personnel, superiors, and decision aids.

Concerning hypotheses frame, all interviewees preferred to work on the assumption that any change in the financial statements is due to a change in the environment i.e. the environmental frame. They said that they do not assume that there is an error in the financial statements unless there is an evidence of this error.

All the interviewees did not show any confirmation bias. They all preferred to follow a balanced strategy searching for all types of evidence specially those who do not form hypotheses because all pieces of evidence are the same to them. One of the interviewees said that if auditors form hypotheses and searches only for confirming evidence - or for disconfirming evidence - then 'they are not doing their jobs good'.

All the interviewees agreed that expertise affects auditors' search for evidence. They said that the more experienced the auditor is, the more efficient he/she can perform any audit task. Their opinions about the difference between experienced and inexperienced auditors in searching strategies were not clear. This is of course due to that they do not form hypotheses when performing the audit process.

When discussing motivational factors and their effect on auditors' search for evidence, all interviewees agreed that auditors' search for evidence will not be affected by either maintaining a consistent set of beliefs or seeking the approval of others, specially that they do not document their 'ideas' or 'directions' in the working papers. Only one interviewee, who forms hypotheses with large-size clients, said that he documents everything even his initial hypotheses, but this would not make him seek cognitive consistency or the approval of others. For the effect of cognitive factors and professional skepticism, they had no clear opinion about these factors and their effect on auditors' search for evidence.

Conclusion

This paper presented a review of the auditing literature concerning auditors' use of confirmatory processes during evidence search and evaluation. Confirmatory processes implies that the auditor formulates a hypothesis and then searches for evidence that confirms this hypothesis. Prior studies on this issue highlighted some factors that could have an effect on auditors' search for evidence. These factors are hypotheses formulation, confirmation bias, diagnostic content of evidence, expertise, motivational factors, cognitive factors, and professional skepticism. Four exploratory interviews were carried out to determine the effect of the previous factors on auditors' search for evidence. However, the results of these interviews are limited and can not be generalised, as they were carried out with auditors who practised auditing in the past but are no more auditing practitioners.

Hypotheses formulation is the most important factor and is considered the basis for auditors' use of confirmatory. If the auditor formulates a plausible hypothesis and follows a confirmatory strategy, i.e. searches only for confirming evidence, the task will be performed in the most efficient and effective manner. Hypotheses formulation consists of two subfactors; source of hypotheses, and hypotheses frame. According to the source of hypotheses, hypotheses could be generated or inherited. Generated hypotheses refers to hypotheses formulated by the auditor himself/herself. Inherited hypotheses, on the other hand, refers to hypotheses given to the auditor from sources like client employees, superiors, or decision aids. Prior studies showed that auditors feel more committed to self-generated hypotheses, and are, therefore, more likely to follow a confirmatory strategy with this type of hypotheses. The exploratory interviews conducted in this study raised another important question which is 'do auditors formulate hypotheses before gathering evidence?'. Three of the interviewees said that they do not form hypotheses and that they search for evidence with an open mind, while one agreed upon forming hypotheses but only for large-size clients. Whether hypotheses formulation is important or not and whether it will improve auditors' decision-making or not, is an issue that still needs further investigation and could be a fruitful area for future research.

Depending on hypotheses frame, auditors could put their hypotheses in one of two frames; the error frame or the environmental frame. Prior studies indicated that because of the conservative nature of auditors, they prefer the error frame. The exploratory interviews showed just the opposite, i.e., that auditors work on the environmental frame. Further research is needed to support one of these conflicting results.

As prior studies indicated, confirmation bias is a factor that directs people in their search for information. However, auditors, unlike others, prefer to follow a disconfirmatory strategy. The exploratory interviews declared that auditors prefer to follow a balanced search strategy. This could be due to that the interviewees did not form hypotheses before their search for evidence. It is therefore important before investigating the effect of confirmation bias on auditors' searching strategies to find out whether auditors form hypotheses or not.

Diagnostic content of evidence is an important factor, specially that some studies indicated that a diagnosing strategy is highly preferable compared with a confirmatory or a disconfirmatory strategy. However, this factor still needs further empirical research. Expertise is one factor that is now receiving much attention by auditing researchers. Results of almost all studies agree that experienced auditors can search for evidence more efficiently without waste of resources. The exploratory interviews support this result.

Motivational factors, cognitive factors, and professional skepticism are the factors that received the least attention by auditing researchers. The exploratory interviews showed that the two sets of motivational factors, cognitive consistency and seeking the approval of others, have no effect on auditors' search for evidence. The opinions of the interviewees concerning cognitive factors and professional skepticism were not clear. This reveals that much research is still needed concerning the effect of these factors on auditors' search for evidence.

In addition to the previous discussion, it is important to note that there is still a need for studies that investigate the joint effect of the previous factors on auditors' search for evidence. Almost all previous studies examined the effect of only one of the stated factors regardless of other factors. Some factors could have different effects when combined with other factors like professional skepticism and hypotheses frame, and confirmation bias and source of hypotheses.

References

American Institute of Certified Public Accountants (1988). *Statement on Auditing Standards No. 56: Analytical Procedures*, New york, AICPA.

Anderson, B.H. & Maletta, M. (1994). 'Auditor attendance to negative and positive information: the effect of experience-related differences', *Behavioral Research in Accounting*, Vol. 6.

Ashton, A.H. & Ashton, R.H. (1988). 'Sequential belief revision in auditing', *The Accounting Review*, Vol. LXIII, No. 4, October, pp. 623-641.

Ashton, R.H., Kleinmuntz, D.N., Sullivan, J.B. & Tomassini, L.A. (1988). 'Audit decision making' In A.R. Abdel-khalik & I. Solomon (eds), *Research Opportunities in Auditing: The Second Decade*, pp. 95-132. American Accounting Association, Auditing Section.

Ashton, R.H. & Ashton, A.H. (1990). 'Evidence-responsiveness in professional judgment: effects of positive versus negative evidence and presentation mode', *Organizational Behavior and Human Decision Processes*, 46, pp.1-19.

Ayers, S. & Kaplan, S.E. (1993). ' An examination of the effect of hypothesis framing on auditors' information choices in an analytical procedure task', *ABACUS*, Vol. 29, No. 2, pp. 113-129.

Bedard, J.C. & Biggs, S. F. (1991). 'Pattern recognition, hypotheses generation, and auditor performance in an analytical task', *The Accounting Review*, Vol. 66, No. 3, July, pp. 622-642.

Biggs, S. & Mock, T. (1983). 'An investigation of auditor decision processes in the evaluation of internal controls and audit scope decisions', *Journal of Accounting Research*, Spring, pp. 234-255.

Bouwman, M.J. (1984). 'Expert vs novice decision making in accounting: a summary', *Accounting, Organizations and Society*, pp. 325-327.

Butt, J.L. & Campbell, T.L. (1989). 'The effects of information order and hypothesis-testing strategies on auditors' judgments', *Accounting, Organizations and Society*, Vol. 14, No. 5/6, pp. 471-479.

Chandler, R.A. (ed). (1994). *Auditing and Reporting 1994/95*, The Institute of Chartered Accountants in England and Wales.

Church, B.K. (1990). 'Auditors' use of confirmatory processes', *Journal of Accounting Literature*, Vol. 9, pp. 81-112.

Colbert, J.L. (1989). 'The effects of experience on auditors' judgments', *Journal of Accounting Literature,* Vol. 8, pp. 137-149.

Davis, J.S. & Solomon, I. (1989). 'Experience, expertise, and expert-performance research in public accounting', *Journal of Accounting Literature*, Vol. 8, pp. 150-164.

Einhorn, H. (1976). 'A synthesis: accounting and behavioral research', *Journal of Accounting Research,* Supplement, pp. 196-206.

Elstein, A.S., Shulman, L.S. & Sprafka, S.A. (1978). *Medical Problem Solving: An Analysis of Clinical Reasoning,* Harvard University Press.

Evans, J. (1987). 'Beliefs and expectations as causes of judgmental bias', in G. Wright & P. Ayton (eds), *Judgmental Forecasting*, pp. 31-47, New York, John Wiley and Sons.

Hackenbrack, K. (1992). 'Implications of seemingly irrelevant evidence in audit judgments', *Journal of Accounting Research,* Vol. 30, No. 1, Spring, pp. 126-136.

Hastie, R. (1980). 'Memory for behavioral information that confirms or contradicts a personality impression' In R. Hastie, T. Ostrom, E. Ebbesen, R. Wyer, D. Hamilton, & D. Carlston (eds), *Person Memory: The Cognitive Basis of Social Perception*, pp. 155-177, Hillsdale, NJ, Lawrence Erlbaum Publishers.

Hogarth, R.M. (1980). *Judgment and Choice*, New York, John Wiley and Sons.

Johnson, E.N. (1994). 'Auditor memory for audit evidence: effects of group assistance, time delay, and memory task', *Auditing: A Journal of Practice and Theory*, Vol. 13, No. 1, Spring, pp. 36-56.

Kaplan, S.E., Moeckel, C. & Williams, J.D. (1992). 'Auditors' hypothesis plausibility assessments in an analytical review setting', *Auditing: A Journal of Practice and Theory*, Vol. 11, No. 2, Fall, pp. 50-65.

Kaplan, S.E. & Reckers, P.M.J. (1989). 'An examination of information search during initial audit planning', *Accounting, Organizations and Society*, Vol. 14, No. 5/6, pp. 539-550.

Kida, T. (1984). 'The impact of hypothesis-testing strategies on auditors' use of judgment data', *Journal of Accounting Research*, Vol. 22, No. 1, Spring, pp. 332-340.

Knechel, W.R. & Messier, W.F., Jr. (1990). 'Sequential auditor decision making: information search and evidence evaluation', *Contemporary Accounting Research*, Vol. 6, No. 2-I, pp. 386-406.

Krogstad, J.L., Ettenson, R.T. & Shanteau, J. (1984). 'Context and experience in auditors' materiality judgments', *Auditing: A Journal of Practice and Theory*, Fall, pp. 54-73.

McMillan, J.J. & White, R.A. (1993). 'Auditors' belief revisions and evidence search: the effect of hypothesis frame, confirmation bias, and professional skepticism', *The Accounting Review*, Vol. 66, No. 3, July, pp. 443-465.

Peters, J.M. (1990). 'A cognitive computational model of risk hypothesis generation', *Journal of Accounting Research,* Vol. 28, Supplement, pp. 83-103.

Popper, K.R. (1977). 'On hypotheses' In P.N. Johnson-Laird & P.C. Wason (eds), *Thinking: Readings in Cognitive Science*, pp. 264-273, Cambridge, England, Cambridge University Press.

Salthouse, T. (1991). 'Expertise as the circumvention of human processing limitations' In A. Ericsson & J. Smith (eds), *Toward a General Theory of Expertise*, pp. 286-300, Cambridge, England, Cambridge University Press.

Simon, D. & Francis, J. (1988). 'The effects of auditor change on audit fees: tests of price cutting and price recovery', *The Accounting Review*, April, pp. 255-269.

Skov, R.B. & Sherman, S.J. (1986). 'Information-gathering processes: diagnosticity, hypothesis-confirmatory strategies, and perceived hypothesis confirmation', *Journal of Experimental Social Psychology*, Vol. 22, No. 2, March, pp. 93-121.

Smith, J. & Kida, T. (1991). 'Heuristic and biases: expertise and task realism in auditing', *Psychological Bulletin*, May, pp. 472-489.

Srull, T. (1981). 'Person memory: some test of associative storage and retrieval models', *Journal of Experimental Psychology: Human Learning and Memory,* November, pp. 440-463.

Staw, B. & Ross, J. (1987). 'Behavior in escalation situations: antecedents, prototypes, and solutions' In L. Cummings & B. Staw (eds), *Research in Organizational Behavior,* pp. 39-78, Greenwich, Conn., JAI Press.

Trope, Y. & Bassok, M. (1982). 'Confirmatory and diagnosing strategies in social information gathering', *Journal of Personality and Social Psychology*, Vol. 43, No. 1, pp. 22-34.

Tubbs, R.M., Messier, W.F., Jr. & Knechel, W.R. (1990). 'Recency effects in the auditor's belief-revision process', *The Accounting Review*, Vol. 65, No. 2, April, pp. 452-460.

7 Early stages of grounded theory in related party disclosures research

Juliet Cottingham

Introduction

Related party transactions are a common and legitimate form of business. However, without appropriate disclosure, their existence can cause published financial accounts to be innocently misleading. SSAP 2 'The Disclosure of Accounting Policies' (1971, p1) states that:

> It is fundamental to the understanding and interpretation of financial accounts that those who use them should be aware of the main assumptions on which they are based.

It is widely acknowledged, (for example Mason, 1979), that users of accounts hold the assumption that all transactions are carried out between independent parties who are free to negotiate terms on an arm's length basis. However, for transactions between related parties this assumption does not hold true as the requisite conditions of free market competition do not exist.

A lack of disclosure concerning related party information can also open opportunities for fraudulent activity. There have been a number of scandals revealed, especially during the last three decades, which have resulted from massive frauds perpetrated through the abuse of related party relationships. Perhaps the most notorious recent scandal was that of Robert Maxwell's empire, in 1992, where approximately £933 million was siphoned off from public companies under Maxwell's control into his own personal empire. However, this has not been the last instance of related party abuse. Even at this time, the Serious Fraud Office is investigating a director and stockbroker of a UK motorbike company who have, allegedly, been using related party relationships in order to defraud the company.

The present research was inspired by the Maxwell scandal, which once again brought the abuse of related party relationships to public attention. The aim of the research is to find possible disclosure requirements which might hinder the opportunities for fraud and stop the misleading nature of financial accounts. The nature of the research is, therefore, prescriptive.

The nature of a research project, to a certain extent dictates, or at least helps determine the research methodology which should be adopted. It is essential that the methodology chosen is appropriate for the aims of the research or the results will not correspond to, or answer the needs of the original research question.

This research into related party disclosures is prescriptive, i.e. aims to suggest what *should* be disclosed, rather than what *is* disclosed, the latter being a positive research approach.

There are many complex links and relationships within the area of related parties and in-depth studies of related parties, their transactions and the problems that arise need to be conducted in order to find the best solutions and disclosure requirements. This requires a qualitative approach. Grounded Theory was adopted as the methodology for this research.

The objective of this paper is to explain how the early stages of Grounded Theory have been applied to the related party investigation. In particular, the method of open coding is exemplified and the identification of properties and their dimensions of those properties are discussed.

Grounded theory

Grounded theory was initially developed by two sociologists, Anselm Strauss and Barney Glaser, whilst conducting research into the awareness of death in dying patients (1965). They published their initial thoughts on the new methodology in 'The Discovery of Grounded Theory' in 1967. This has since become a central text for researchers using grounded theory. However, both authors have added to this original work with joint and individual publications (Glaser 1978, Strauss 1987, Strauss and Corbin 1990). Perhaps the most notable of these is the collaboration of Strauss with Juliet Corbin in 1990: 'Basics of Qualitative Research: Grounded Theory Procedures and Techniques' which provides a more practical approach on how to conduct grounded theory research, whereas earlier publications were more conceptual in their address. The use of Grounded Theory has grown and developed. Although originally used by sociologists, its application has in no way been limited to this field. 'Grounded theory can be used successfully by persons of many disciplines' (Strauss and Corbin, 1990, p26).

A number of research projects using a grounded theory have been completed including Trimble et al, 1972; Riley and Sermsri, 1974; Conrad, 1978; Turner, 1981 and 1983, Segev 1988, Compton, White and DeWine, 1991; and

Gummesson, 1991. However, its application in accounting has been limited. Perhaps the most successful application in accounting research to date was by Gibbins, Richardson and Waterhouse (1990).

However, grounded theory does have a useful role to play in accounting research. Grounded theory was chosen above other qualitative methodologies for two main reasons. Firstly, the central aim of the grounded theory methodology is the construction of a theory. This ensures that the research is not conducted within a constrictive and / or ill-fitting preconceived theory. The theory developed by a grounded methodology is derived solely from the data under study: the theory should be allowed to evolve and emerge from the data. Strauss and Corbin (1990, p23) defined a grounded theory as one that is:

> discovered, developed, and provisionally verified through systematic data collection and analysis of data pertaining to that phenomenon. Therefore, data collection, analysis, and theory stand in reciprocal relationship with each other. One does not begin with a theory, then prove it. Rather, one begins with an area of study and what is relevant to that area is allowed to emerge.

Theory construction seemed appropriate for the present research. Preliminary investigations into existing theories (including Watts and Zimmerman 1979, Cooper and Sherer 1984, and Nobes 1991), although providing useful and interesting insights into limited sections, revealed none which were totally suitable or which fully encompassed the area under study. Rather than having the research restrained and constricted by an ill-fitting preconceived theory, it was more appropriate to use grounded theory and build a new theory, tailor made to the individual circumstances of the research topic.

Secondly, grounded theory is a phenomenological approach which is concerned with the actions and interactions which are performed to manage or correct a central idea or happening - the phenomenon (Strauss and Corbin, 1990). This is particularly appropriate for examining regulation and policy setting. The development of regulation and policies *is* a responsive action to a phenomenon (Cottingham, 1995). Within the related party research the phenomena are the misleading property of accounts and the possibilities for fraud, about which the research aims to discover 'corrective' actions and interactions. The key elements in grounded theory, as identified by this research, are interpretation, creativity, discovery, grounding and construction.

Interpretation is an essential part of grounded theory (Pidgeon et al., 1991). It is the researcher's ability to interpret the data that enables a theory to develop. Without interpretation, the resulting finished product would be a descriptive report with little or no analysis. The philosophy behind such a descriptive approach would be the underlying aim to present a faithful representation to the audience: a representation which would be free from the researcher's bias and clear of misinterpretation.

In effect, the researcher acts as a conductor of information which enables the information to flow, in its original form, to the audience, thus enabling the audience to decipher and translate the information for themselves. Content analysis is an example of this type of descriptive research. Stern (1994), indeed, criticises many researchers for calling themselves grounded theorists when they are actually using content analysis which, as normally undertaken today 'falls out of the arena of interpretative research' (p214).

The aim for a grounded theory researcher is to construct theory and present theory to the audience, not to regurgitate the original data. The role of the researcher is not that of merely being a gateway for information to flow through, but to analyse the data at a conceptual and abstract level. This cannot be done without the data being interpreted. The researcher specifically aims to, and takes full responsibility, for translating the data and presenting it to the audience in its interpreted form.

Creativity is essential to a researcher's abilities (Stern, 1994; Strauss and Corbin, 1990). When interpreting information, it is necessary for the researcher to be able analyse the information and gain insight from the information which is not always obvious or apparent at first glance. Without creativity, the researcher will not be able to see past assumed knowledge or will not be able to break from traditional viewpoints to find new interpretations. Creativity 'force(s) the researcher to break through assumptions and to create new order out of the old' (Strauss and Corbin, 1990, p27). To aid creativity, researchers should be advised to try and enhance their theoretical sensitivity.

Theoretical sensitivity is a researcher's ability to see into and through the data presented and see past the beliefs and assumptions with which he or she has been brought up. Often people are biased by views that they subconsciously hold, or by interpretations which they expect to find in the data. Any views that are held prior to the research may restrict the researcher's perceptions of the phenomenon that is being studied. This could lead to important links and relationships not being discovered, or inaccurate deductions being made about the data. 'Specific knowledge, alas, is not only necessary but at times constitutes mental baggage that impedes this kind of intellectual creativity' (Strauss and Corbin, 1990, p29).

However, by enhancing one's theoretical sensitivity, one can start to overcome these biases, aiding creativity. This creativity is essential if the researcher is going to make discoveries.

Discovery is the act of finding something new. Discoveries may be concerned with previously undetected links and relationships that exist within the data, or fresh or new understanding of the meanings of events and patterns in the data. Discovery is concerned with a novel perception of what is contained within the data. Without discovery, a theory cannot emerge from the data, and as such, it is a fundamental part of grounded theory (Hutchinson, 1986). However, although these discoveries cannot be made without creativity, they must be verified in the data to ensure that they are true: grounding them in reality.

Grounding is the embedding of thoughts, ideas and hypothesis in the data. It is the grounding that ensures that the research is rigorous and the resulting theory is solid and valid (Strauss and Corbin, 1990). Creativity is the deductive process of the researcher. However, to corroborate these deductive thoughts and suggestions, the researcher must revert to inductive processes and test the postulates in the data. The data will either support or refute the postulates. Some postulates may need modification. However, once supported by the data, they can be made into hypothesis, investigated more fully and eventually incorporated into the final theory. The grounding of the discoveries ensures that the interpretations are consistent with the phenomenon being studied. It also distinguishes grounded theory from other theories which rely on the 'a priori' deductions and conditions: mostly associated with positivistic theories.

Construction is an extremely important part of grounded theory. Grounded theory is a methodology that has the development of theory as its main aim, and as such, construction of that theory is a central theme that is ever present during grounded theory research. The theory is constructed from the full integration of the various concepts, themes and discoveries and interlinking relationships which exist within the data. All the ideas and tested hypotheses should be interwoven into a close knit description and explanation of the phenomenon. It is this construction of theory, and interpretation of data, that sets grounded theory apart from other interpretative research methodologies (Strauss and Corbin, 1994). It is also this construction of a theory which makes grounded theory an interesting challenge for researchers.

Grounded theory procedures

Grounded theory consists of various levels of coding: open, axial and selective coding, which seeks to sort and categorise data.

Open Coding

Open coding, or substantive coding (Strauss, 1987; Lester and Hadden, 1980) is the initial stage of a grounded theory, although it is a process which is continued through out the research as new data is introduced. Open coding is the process of breaking down and labelling units of information, making the information easily recognisable and easier to manage. It also involves the examination and comparison of information and the grouping of similar ideas or *concepts* into categories.

Axial coding

Axial coding is the rearrangement of the data into different patterns in order to discover relationships between different concepts and categories. The prime model for doing this is the paradigm model (Strauss and Corbin, 1990) which links the data to emphasise causal conditions, the phenomenon, actions and interactions, and the consequences of the actions and interactions.

Selective coding

Selective coding is where the final theory is constructed, where the 'story is told' both descriptively and conceptually. During the process of selective coding all the concepts and categories are systematically linked to the core category and all the relationships validated.

Although each coding stage is a separate and distinct process in theory, in reality it is difficult to isolate the stages and they are often carried out alongside each other. This paper is primarily concerned with the early stages of grounded theory: open coding, and how it has been applied to research into related party regulations.

Process and application of open coding

Process of open coding

At the heart of any grounded theory lies the data from which the theory was created. The theory must be grounded in the data, and the importance of the data is, therefore, implicit. Incomplete, flimsy data will lead to an incomplete, flimsy theory. Within a grounded theory, the sources of data can be numerous and varied, ranging from literature to archival manuscripts, newspaper articles to interviews and observation (Strauss and Corbin, 1990; Eisenhardt, 1989; Hutchinson, 1986).

Triangulation of data sources: 'the use of multiple methods in the study of the same object' (Denzin, 1970, p301) can offer a variety of insights of a phenomenon and help the emergence of the theory. Eisenhardt (1989) argues that 'the triangulation made possible by multiple data collection methods provides stronger substantiation of constructs and hypotheses' (p538). Also, the use of multiple sources of data can reduce the level of misinterpretation or bias that may be present in any one given data source (Hutchinson, 1986). Once the data has been collected, it must be analysed and categorised - open coding. As with any form of construction, a good solid base and foundation is required. Open coding can be likened to the preparation of the bricks with which the resultant theory will be built. It is, therefore, an essential and important part of a grounded theory method.

The first stage of a grounded theory is to study the data, whatever its source. Several elements should become apparent to the attentive researcher who will need to identify, separate and code the raw data. This is accomplished by classifying the different elements into distinct concepts which can be identified and which can be developed in terms of their properties and dimensions. Similar, individual concepts should then be grouped together into categories and subcategories. These categories and subcategories should also be labelled and should be more abstract than the concepts of which they comprise.

The labels by which the concepts and categories are known, are entirely subjective and the choice of the researcher. This can be one example of a researcher's creativity! The label which is attached to each concept or category should reflect the nature and the content of the concept or category. As the concepts are grouped into more abstract categories, so too should the labels become more conceptual. Labels can come from a variety of sources: technical literature, interviewees and informants - 'in vivo' codes (Glaser, 1978, p70; and Strauss, 1987, p33) - or from the researcher's own imagination and vocabulary.

Code labels which may be meaningless to readers of the research due to a technical content or unfamiliar 'jargon' should be explained so that the reader will understand what is contained within the label, without any misinterpretations. Where common terms are used the researcher should make explicit the specific meaning meant by himself/herself so that a reader who has a prior association with the term is not biased by this previous knowledge.

The observation and cataloguing of raw data into concepts and categories is one part of open coding. The other part of open coding is concerned with the identification of the attributes or characteristics pertaining to a concept or a category - the properties; and finding their dimensions - where the properties are positioned along a continuum (Strauss and Corbin, 1990). Each observed example of the concepts should be recorded with details of the properties and where the specific example is situated on the dimension range. This is best explained with an illustration. It should be made clearer in the next section - the application of open coding.

Application of open coding

The open coding process within the research into the regulation of related party disclosures established a number of codes which were grouped into concepts, categories and subcategories, and their properties and dimensions determined. The sources of data for these codes was extremely varied and included both primary and secondary data.

Data sources The primary sources consisted of manuscripts, participant observation, non participant observation and interviews.

The manuscripts included publications of regulations; letters commenting on regulation, specifically ED 46 (ASC, 1989); archival manuscripts from the ASC archive held at John Rylands Library, Manchester; and newspapers. The participant observation consisted of membership of an ASB working party and the non participant observation included attendance at court hearings.

One formal interview has been completed. This was a forty minute interview with a leading member of the ASC, the nature of which was confirmatory rather than exploratory - ideas that had developed and grown as a result of previous research and coding were queried and either confirmed or denied: the inductive verification of researcher postulates. Another nine interviews have been arranged with partners of auditing companies.

Coding The coding was done on a systematic basis. Initially a line by line approach to open coding was applied to the data. However, this was found to be time consuming, messy and ineffective as the first step of coding. Each type of data consisted of so many different aspects of the research that on a practical level, it was difficult to write all the codes necessary next to the text, even where extra large margins were designed on specifically written transcripts.

A new style of coding was adopted whereby paragraphs were coded for general themes, for example Regulation, Harmonisation and Auditing. These paragraphs were then transferred onto computer files under the theme titles. Paragraphs with a number of theme titles were copied in their entirety into as many 'theme files' as necessary and it was at this stage that the line by line open coding was attempted. This method had the advantage of fewer codes per file and an easier coding system due to the theme files containing boundaried ideas. Paragraphs which were included in more than one theme file were only coded for the theme in question. Each paragraph was registered with a note of its source.

Through out the open coding stage, perpetual questioning and constant comparisons were continued to ensure theoretical sensitivity.

Codes	
Workability Support for regulation Scope	We are concerned that no undue burdens should be placed upon companies and think that the application of the proposed standard to small companies could impose a reporting burden which is not justified.
Scope / Implementation Related party definitions Implementation Related party transactions definitions Workability Legal regulation Support of regulation	We think that small companies are likely to have just as many related parties as large one, the likely lower number of shareholders holding 10% of the voting rights. However, the need to identify all transactions with those parties and review them for abnormality would impose significance compliance burdens on small companies. There is also a rather lesser degree of public interest in small companies and we think that, in the particular context of the exposure draft, the public interest is adequately covered by the statutory disclosure requirements without the imposition of additional requirements by an accounting standard.

Figure 1 - Example of line by line coding of data

Similar items were included under the same label whereas new events, perceptions or phenomena were given different codes. Some of the initial codes were modified or deleted later on in the research. Some were joined together as one concept and others were grouped together into categories.

A rigorous examination of ED 46 'Related Party Transactions' (ASC, 1989) and IAS 24 'Related Party Disclosures' (IASC, 1984) proved wealthy sources of a variety of information which needed to be coded. Among the codes developed from the exposure draft and international standard were UK Regulation, International Regulation, Related Parties, Related Party Transactions, Definitions, Disclosure, Aggregation, Materiality, Scope and Authority. These were mostly headings or terms that were included in the statements, although the latter came from the researcher. Other regulations yielded the new codes of Accounting Regulation, Market Regulation, Legal Regulation and Other Regulation.

Analysis of the letters in response to ED 46 lead to the creation of other new codes, including International Harmonisation, Support of Regulation and Workability. The reviews of ED 46 also added information and properties to the codes which had been already adopted and helped the positioning of ED 46's properties on their dimension ranges. The archival documents contained in the ASC archive added information on both the ASC and the development of ED 46, but were mostly labelled according to existing codes.

The codes concerned with fraud were stimulated mostly from newspaper articles and secondary data sources, for example Mason 1979. They included Fraud, Aims of Fraud, Level of Disclosure, Related Party, Related Party Transaction Terms, Related Party Transaction Effects, Fraud Perpetrator, Level of Domination and Inaccurate Disclosure. These codes were used mostly for labelling the properties of the various examples of fraud cases. The area where data is lacking, at present, is Misleading Accounts. Although the misleading nature of accounts due to undisclosed related party information is acknowledged by several sources including Mason, 1979 and Brown, 1980; there are few published cases of accounts which have been innocently misleading and where actual examples of published financial accounts are misleading, it is difficult to establish this fact. The interviews with the auditing company partners are hoped to remedy this gap. Other codes were yielded from the secondary sources of data. Away from the coding of data, the various codes were organised into a hierarchy of abstraction of categories, subcategories and concepts.

Fraud, Misleading Accounts, Accounting Regulation, Stock Market Regulation, Legal Regulation, Tax Regulation, Other Regulation and Comments on ED 46 were maintained as concepts. The first two were linked to the Core Category of Related Parties by the Problems of Non Disclosure category. The various regulation concepts were grouped under the subcategories of UK Regulation and International Regulation, which both came under the heading of Existing Related Party Regulation. This is opposed to the category of Recommended Related Party Regulation which is a category to be developed with the construction of the theory.

Properties were assigned to each of the concepts and categories. The properties are the characteristics or attributes of each of the codes. The properties should have a dimension continuum or range upon which the property of individual examples of the concepts or category can be situated. For example, the various types of regulation had similar properties, which included scope, definitions, level of disclosure, level of international harmonisation, level of aggregation, level of standardisation (Nobes, 1991), authority and workability. These properties were then broken down into their dimensions: dimensionalization (Strauss and Corbin, 1990), as seen in figure 2.

Scope	Limited scope	Complete scope
Definitions	Vague	Precise
	Narrow	Broad
Disclosure levels	Low	High
Level of international harmonisation	Low	High
Level of aggregation	Low	High
Levels of standardisation (Nobes)	Low	High
Authority	Weak	Strong
Workability	Low	High

Figure 2 - Regulation Properties and Dimensions

The various examples of related party regulations were re-examined and their properties registered on the continuums. The placing of the dimensions on the scales for ED 46 and FRED 8 were determined by the comments from the reviewers. The markings were placed relative to each other: because the scales are not quantitative, the importance lies with the relativity, not the absolute measures. Other regulations, where there were no commentators views, were placed on the dimension scales comparable to ED 46 and FRED 8 based on their content.

Scope refers to the remit or the targeted audience of the regulation. The Stock Exchange has a limited scope, only requiring the listed companies to fulfil its requirements, whereas an accounting standard would apply to the majority of limited companies, barring any exemptions which would be incorporated in the standard.

The property of *Definitions* can be broken down into discrete definitions e.g. Definitions of Related Parties, Definitions of Control, Definitions of Significant Influence and Definitions of Related Party Transactions. Each would have the two dimension ranges of vague/precise and narrow/broad. The first dimension range is a measure of the ambiguity contained within the definition, the latter a measure of whether the range contained within the definition is all encompassing or only applies to selective items. For example for the definitions of related parties, ED 46, bar a limited number of exceptions was designed to regulate the disclosures of all related parties, whereas the stock exchange regulations or company law are only concerned with limited types of related party.

Disclosure Levels or (Levels of Disclosure) is self explanatory, as is *Level of Aggregation.* The former refers to the amount of disclosure which is required by each form of regulation and the latter refers to the amount of aggregation of information is allowed within the regulations. *Level of Harmonisation* again needs little explanation except to mention that this property is only being applied to accounting standards, rather than other forms of regulation, and that IAS 24 is being used as the control against which the other standards are being compared. *Level of Standardisation* was a property that emerged from earlier investigations into prior theories. Only applied to UK accounting standards, it refers to the level of choice or freedom for companies that is embedded in the exposure drafts and resulting standards. *Authority* refers to the amount of 'clout' that is behind each regulation. Two extreme examples are exposure drafts which are not enforceable at all as they are not yet regulation which has to be complied with; and company law which has the backing of the whole UK legal system behind it.

Workability refers to the practical issue of complying with regulation. This is an important property of exposure drafts, and should be borne in mind with the ultimate solutions and recommendations which are made within the final research theory. This can be broken into two areas, which sometimes overlap: accounting problems i.e. problems for accountants within a company drawing up final published accounts and auditing problems i.e. problems for auditors who may have similar problems to the accountants and also additional problems due to lack of access of knowledge and/or co-operation.

This process of finding the properties and identifying their dimension ranges was repeated for the other concepts and categories. As of yet, the Misleading Account's properties and dimensions have not been investigated but the interviews should soon rectify that discrepancy. However, Fraud properties have been classified as Aims of Fraud, Level of Disclosure, Related Party, Related Party Transaction Terms, Related Party Transaction Effects, Fraud Perpetrator, Level of Domination and Accuracy of Disclosure.

Conclusions

Grounded theory offers a new and exciting methodology for accounting researchers. Although more widely used in other research areas, it has the potential to become a major part of accounting research. It is especially useful for those investigation regulation or policy setting. This paper, although giving a brief outline to grounded theory as a whole, has mostly concentrated on the open coding stage, yet already, the complexity and the power of the methodology are becoming clear. The dissection and the investigation of the data at its most basic has forced prior perceptions to be re-evaluated, and revealed elements which could so easily have been missed or ignored as irrelevant.

However, although grounded theory methodology has proved an inspiration and a challenge, it has also proved to be a time consuming and laborious process. Also, the easy 'step by step' approach suggested by Strauss and Corbin has been heavily criticised by Barney Glaser the original co-founder of Grounded Theory. Glaser (1992) suggests that the procedures recommended by Strauss and Corbin forces the development of theory, rather than letting it emerge from the data. In personal correspondence to Anselm Strauss, he suggests the book 'distorts and misconceives grounded theory'. Further research will have to be undertaken to investigate these claims.

The use of grounded theory, to date, however, has proved a worthwhile exercise. A much clearer and broader understanding of the issues and problems surrounding related parties and the possible regulation of related party disclosures has evolved from the research undertaken. The next stage of the research is already planned and hopes are high for a successful completion of the research. It is to be hoped that with the completion of the research will come a fully developed, rigorous theory and an encouragement for other accounting researchers to attempt a grounded theory methodology.

References

Accounting Standards Board (1994), *Financial Reporting Exposure Draft 8: Related Party Disclosures*, March.

Accounting Standards Committee, Archive at John Rylands Library, Manchester.

Accounting Standards Committee (1989), *Exposure Draft 46: Related Party Transactions*, April.

Accounting Standards Committee (1990), *Comments received on ED 46*.

Brown, H. R. (1980), *Background Paper on Related Party Transactions*, Institute of Chartered Accountants of England and Wales.

Compton, C. D., White, K. and DeWine, S. (1991) 'Techno-sense: Making Sense of Computer-Mediated Communication Systems', *The Journal of Business Communication* 28:1 Winter pp23-43.

Conrad, C. F. (1978) 'A Grounded Theory of Academic Change', *Sociology of Education,* 51, pp101-112.

Cooper, D. J. and Sherer, M. J. (1984) 'The Value of Corporate Accounting Reports: Arguments for a Political Economy of Accounting', *Accounting Organisations and Society*, v.9, No 3/4, pp207-232.

Cottingham, J. (1995) *Grounded Theory: a working example*, BAA Conference paper (unpublished).

Denzin, N. K. (1970) *The Research Act: A Theoretical Introduction to Sociological Methods*, Chicago: Aldine.

Eisenhardt, K. M. (1989) 'Building Theories from Case Study Research', *Academy of Management Review*, v.14, No. 4, pp532-550.

Gibbins, M., Richardson, A. and Waterhouse, J. (1990) 'The Management of Corporate Financial Disclosure: Opportunism, Ritualism, Policies and Processes', *Journal of Accounting Research*, Vol. 28, No 1, Spring pp121-143.

Glaser, B. (1978) *Theoretical Sensitivity*, Mill Valley, CA: Sociology Press.

Glaser, B. (1992) *Basis of Grounded Theory Analysis*, Mill Valley, California: Sociology Press.

Glaser, B. And Strauss, A. (1965) *Awareness of Dying*, Chicago: Aldine.

Glaser, B. and Strauss, A. (1967) *The Discovery of Grounded Theory*, Chicago: Aldine.

Gummesson, E. (1991) *Qualitative Methods in Management Research*, Sage Publications.

Hutchinson, S. A. (1986) "Education and Grounded Theory" *Journal of Thought* v.21, No 3, pp50-68.

International Accounting Standards Committee (1984) *International Accounting Standard 24: Related Party Disclosures*.

Jenson, M. C. and Meckling, W.H. (1976) 'Theory of the Firm; Managerial Behaviour, Agency Costs and Ownership Structure', *Journal of Financial Economics*, 3, pp305-360.

Lester, M. and Hadden, S. C. (1980) 'Ethnomethodology and Grounded Theory Methodology: An Integration of Perspective and Method', *Urban Life*, v.9, No.1, April, pp3-33.

Mason, Alister K. (1979) *Related Party Transactions. A research study*, CICA

Nobes, Christopher (1991) 'Cycles in UK Standard Setting', *Accounting and Business Research*, v.21, no 3, pp265-274.

Pidgeon, N. F., Turner, B. A. and Blockley, D. I. (1991) 'The use of Grounded Theory for conceptual analysis in knowledge elicitation', *International Journal of Management - Machine Studies*, 35, pp151-173.

Riley, J. N. and Sermsri, S. (1974) '*The Variegated Thai Medical System as a Context for Birth Control Services*' Working Paper No 6, Institute for Population and Social Research, Mahidol University, Thailand.

Segev, E. (1988) 'A Framework for the Grounded Theory of Corporate Policy', *Interfaces*, 18:5, pp42-54.

Stern, P. N. (1994) 'Eroding Grounded Theory' in *Critical Issues in Qualitative Research Methods* (ed. Morse, J. M.), Sage, California, pp212-223.

Strauss, A. (1987) *Qualitative Analysis for Social Scientists*, New York: Cambridge University Press.

Strauss, A. and Corbin, J. (1990) *Basics of Qualitative Research: Grounded Theory Procedures and Techniques*, Sage Publications.

Strauss, A. and Corbin, J. (1994) 'Grounded Theory Methodology: An Overview' in *Handbook of Qualitative Research* (eds. Denzin, N. K. and Lincoln, Y. S.) Sage, California, pp273-285.

Trimble, E. G., Cherns, A. B., Jupp, B. C. and Turner, B. A. (1972) *The Effectiveness of Cost Planning and other Cost Control Techniques in Hospital Construction. Final Report to the Department of Health and Social Security*, Loughborough University.

Turner, B. A. (1981) *Quality and Quantity*, Elsever Scientific Publishing, Amsterdam.

Turner, B. A. (1983) 'The Use of Grounded Theory for the Qualitative Analysis of Organisational Behaviour', *Journal of Management Studies*, 20(3), pp333-348.

Watts, R. L. and Zimmerman, J. L. (1979) 'The Demand for and Supply of Accounting Theories: The Market for Excuses', *The Accounting Review*, v. 54, April, pp273-305.

8 Private shareholders and the summary financial statement: The experiences of one company

Ann Hansford and Roger Hussey

Introduction

Fully listed public companies are permitted, under section 251 of the Companies Act 1985, to send summary financial statements instead of the full report and accounts to shareholders. The method for determining whether a shareholder wishes to receive such a document and the form, content and auditors' statement for a summary financial statement are contained in Statutory Instrument 1990 No 515 which came into force on 1 April 1990. Summary financial statements are not unique to fully listed companies as, under the Building Societies Act 1986, such documents must be sent by building societies to their members and other certain parties 21 days before the annual general meeting.

The possibility of simplifying the financial reports sent to shareholders first started to gain ground in the mid-1970s. The Corporate Report (ASSC, 1975), published by the then Accounting Standards Steering Committee, strongly supported the production of a simplified version and special interest extracts of annual reports and accounts. A subsequent study by Hammill (1979) for the Institute of Chartered Accountants in England and Wales concluded that there was sufficient argument for at least experimenting with simplifying the financial information given to shareholders. However, it was the privatisation of such organisations as British Telecom, Trustee Savings Bank and British Gas, introducing millions of individuals to shareholding for the first time, that led to pressure for a change in company legislation.

In 1987, Sir John Read, who was then chairman of Trustee Savings Bank, argued that public companies should be allowed to send an abbreviated version of the full report and accounts to shareholders, but still issue the complete document to those who required it (Martin, 1989). This proposal received considerable support. The Department of Trade and Industry (DTI) sounded out a number of representative organisations, including the major professional accountancy bodies, the Confederation of British Industry (CBI), The International Stock Exchange, the Bank of England and the Wider Share Ownership Council. The response was favourable. On 25 March 1988 the Government announced its intention to introduce a provision in the Companies Bill 1989 permitting companies to issue summary financial statements. Clause 15 of the Companies Act 1989 inserted a new section 251 into the Companies Act 1985 which allows the Secretary of State to issue statutory instruments dealing with the detail of summary financial statements.

Despite the enthusiasm expressed for summary financial statements, there was no evidence as to what the reaction of shareholders would be. The rationale for the documents was, in part, the various studies which demonstrated that private shareholders had difficulty in understanding the full financial statements and tended to show little interest in them. The contents of the summary financial statement were therefore very much an abbreviation of the full document with no attention paid to identifying information which would be of interest to the private shareholder nor was any attempt made to simplify it.

This paper examines the legislative background to summary financial statements and the earlier studies which had been concerned with private shareholders reactions to the full report and accounts. The main part of the paper discusses the early results of an investigation of private shareholders reactions in a major company which issues summary financial statements.

The legislative background

In August 1989 the Department of Trade and Industry issued a consultative document seeking views on the mechanisms to be used in ascertaining whether a shareholder wishes to receive a copy of the full report and accounts or a summary financial statement; also the minimum requirements for their form and content. The DTI stated that the arguments in favour of summary financial statements were as follows:

- Many shareholders were not interested in all the detail given in the full report and accounts.
- A more easily understood summary financial statement would be welcomed by shareholders.
- Companies would have the opportunity to improve their communications with shareholders.
- Companies would be relieved of the cost of sending unwanted, expensive annual reports to shareholders.

The regulations in respect of summary financial statements which the Secretary of State was empowered to make under section 251 of the Companies Act came into force on 1 April 1990. The regulations are concerned with fully listed public companies, including banks and insurance companies, issuing a summary financial statement for a financial year commencing on or after 23 December 1989.

Assuming that a company is not prohibited by its articles from issuing a summary financial statement, it may send them to members in place of the full report and accounts if the following conditions are met:

- The company must have ascertained that the member does not wish to receive the full accounts and reports (section 251(2)).
- The period must not have expired for laying and delivering the full accounts and reports (section 244).
- The summary financial statement must be approved by the board of directors and signed on behalf of the board by a director, whose name must be stated.
- In the case of companies which are not required to prepare group accounts and those which are, the summary financial statement must include, in a prominent position, the following 'health warning': 'This summary financial statement does not contain sufficient information to allow for a full understanding of the results and state of affairs of the company. For further information the full annual accounts, the auditors' report on those accounts and the directors' report should be consulted.'

There must be a conspicuous statement of members' rights to demand, free of charge, a copy of the company's last full accounts and reports. These rights are contained in section 239 of the Companies Act 1985.

A printed pre-paid card or form must accompany the summary financial statement. This should allow the member to indicate by ticking a box whether s/he wishes to exercise the right under section 239 to receive the full accounts and reports for the financial year covered by the summary financial statement and whether the member wishes to receive the full accounts and reports for future financial years. The form and content of summary financial statements vary according to classification of the issuing company. There are four categories:

- fully listed public companies and groups other than banking and insurance companies and groups;
- banking companies and groups (a banking company is a company which is authorised under the Banking Act 1987);

- insurance companies and groups (an insurance company is a "person or body of persons (whether incorporated or not) carrying on insurance business" Insurance Companies Act 1982);
- fully listed public limited companies including banks and insurance companies issuing a summary financial statement for a financial year commencing prior to 23 December 1989.

The principal requirements for companies in the first category are:

(i) directors' report showing:

business review;
important post balance sheet events;
likely future developments in the business;
list of directors' names.

(ii) summary profit and loss account, including amounts for preceding financial year;
(iii) directors' emoluments (at end of profit and loss account);
(iv) summary balance sheet, including amounts for preceding financial year;
(v) 'health warning' in a prominent position;
(vi) statement of members' rights under section 239;
(vii) signature of a director on behalf of the board with the name stated;
(viii) a statement as to whether the auditors' report on the annual accounts was unqualified or qualified, and if qualified, the report in full together with any further material needed to understand the qualification;
(ix) a statement whether the auditors' report on the annual accounts contained a statement under section 237(2) (accounting records or returns inadequate or accounts not agreeing with records and returns) or section 237(3) (failure to obtain necessary information and explanations), and if so, set out the statements in full;
(x) a statement by the auditors of their opinion as to whether the summary financial statement is consistent with the full report and accounts and complies with the Companies Act 1985 section 251 and with the regulations made thereunder.

Previous research

In the UK, USA, Australia and New Zealand surveys have been conducted which examine the preferences of the unsophisticated investor, normally considered to be the private shareholder. The sources of information the investors claim to use for making investment decisions have been of particular interest to researchers. A study in the USA by Baker and Haslem (1973) allowed the authors to conclude that 'financial statements are relegated to a position of minor importance'.

Other surveys have also considered the importance of annual reports to investors, but the results are somewhat contradictory, with financial statements obtaining a higher ranking than in the Baker and Haslem study. In explaining these differences Chang and Most (1977) suggest that the assumption used in the surveys that private shareholders may be considered as a separate homogeneous group is misleading. The variables that could affect the responses are not only the age, education and occupation of the recipients, but also the number of corporate securities held and the relationship between the size of the portfolio and the total amount of the individual savings.

There is also some inconsistency in the surveys on the actual level of readership of the annual report. However, one definite conclusion drawn is that the chairman's statement is claimed to be the most widely read part of the annual report and accounts. In most of the surveys a sizeable proportion of unsophisticated users, but not the majority, claim to read the profit and loss account and balance sheet thoroughly. In the Lee and Tweedie study (1975) the figures were 46.5 per cent and 34.0 per cent respectively. These results must be treated with some caution in view of the same study's findings that a significant proportion of individual shareholders appear to have a poor understanding of accounting information, but fail to recognise this.

The major investigations in the UK into private shareholders' understanding of financial information were conducted by Lee and Tweedie in 1975 and 1977. In the 1975 study a questionnaire was used and the respondents evaluated their own understanding; some 68 per cent claimed to have no difficulty with comprehension. In the 1977 study interviews were conducted and a more rigorous questioning took place. The researchers concluded that shareholder respondents' actual knowledge was well below their perception of their ability.

A similar study by Winfield (1978) in Australia found that although 80 per cent of respondents claimed to understand accounting information, the application of comprehension tests revealed that approximately half these shareholders demonstrated a poor understanding.

As well as the conceptual problems, particularly the difference between cash and accruals bases of accounting, the terminology used by accountants causes many problems. This restricts the reader's comprehension of the accounts. Studies by Mitchell (1982) and Gorb et al, (1989) demonstrate that the unsophisticated readers experience a range of problems in attempting to understand financial statements.

Baker and Haslem (1973) argued that the full report and accounts should be structured with summary financial statements and specific information relevant to the average investor separated from that section of the report directed at the professional analyst. Lee and Tweedie (1977) recommended that the present system of financial reporting should be simplified and identify areas where simplification could be helpful. These improvements were recommended to be introduced into the full report and accounts without any attempt at summarising it.

Although the above studies demonstrate that the full report and accounts as presently constructed is not the most appropriate document for many unsophisticated users, they tell us little about the possible reaction of shareholders to summary financial statements. A number of surveys have been conducted in prospect of the legislation which may give some indications. A survey quoted by Hussey (1990) was conducted by a major UK company in 1989, before the regulations came into force, found that 83 per cent of the shareholders responding stated that they would prefer a summary report in future years (Hussey, 1990). Also in 1989, the Trustees Savings Bank proposed to introduce a short form annual report which would aim to be less technical. At their annual general meeting on 30 March 1989, 70 shareholders were interviewed from an audience of approximately 450. The results suggested that shareholders would welcome a summary financial statement.

Although figures are not available, another company, British Telecom, was persuaded that shareholders would react favourably to a summary financial statement. In their Notice of Annual General Meeting 1990, resolution 10 states: 'Research amongst British Telecom shareholders indicates that the majority would prefer to receive shorter and simpler accounting information. British Telecom intends, therefore, to use the opportunity provided by the change in the law to meet the requirements of its shareholders.'

A recent study (Epstein and Pava 1995) examined experiences in the USA, but the low response rate and the limited nature of the questions limits the value of the study.

Methodology

Negotiations were conducted with a large listed company issuing summary financial statements to conduct a survey of a sample of shareholders receiving these documents instead of the full report and accounts.

The company agreed on the understanding that they would remain anonymous and have a measure of control over the questionnaire used. The summary financial statement issued by the company was part of a larger document entitled the Annual Review and that title will be used in the remainder of this paper.

The research instrument was based to a large extent on that used by Lee and Tweedie (1975), but it was realised that this was not entirely suitable for the summary financial statement. Accordingly focus groups were held within the company to refine the questions. Although the members of the focus groups were employees they were also shareholders and they were asked to offer their opinions as from the stance of shareholders. Following the focus groups it was possible to pilot the questionnaire. This led to some alterations and the company also desired to make some changes.

A systematic sample of 2,000 shareholders was taken. The questionnaires were sent with a covering letter and after 4 weeks delay a follow up letter was despatched to non-respondents. The response rate was 26.1 per cent.

Analysis and discussion

In this section we concentrate on the initial analysis of the responses. In particular we examine the perceived functions of the Annual Review, the level of readership, the level of understanding and the amount of information required.

The Annual Review for the company concerned is a 28 page document split into 13 sections. The overall appearance of the Annual Review is attractive with the text being broken by pictures, simple graphs and photographs of the company's products. It is produced on good quality paper with colour featuring on 23 of the 28 pages.

The first section is *The Year at a glance***.** This is a first page in the Annual Review and it contains information on pre-tax profit, dividends per share and earnings per share. The information is clearly set out in both figures and as simple bar charts. The bar charts compares each of the three items with the previous year. There are clear, straightforward notes at the bottom of the page giving the composition of the total profit between different areas of the business together with notification of a major business acquisition during the year. The figures are given in large clear white print which stands out from the green background.

The *Chairman's Statement* covers pages 2 and 3. The statement is clear and easy to read. There is a photograph of the Chairman together with a bar chart showing the dividends over the last five years which breaks up the narrative. It presents an overview of the different areas of the business and makes reference to the Group's pre-tax profit. Finally, it refers to the dividend for the year recommended by the Board.

The *Chief Executive's Review* is 12 pages long and contains a more detailed review of the different areas of the business during the year. Colour is used on all 12 pages with photographs of the different products, logos and simple bar and pie charts. There is a colourful map of the World showing sales volume by area. This review concentrates on the types of sales, geographical location of the sales and information on new markets.

The *Finance Director's Review* contains a review of various aspects of the Group's results. It is 6 pages long with less colour than the previous Review and Statement with larger blocks of text. There are bar charts to illustrate net debt/equity, interest cover and the maturity profile of debt.

The *Board Committees and Policies* section is a single page of narrative. Three of the Board committees are referred to and there is a paragraph on each one explaining briefly the items considered by these committees during the year. The Board policies section includes items on employee policies, equal opportunities, community involvement and environmental issues.

The *Summary Financial Statement & notes* amounts to 2/3rds of a page and contains the 'health warning' referred to in the section above on the legislative background. It also contains details of contingent liabilities and a brief note stating that the auditors' report on the full accounts has not been qualified.

The *Auditors' statement* is very brief. It states that the summary financial statement is the responsibility of the Directors, but the auditors confirm that the statement is consistent with the Directors' Report and Accounts.

The *Summary Group Profit & Loss Account, Statement of Recognised Gains & Losses* and *Summary Group Balance Sheet* cover 2 pages in total. The comparatives are given for the previous year, with the current year figures given in green which makes them stand out.

The *profit & loss* account identifies the revenue for the year as split between different sections of the business, together with the makeup of the profit figure. Operating profit, profit before tax and profit for the year are each presented in bold type to stand out from the other text.

The *Statement of recognised gains & losses* is very short, amounting to three items.

The *Summary group Balance Sheet* covers one page with a clear distinction between assets and liabilities. Within these sections the assets and liabilities relating to the three broad areas of the business are identified and presented in bold type. There is one figure for fixed assets and one for current assets without further analysis. Investments are split between two different areas of the business and so two figures are given for this, but without further details. The section on *Other Financial Information* covers 1 page and includes some figures together with narrative. Details of dividends are given together with brief details on Director's emoluments. The total amount paid to the Directors is given with the Chairman's actual emoluments specified.

The *Board of Directors* section is a page long and includes a picture of three of the Directors. Brief details of all the Directors are included, age, date appointed and area of responsibility.

The *World of Xplc* is the final page of the Annual Review. It includes colourful bar charts showing the revenue by area and profit by area for the year and for the previous four years. The various group companies are identified together with very brief details of the type of sales and services undertaken by the each of these companies.

The functions of the annual review

The expectations of the shareholders receiving the Annual Review were the subject of the first question on the questionnaire. Seven alternative functions or purposes were given together with the opportunity for shareholders to add further items. The outcome of the analysis is given in the following table. Most of the respondents ticked more than 1 item with some identifying up to 4 of the given functions as important for them.

TABLE 1
Responses to the question: What are the most important functions of the annual review for you? (more than one can be ticked)

FUNCTION	Number of respondents	Percentage of total
To know the amount of the dividend	346	66.3%
To assess the performance of the company	339	64.9%
To keep abreast of company developments	281	53.8%
To understand the strategy & policies of the company	212	40.6%
To aid future share trading decisions	122	23.4%
To feel involved with the company	106	20.3%
To identify members of the Board	81	15.5%

The greatest number of respondents, 346 (66.3%) identified knowing the amount of the dividend as an important function of the Annual Review for them. Interestingly 339 (64.9%) selected assessment of the performance of the company as important. It must be questionable whether the Annual Review can perform this satisfactorily. Despite the fact that the Annual Review & summary financial statement are required by the legislation to carry a statement to the effect that they should not be used for decision making 122 (23.4%) of the respondents identified this as an important function.

Level of readership

This was assessed by identifying each item in the Annual Review and asking the shareholders to specify whether they had read it, glanced at it or had not read it at all. The results are set out in the following table.

TABLE 2

Responses to the question: For each of the following sections of the annual review indicate whether you have read it thoroughly, glanced at it or not read it at all.

READERSHIP	Read thoroughly	Glanced at it	Not read
Year at a glance	241	214	19
Chairman's Statement	292	161	38
Chief Executive's Review	149	180	84
Finance Director's Review	120	192	99
Board Committees & policies	34	156	169
Summary Financial Statement & notes	133	211	78
Auditors' Statement	48	140	190
Summary group profit & loss account	131	209	85
Statement of recognised gains & losses	77	196	122
Summary group Balance Sheet	82	193	119
Other Financial information	43	176	153
Board of Directors	69	186	128
The World of Xplc	148	220	71

The Chairman's Statement was the most thoroughly read item with 292 (55.9%) of the respondents having read it thoroughly and 161 (30.8%) having glanced at it. These findings support earlier studies on shareholder readership of the full Report and Accounts.

The item attracting most attention was The Year at a Glance with 241 (46.2%) having read it and 214 (40.9%) having glanced at it. The position of this section, immediately inside the front cover of the Annual Review and before the Chairman's Statement, means that shareholders will be aware of the section. The clear and straightforward presentation of the information on the dividend, profit per share and earnings per share in The Year at a Glance would appear to be effective. Table 1 shows that knowing the amount of the dividend is an important function of the Annual Review for more of the respondents than any other and this is provided simply and quickly by The Year at a Glance section.

The readership levels vary in the sections relating directly to the Summary Financial Statement. The summary financial statement and notes and summary profit & loss account attract the highest readership levels, but only 133 (25.5%) and 131 (25.1%) respondents claim to have read them thoroughly. The arrangement, presentation and content of the information in the Summary Financial Statement & notes and Auditors' Statement, as described above, is of a different type to other sections of the Annual Review and is not so immediately attractive to the reader. The Summary Profit & Loss account, Statement of recognised gains & losses and Summary Balance Sheet are set out on 2 facing pages, in that order. More of the respondents are likely to glance at the balance sheet and statement of gains/losses, 196 (37.5%) and 193 (37%) respectively than read them thoroughly, 77 (14.7%) and 82 (15.7%) respectively.

The Other Financial Information section is read thoroughly by only 43 (8.2%) of the respondents. This is positioned at the end of the Summary Financial Statement sections and includes further information on the dividends together with outline details of the Director's emoluments and specific details of the Chairman's emoluments. Given the recent publicity on such issues it is a surprisingly low readership level. The positioning and heading of the information may be significant in this respect.

Taking the entire Annual Review the section identified as not read by the largest number of respondents is the Auditors' Statement which states that the Auditors confirm that it is consistent with the full Report & Accounts. It is very brief and at the bottom of a page of text.

Understanding

The shareholders in the study were asked to assess their own level of understanding of financial information before looking in detail at each section of the Annual Review. Table 3 shows the responses to their own assessment and table 4 requires them to assess each of the 13 sections as very easy, easy no opinion difficult or very difficult.

TABLE 3
Responses to the question: How would you assess your general understanding of financial information?

ASSESSMENT OF GENERAL UNDERSTANDING	Number of respondents	Percentage of total
Very good	39	7.5%
Good	124	23.8%
Adequate	286	54.8%
Poor	46	8.8%
Very poor	9	1.7%

The majority of respondents 286 (54.8%) opted for the middle assessment category - adequate. Shareholders were reluctant to assess themselves as very good with only 39 (7.5%) placing themselves in that category and even fewer assessed themselves as very poor, 9 (1.7%). However, 124 (23.8%) assessed themselves as the second category, good, compared to 46 (8.8%) placing themselves in the fourth category, poor.

TABLE 4
Responses to the question: How easy do you find it to understand the following items in the annual review?

UNDERSTANDING OF ITEMS IN THE ANNUAL REVIEW	Very easy	Easy	No opinion	Difficult	Very difficult
Year at a glance	155	240	48	11	2
Chairman's Statement	141	255	58	9	3
Chief Executive's Review	89	198	115	15	5
Finance Director's Review	47	171	154	30	8
Board Committees & policies	37	122	191	20	8
Summary Financial Statement & notes	47	168	124	50	12
Auditors' Statement	39	115	173	47	15
Summary group profit & loss account	42	176	119	59	14
Statement of recognised gains & losses	32	131	154	63	16
Summary group Balance Sheet	34	145	144	52	19
Other financial information	33	108	175	41	11
Board of Directors	73	142	155	13	4
The World of Xplc	100	206	100	5	4

The Year at a Glance and the Chairman's Statement were found to be very easy, 155 (30%) and 141 (27%) respectively, or easy, 240 (46%) and 255 (48.9%) respectively, by the respondents. Just over 75% of the respondent found each of these two sections to be either easy or very easy to understand. The level of understanding for the Summary Financial Statement sections attracted a very different response. For all six sections, summary financial statement & notes, auditors statement, summary group profit & loss account, statement of recognised gains/losses, summary balance sheet and other financial information less than 10% of the respondents found them very easy. The summary group profit and loss account was the one with the greatest total number of respondents who found it either easy or very easy, 218 (41.8%). Other financial information, with 141 (27%) of the respondents finding it easy or very easy, was the one with the lowest level of understanding of the six summary financial statement items.

The numbers of respondents assessing the Finance Director's review as very easy or easy were similar to the summary group profit & loss account, which had the most such responses of the six summary financial statement items. For the Finance Director's review 47 (9%) found it very easy whilst 171 (32.8%) found it easy. The comparable figures for the profit and loss account were 42 and 176. They are very different types of item. The Finance Director's review is 6 pages long as opposed to the profit & loss account which covers three-quarters of a page. The profit & loss account consists of brief labels to the figures, whereas the Finance Director's review gives far more detailed background and narrative to explain the results. Despite these clear differences, the same number of respondents, 218 (41.8%), found them either very easy or easy.

It was reassuring to note that few of the respondents found items in the Annual Review very difficult. The summary balance sheet had the greatest number of respondents assessing it as very difficult with 19 (3.6%) as compared to the year at a glance having 2 (0.3%).

Amount of information

In this section we classified the 13 items of this Annual Review into 5 main groups, as given in table 5. This will aid comparison with the other two companies in the study. The results are given in table 5.

TABLE 5

Responses to the question: Do the following sections of the annual review contain too much, the right amount or too little information?

AMOUNT OF INFORMATION	Right amount	Too much	Too little
Year at a glance	414	25	9
Chairman's Statement	392	32	11
Chief Executive's Review	317	49	11
Finance Director's Review	296	68	9
Summary Financial Statement	338	41	9

The Year at a glance was the section that the largest number of respondents considered to contain the right amount of information, 414 (79.3%), followed by the Chairman's Statement, 392 (75.1%). From table 2 these two items are the ones shareholders were most likely to either read thoroughly or glance at.

The Finance Director's review had the fewest number of respondents assessing it as having the right amount of information 296 (56.7%) and the largest number of respondents, 68 (13%), assessed it as having too much information. Table 4 indicates that the level of understanding of the Finance Director's review is lower than for the Chief Executives review and the Chairman's statement and is at a similar level to the summary financial statement. Responses to this final question indicates that the respondents found the Finance Director's review was the most likely item to contain too much or not the right type of information.

Conclusions

Summary financial statements were introduced in the belief, at least in part, that the abbreviation of financial information to private shareholders would make it more understandable and encourage the shareholders to read it. There has been no published study on the effectiveness of summary financial statements in the UK to date and the findings from this paper have raised a number of issues.

First, the importance attached to the Chairman's statement for the shareholders confirms previous studies of the full report and accounts. As there has been no alteration in this piece of information, legislation has not brought about change. Shareholders assess their own understanding of financial information positively with two and a half times more shareholders assessing their understanding as good rather than poor. These results yet again confirm the findings from earlier studies, but as the data is based on the shareholders' own assessment some caution must be exercised.

The level of understanding of the Annual review ranges widely between different parts of the document. The six summary financial statement items in this company's Annual review compare unfavourably with other parts of it, as does the Finance Director's review. It would not appear, therefore, that the abbreviation of financial information has made it more comprehensible in comparison to other information provided to shareholders.

The level of readership of the items in the Annual review is dependent on the type of item under consideration. The more narrative, user-friendly sections, Chairman's statement, Chief Executives review are more likely to be read than the summary financial statement items. These statements have been unaffected by the legislation.

The current study has been based on the results from one company and its particular version of the summary financial statement. Further statistical analysis of these findings may demonstrate, as other studies have suggested, that certain attributes of the shareholder may affect readership levels and understanding. The extension of the survey to other companies would permit a comparative analysis to be conducted which would provide greater insight into the impact of the abbreviation of financial information.

A full review will only be possible once the data has been processed for the other two companies and comparisons between all three can then be made.

References

Baker H and Haslam J A 'Information Needs of Individual Investors' *Journal of Accountancy*, November 1973.

Chang L and Most K S 'Investors Uses of Financial Statements - An Empirical Study' *Singapore Accountant*, 1977.

Epstein M J and Pava M L 'Individual Investors' Perceptions on the Summary Annual Report: A Survey Approach' *Journal of Applied Business Research*, Vol 10 no 3 1995.

Gorb P, Burns R, Clarke F, Ludholm D and Ross D *What Do Investors Really Want To Know?* (Wolff Olins/ Hall 1989).

Hammill A E *Simplified Financial Statements, A Study prepared for the Accounting Standards Committee* (Institute of Chartered Accountants in England & Wales, London, 1979).

Hussey R 'Shareholders in the Driving Seat' *Accountancy Age* 8 March 1990.

Lee T A and Tweedie D P 'Accounting Information: An Investigation of Private Shareholder Understanding' *Accounting and Business Research*, Winter 1975.

Martin D M *How to prepare the Annual Report* (Director Books, Cambridge, 1989).

Mitchell F 'Communicating Financial Information - The Private Sector Experience' *Local Government Studies*, March/April 1982.

Winfield R R 'Shareholder Opinions of Published Financial Statements' in Courtis J *Corporate Annual Report Analysis* (AFM Exploratory Series no.5, Armadale, University of New England, 1978).

9 The problems of accounting for intangible assets in the food and drink industry

Audra Ong

Introduction

Intangible assets have long played a major role in business strategy and marketing. As industry structures in the Western world shift towards information/technology-intensive industries (such as pharmaceuticals, bioengineering, global communications) and towards the creation of added value through product differentiation (branded consumer goods industries), the strategic management of these assets for competitive advantage has become increasingly important for the modern corporation.

Industrialists and management gurus argue that the profitability of modern business is more dependent on intangible assets (e.g. a powerful brand name, a patented technology, a proprietary database, company reputation, employee know-how) than on tangible assets such as property, plant and machinery. The importance attached to intangibles as a core competence for business success are confirmed by captains of industries:

> If this business were to be split up, I would be glad to take the brands, trademarks and goodwill. You could have all the bricks and mortar and I would fare better than you. (John Stuart, former CEO, Quaker.)

> Brands are the priority for securing the profit base for the 1990s. (Tony O'Reilly, Chairman and CEO, HJ Heinz.)

> Buildings age and become dilapidated. Machines wear out. Cars rust. But what lives on are brands. (Sir Hector Laing, United Biscuits.)

Itami argues that when a firm exploits its invisible assets, *synergy* is achieved when resources accumulated in one part of the company are used simultaneously and at no additional expense by other parts (i.e. to get a 'free ride'). For instance, Ajinomoto, the Japanese condiments company, (with its invisible assets in condiments marketing and production), had developed a strong brand image and distribution network. It has entered the mayonnaise market successfully when other companies failed. The Ajinomoto acid amino technology developed for condiments was also used in pharmaceutical products. The synergy from invisible assets enabled the enterprise to build a competitive position at lower cost via the utilisation and the 'stretching' of it's core competencies.

The accounting view of intangible assets

Definition and nature of intangible assets

The accounting profession in its publication defines an intangible asset as one that is 'non-monetary in nature and without physical substance.' (*ED 52 Accounting for Intangible Assets, 1990*). There are three main types of intangible assets - R & D; goodwill and intellectual property. The latter includes patents, trademarks, copyrights, registered designs, know-how and trade secrets. The Companies Act deliberately left room within the classification for new commercial practices by adding the phrase 'similar rights and assets' in the balance sheet. This definition would encompass items such as brands, publishing rights and newspaper titles.

Although accountancy conventions allows the valuation of patents and trademarks, perplexity remains over what constitutes an intangible asset and therefore is eligible to be capitalised in the balance sheet. Because of the separability criteria, ED 52 implies that brands are unlikely to be valued on it's own in the balance sheet. It states that the term brand is used to describe goodwill. ED 52 also states that intangible fixed assets should be deemed to have a finite useful economic life.

In addition, descriptions for intangible assets are broad and the inconsistency of existing accounting conventions highlighted in the Companies Act 1985 and ED 52 as well as flexible legal requirements have permitted a variety of alternative practices to co-exist. A perplexing issue is the valuation of intangible assets for balance sheet purposes, particularly brands. For instance, the Companies Act 1985 allows both acquired and home-grown brands at historical or current cost valuations.

This implies that brand names can be revalued or devalued. This conflicts with ED 52 which rules out revaluation and home-grown intangibles (Elliott & Elliott, 1993).

Several organisations and individuals have attempted to set out the characteristics of an intangible asset which allows it to be capitalised.

The range of possible descriptions for intangible assets, however, is broad and several organisations have attempted to set out the characteristics of an intangible asset which can be capitalised in the balance sheet. Touche Ross (1993) classifies intangibles into three groups depending on its degree of separableness as illustrated below:

TANGIBLE →	**INTANGIBLE,** → **but separable**	**INTANGIBLE, not separable**
eg. plant & machinery	eg. patent	eg. goodwill

The characteristics of different intangible assets demonstrate that while some have attributes that are similar to a tangible asset - ie. they are legally discrete and their costs can be fully ascertained - others show attributes that are similar to goodwill in that they are 'part of the underlying business'.

Arthur Andersen (1992) states that an intangible asset must possess the following attributes for valuation purposes:

* non-physical in nature;
* capable of producing further economic benefit;
* protected legally or through a de facto right;
* readily identifiable and capable of being separated from other assets employed in the business.

They analyse intangible into four classes:

* *Brands* eg. consumer good brands, trademarks, corporate names;
* *Intellectual Property* eg. patents, copyrights, technology, know-how;
* *Publishing Rights* eg. magazines, books, mastheads, film and music rights;
* *Licences* eg. TV and radio, airline slots, franchises, distribution rights.

Intangible assets which do not have property rights are defined as 'knowledge' (Hall,1989,1991). This includes reputation, personal, organisational networks, experience of skilled employees. Where there are legal rights, these are known collectively as Intellectual Property Rights. Irish (1992) identifies six types in the UK which include patents, trademarks, copyright, design rights, registered designs and know-how. According to Hares & Royle (1994), intangibles can be classified into four groupings - two of which are 'on-going' and two of which may occur in the 'future'.

The further into the future, the more difficult it is to identify, measure and value. The following diagram highlights the nature of intangible assets:

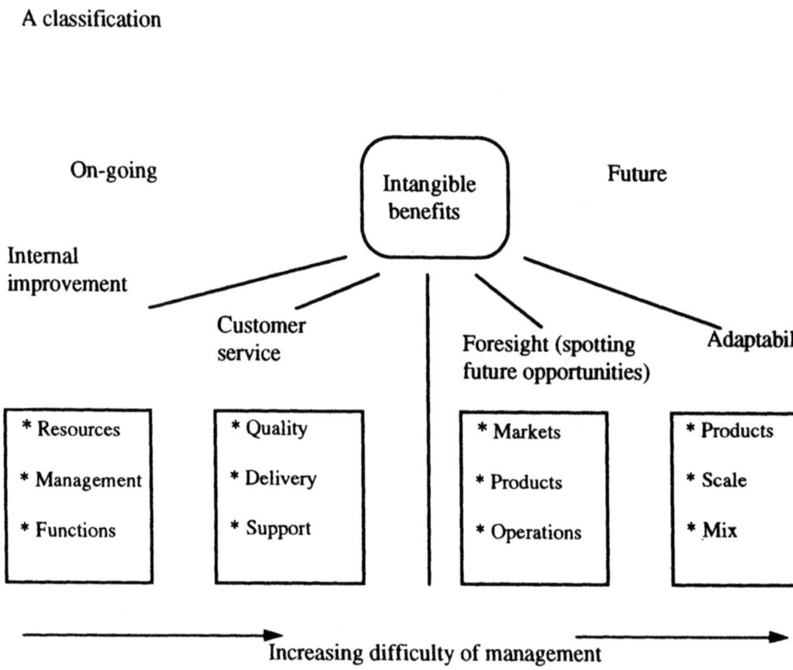

Figure 6.1: What are intanglibles

An intangible benefit can result in any combination of the following:

* A higher price for a premium product or service;
* More sales from an existing product or service;
* Retained custom;
* Opportunity savings;
* New business/sales from a new product/service.

The fact that some categories of intangibles are inter-related makes it difficult to define their boundaries without distorting the 'true and fair view' of accounting information (Arthur Andersen, 1992; Kapferer, 1992).

The debate is further complicated by the fact that some categories of intangibles are inter-related. For example, a brand consists of a blend of 'ingredients' or attributes - both tangible and intangible. Arthur Andersen (1992) claims that a brand possess four components: the trademark, the get-up eg. packaging, the product component eg. secret recipe and brand image cultivated through its 'marketing profile'.

In the UK, consideration of intangible assets is dominated by the uncertainty over the accounting treatment of goodwill (Egginton, 1990). There are those (Nobes, 1989) who argue that it should be capitalised and amortised over several years and others who believe that there are good arguments for leaving it on the balance sheet unless there is a permanent diminution in value (Stacey & Tweedie, 1989; Baxter, 1993). Finally, there are some who argue that goodwill should be written off against reserves as its value is uncertain. These different viewpoints have led to dissatisfaction with *SSAP 22 Accounting for Goodwill* which defines it as 'the difference between the value of the business as a whole and the aggregate of the fair values of its separable net assets.'

However, this definition allows considerable scope for interpretation. Goodwill has been defined by Rutteman (1990) as a residual i.e. 'what is left over when all identified as separable assets have been acted for'. This views goodwill as a 'tidying up" book-keeping procedure rather than fully addressing its complex nature and valuation which, according to Nelson (1953), 'is about as fickle as the human nature of which it is an aspect'. Baxter (1993) states that the name 'goodwill' suggests 'something too nebulous and fickle to be put alongside trustworthy assets'(G. Sarjeant, The Times, 20 December 1993). Thus, valuation of goodwill at any point in time is an extremely difficult and subjective process

Regulatory requirements

In the UK, the ASC initially responded to the emerging practice of intangible asset capitalisation, particularly brands, with a Technical Release TR738 (1989), which sought to provide interim discouragement to the practice, pending the investigations of various 'conceptual issues' involved - especially on the capitalisation of *internally* generated intangibles by RHM plc. Curiously, the International Stock Exchange (1989) almost simultaneously issued a statement that intangible assets such as brands may be included for class test purposes provided that they have been included in the accounts without audit qualification.

TR 780 and ED 47 (1990) were subsequently issued. TR 780 states that brands, whether acquired or internally created, are indistinguishable from brands. ED 47 was greeted with hostility from the business community when it proposed that the immediate write-off of goodwill as permitted by SSAP 22 should be prohibited and that goodwill should be capitalised and amortised. The ASC, before it dissolution, issued ED 52 in May 1990 (based on TR 780). ED 52 sets out specific recognition criteria for an intangible asset to be valued in the balance sheet. Intangible assets are only capitalised if:

*   the historical cost is ascertainable
*   assets are distinguishable from goodwill
*   cost is measurable independently of goodwill, other assets and earnings of relevant business.

In the UK, *SSAP 22* uses the term *separable intangible assets* to identify those other than goodwill. The practice now, particularly internationally, is to refer to intangible assets other than goodwill as identifiable intangible assets. By identifying such items as intangible assets as being separate from goodwill, they do not fall under the requirements SSAP22 where goodwill has to be either written off immediately to reserves (the preferred method) or amortised over its useful economic life (subject to an arbitrary maximum method) to the profit and loss account. The intangible assets may therefore remain on the balance sheet indefinitely, unless there is a permanent diminution in value.
SSAP 22 recommends that purchased goodwill should be either:

a) written off against reserves immediately upon its acquisition to ensure consistency and prudence with the accepted practice of not including inherent goodwill in the financial statements, due to its volatile, uncertain and subjective nature; or
b) the standard also allows companies the option of treating goodwill as an asset and amortising it via the Profit & Loss Account over its useful economic life (in line with the accruals concept).

SSAP 22 is therefore not in line with IAS 22 which only allows one method for goodwill accounting i.e. capitalisation and amortisation. According to Alexander & Archer (1992), 'the varying treatment of goodwill is one of the most serious hindrances to the comparability of financial statements'.

Criticisms of SSAP 22

*   Capitalisation and amortisation of goodwill will have adverse effects on certain performance indicators e.g. EPS and ROCE ratios.
*   An immediate write-off against reserves undermines the strength of the balance sheet as it reduces shareholders' funds - an illogical consequence for a successful acquisition. This method also encourages the use of negative goodwill reserve accounting. In reality the goodwill is never eliminated at all and remains on the balance sheet on a permanent basis. The negative goodwill figure just gets larger each time an acquisition takes place. A motivation for this method occurs when there are insufficient retained funds against which to write off goodwill.

Observations of the 1994/95 Reports & Accounts of companies in the companies revealed that this is a common practice eg. Matthew Clark has negative goodwill reserves. Some companies such as John Lusty create negative goodwill reserves as their negative retained earnings cannot absorb large amounts of goodwill. Other corporations such as Grand Metropolitan, United Biscuits and Guinness have sufficient retained profits but choose instead to create a separate negative goodwill reserve - presumably to avoid depleting retained funds.

The ROCE ratio will be meaningless when the denominator is a negative figure. SSAP 22 does not provide any guidance as to which reserves should be used to write off goodwill. This has led to companies using various reserves and even concocting some in order to escape the reduction of retained earnings

* The useful economic life is highly subjective and has therefore provided considerable scope for choice in the amortisation period e.g. Independent News use a 40-year amortisation period, presumably as this minimises the effect on earnings per share.
* Inconsistent treatment between purchased and internally generated goodwill.

Recent regulatory pronouncements

In December 1993, the ASB issued a Discussion Paper *Goodwill and Intangible Assets* which highlighted six methods for accounting for purchased goodwill. Two have received support from the ASB members i.e.:

* a combination of capitalisation and predetermined life amortisation (not exceeding 20 years); or capitalisation and annual review for any permanent diminution using the ceiling test; and
* transfer to a separate write-off reserve on acquisition

The shortcomings of the Paper are that no definitive guidance has been given on intangible assets other than the proposed "ceiling test" for determining the carrying value of purchased goodwill. This method does not, however, provide consistency of treatment between purchased goodwill and internally generated goodwill.

The recent release of the *IASC's Exposure Draft, E50 Intangible Assets* also fueled critical comments as it proposes a 20-year limit on the useful life of capitalised intangible assets for amortisation purposes. Interbrand described E50 as 'over-prudent, unworkable and contradictory' (Accountancy, July 1995, p. 112).

Criticisms of the ASB Working Paper (1995) 'Goodwill & Intangible Assets'

Due to lack of consensus, a working paper of the same title was issued in June 1995 and a public hearing was held in September the same year. There has been a considerable 'U-turn' from the approach stated in the original Discussion Paper. The working paper suggests that acquired intangibles (including brands) should be recognised if a 'fair value can be ascertained by management'. In all cases, these assets must be reviewed for impairment at each year end. This is to ensure that they are not carried in the balance sheet at above their recoverable amount. Recovery amount is the higher of net realisable value and value in use - the latter being the net present value of future cash inflows expected to be generated by the asset. The extent for this review would be minimal for goodwill and intangible assets having a life not exceeding 20 years. For those exceeding 20 years or an indefinite life a fuller review would be required, involving an assessment of future cash flows.

The impairment tests are based on those given in the US standard *FAS 121 Accounting for the Impairment of Long-lived Assets & for Long-lived Assets to be Disposed Of.* The ASB is currently working on its own impairment standard, to be released after the public hearing on goodwill. It is expected to be more restrictive than FAS 121, to prevent any bending of the current impairment rules.

The Paper focuses only on purchased goodwill and purchased intangible assets. It has yet to solve the anomalies of goodwill and other intangible assets. It raises as many questions as it tries to solve. The ASB's compromise may find general acceptance as the objections of acquisitive companies are accommodated but there are conceptual shortcomings and their proposals are more permissive than the current existing UK rules. Respondents of the Working Paper have expressed shortcomings of the Working Paper. The shortcomings include the following:

* The working paper states that 'intangible assets' should be recognised separately from purchased goodwill where management *believes* that fair value can be measured reliably. If fair value cannot be ascertained, then the assets should be treated as part of the goodwill balance. 'Management belief' is highly subjective and inauditable. How do we test the reasonableness of management belief? The ASB uses measurability as a recognition criteria, although recognition is logically prior to measurement. Also, it doesn't define separable intangible assets (such as legally protected intellectual property rights) and those that are non-separable. This could result in the recognition of non-separable intangibles which are in fact a subset of goodwill.

* It also does not provide specific guidance on the determination by a company of the *useful economic life* of a purchased goodwill. How is the finite life to be ascertained? Companies may tend to opt for the maximum amortisation period without assessing realistically the carrying value of the asset and its remaining economic life. Disclosure is needed on the *period* chosen and the reasons for choosing that period.
* The Working Paper states that the presumption of useful economic life can be *rebutted*. This is akin to opening the Pandora's Box. Only certain categories of intangibles (i.e. patents, licenses and copyrights) have indefinite life and which continue to give practical and identifiable advantage to the business - subject to certain legal technicalities being adhered to (e.g. are they renewable?). The proposal fails to distinguish between *indefinitely* long (infinite) lives and *indeterminate* life. Companies may invoke an 'indefinite life' in situations where the assets have an indeterminate useful economic life.
* Permitting goodwill to be held indefinitely in the balance sheet is against the concept of prudence. The 'value' of goodwill at any one time is only maintained by continuing efforts and expenditure. Purchased goodwill can have an indeterminate life but not an infinite life. It is unrealistic to expect that actions and expenditure taken more than 20 years ago on goodwill are likely to be still sufficiently identifiable as to justify a rise in an advantage to the business - unless it is subsequently topped up (Any *topping - up*' counts as *internally generated goodwill. Should this then be capitalised?*).
* The reluctance shown by UK companies in the past to accept the dominant international practice whereby goodwill is carried forward and amortised suggests that many will want to assert an indefinite life for the goodwill carried in the balance sheet. Auditors will have difficulties rebutting an acquirer's rebuttal of finite life. The Paper provides no guidance on how this should be audited.
* Another issue of contention is the *non-recognition of internally generated goodwill* by the ASB. Several implications arise from this:

  Purchased goodwill is the *added value* created by previous management over and above the net assets measured by accounting convention. *The contribution of previous management on the on-going market value of a company diminishes with time and is gradually replaced by internally generated goodwill.* This means that acquirers would eventually include self-generated goodwill in the balance sheet - but companies pursuing organic growth would not have done so.

This implies that the *earnings* figure of companies in similar industries would not be comparable - those of acquirers being higher. The accounting treatment will create managerial motivations towards acquisitions rather than internal growth or internal investment.

FRS 6 Acquisitions & Mergers and *FRS 7 Fair Values in Acquisition Accounting* were issued in September 1994 but do not deal fully with the valuation of intangible assets.

Research questions and problems

The last few years have seen considerable debate within the accounting profession and business community over the issue of accounting for intangible assets and intellectual property for financial reporting purposes in the UK (Tweedie & Blanchet,1989; Barwise et al,1989; Power 1990; Egginton,1990; Arthur Andersen, 1992; Hussey, 1994). The financial reporting of goodwill and other intangible assets such as brands, trademarks, licenses, publication titles have proved to be a controversial and polemical area. Many companies have valued and capitalised these assets on the balance sheet but there is considerable diversity, as well as uncertainty in accounting treatments.

A survey conducted by Coopers & Lybrand (1990) showed that many of the corporate respondents had some difficulty in reaching decisions on certain aspects of intangibles e.g. deciding on a reliable measure of value caused the greatest problems. Another survey by Company Reporting (March 1992) found that disclosure for intangible assets remains a minority practice. Recent surveys by Hussey (1994) demonstrate that preparers of accounts in different organisations adopt different accounting policies for similar transactions. The Companies Act 1985 requires separate disclosure for intangible fixed assets, but does not define them and extant accounting standards are vague and incomplete. The following highlights some of the key issues and problems of accounting for intangible assets:

* What are the *methods* for *valuing* intangible assets and goodwill? What *criteria* should be used for the *recognition* of both acquired and self-generated intangible assets?
* What are the *valuation methodologies* and *accounting treatment* used by companies in the food and drink industry as regards to intangible assets? Is there a *correlation* between intangible asset treatment and age, size, turnover, profitability, gearing or other factors?
* What are the *publicly disclosed* and *internally* operated *accounting treatments* used in the food and drinks industry? How do the practices of *different* companies compare?

* Are the economic benefits derived from one category of intangible assets *separable* from those contributed by another (intangible) as well as from tangible assets? Which *type* of intangible assets and under what circumstances are they capable of being discharged separately without disposing of the business as a whole?
* What *information* concerning intangible assets should be disclosed in the published financial statements and the *extent* of disclosure.

Arguments for recognising and capitalising intangible assets in the balance sheet

It is argued that not to recognise the existence of intangible assets where they are present is misleading (Bryant, 1989). The absence of a proper framework for intangible asset accounting has meant that there is often a significant understatement of such assets, even though a business is using them to make profit - which are generated by intangibles with no record of existence although they enhance the company's ROCE ratio (Hussey, 1994). Where the assets have been acquired, the immediate write-off will depress profits in the year of acquisition and flatter them in future years as the benefits are realised. Arthur Andersen (1992) argued that 'there are indeed methodologies for valuing intangible assets that are well understood and applied by many different types of practitioners, both in the UK and overseas.' (p.iii). The advantages of recognising and valuing intangible assets, particularly brands, include the following:

1 Brands are valuable

Hugh sums are paid for brands. Brand identities can be rented or licensed. For example, Sunkist, receives £10m per year in royalties for allowing companies such as Cadbury Schweppes, General Mills and Lipton to use its brand names (Doyle, 1994). Developing brand equity is a central issue for top management because it is a key determinant of corporate value. The average British and American company is valued by the stock market around twice the net assets. However, companies with portfolios of strong brands are valued by the stock market at 4 times the net assets (Financial Times, 23/11/91) as illustrated below:

TABLE 1
Ratio of market cap of ordinary shares to net assets (book value)

UK Companies	*Valuation ratio (1992)*
Reckitt & Colman	4.28
Cadbury Schweppes	3.89
United Biscuits	3.33
Guinness	2.89

Source: Strategic Management - Fast Track MBA Series (1993) by Craig, J. & Grant, R., p. 51

US Companies	*Valuation ratio (1989)*
Coca-Cola	9.62
Kellogg	5.46
HJ Heinz	4.71
Pepsi-Cola	4.57
Philip Morris	3.59
Campbell's Soup	3.57

Source: Business Week, December 25, 1989 - adapted from Contemporary Strategic Analysis (1991) by R. Grant, 1991, p. 105

2 Effect on management and investor decision-making

Disclosing brands on the balance sheet make published accounts more commercially 'realistic' and to provide information which might be of benefit to readers and for strategic decision-making for management. For instance, in the 1990 accounts for Guinness, the acquired brands of £1,375m represented 36 per cent of the total fixed assets of £3,814m. It can be argued that the inclusion of brands provides a 'truer' picture of the company's total assets.

Although brand valuation in themselves provide no new substantive information, the very act of disclosing the valuation may itself convey information to the market. It may signal, for example, that management believes its shares are undervalued; or that the company is on the acquisition trail; or that it feels vulnerable to take-over and believes this will bolster its defenses. Following the bid from Goodman Fielder Wattie, (an Australian foods group), RHM valued its brands at £678m. This transformed its balance sheet with net assets rising from £265m (in 1987) to £979m (in 1988). The bid eventually lapsed. Later, RHM announced that it had purchased Nabisco's UK breakfast cereals.

3 Shareholders funds

An immediate goodwill write-off results in a reduction in net tangible assets, even though the market capitalization of a company increases. This is a problem for heavily acquisitive companies - the more they acquire, the lower their net worth became and the less freedom the directors would have. One way to maintain the asset base and avoid a depletion of reserves is to divide the purchased goodwill into two parts - brands and pure goodwill. This reduces the amount of purchased goodwill to be written off against reserves on acquisition.

4 Effect on borrowing powers and stock exchange implications

Companies which write off large amounts of goodwill against their reserves may fall foul of the Class 1 test under Stock Exchange regulations. Cadbury-Schweppes claimed that this was the reason why they introduced brands on to the balance sheet. This would also explained why, just prior to buying Pillsbury in 1989, Grand Metropolitan valued the Smirnoff brand at about £588m on the balance sheet. Had it not done this, it might well have had to seek shareholder approval for the massive $5.5 billion Pillsbury acquisition.

5 Effect on ratios

Gearing ratios are widely used to evaluate the financial structure of a company. Immediate write-off of goodwill against reserves distorts this figure, but the inclusion of brands as intangible assets minimises this distortion by providing a more realistic value for shareholders' funds and 'strengthening' the balance sheet - thus providing the opportunity to absorb goodwill from future acquisitions.

6 As collateral

To pay for acquisitions and joint ventures, consumer products companies use brands as collateral. An ultimate example of borrowing money based on the value of a company's brands, rather than on its capital structure, is RJR Nabisco. In 1989, Kohlberg Kravis Roberts led an unprecedented $26 billion leveraged buy-out of RJR based mainly on the value of RJR's brands - not the $5.8 bn in equity the company had on its balance sheet at the time.

This trend is quite prevalent in the States. In 1991, Citibank engineered a $480m deal financing Borden using the company's brands as collateral. Sara Lee has relied on the technique in the past. The transaction involves the issuance of bonds backed by the value of a consumer brand known as 'special purpose vehicle-related' financing. The $480m is classified as long-term debt and is repaid to Citibank in a bullet repayment after five years.

7 Identify the changing value of brands in the market - place

Recognising brands allows companies to make commercial investment decisions without succumbing too much to short-term pressures. Brand-building requires a long-term focus and at present, brand investments are treated as costs in the accounting books. In order to develop safeguards to short-termism, companies have introduced 'brand equity managers'.

Moorhouse (1990) claims that 'putting brands on the balance sheet forces a company to look at their value as well as to profits. It serves as a reminder to management of the value of the assets for which they are responsible....those companies which recognise brands on the balance sheet will be better and stronger for it.' Brand valuation can move financial statements away from *'stewardship reporting'* to 'pro-active financial management, which involves forward-looking subjective judgments, often based on intangible values ie. on gains that are as yet unrealised and thus do not find their way into a set of financial accounts' (Allen, 1990).

Arguments against capitalising intangible assets

Opponents of these practices advocate a strict adherence to the prudence concept, particularly on brand valuation due to subjectivity and inconsistency in valuation practices and lack of agreement on separability issues for financial reporting purposes. For instance, research conducted by the London Business School (Barwise et al., 1989) oppose the incorporation of intangible asset . Their conclusion was that 'the present flexible position, far from being neutral, is potentially corrosive to the whole basis of financial reporting...... Subjective judgments mean that there is a fundamental conflict between economic validity and the degree of objectivity needed for financial reporting.'

Damant (1992) argues that an intangible asset may be only be capitalised at cost where this is justified in order to match expenditure with revenues, such as research and development. Alternatively, if the intangible asset has an opportunity cost, it may be sold to another person and entered on the balance sheet at its market value or other arm's length value eg. milk quotas and airline franchises. Damant argues that these values have the merit of being independent of the future economic benefits generated by the asset. He considers that any valuation method based on future cash flows is illogical because it is the responsiblity of the users to make their own predictions. Arguments against the accounting of certain intangibles (e.g. brands) have been explored. In particular, 4 main issues are discussed below.

1 Separability

Separability is deemed a pre-condition to the recognition and valuation of an intangible asset (Tonkin and Robertson, Financial Reporting, 1991). The fundamental problem when valuing certain intangibles, especially brands, is that there is no 'open market' for these assets. Identifiable assets [or liabilities] must be capable of being disposed of or discharged *separately* without disposing of a business as a whole (Companies Act 1985 Sch 4; SSAP 22:27). Touche Ross (1993) argues that separability of assets typically lies on a spectrum.

Arthur Andersen (1992) suggests that in order to 'assess the degree of separability, the valuer should consider the feasibility of transferring the asset to a hypothetical (or actual) third party.....if an arm's length contract can reasonably be established that enables the third party to exploit the asset commercially, then the asset is separable'.

Also, intangible assets are also used in conjunction with other assets in order to yield economic benefits. e.g. manufacturing and selling chocolate bars require tangible assets (plant and machinery) and intangible assets (know-how, franchises, image). Moreover, the value of one intangible (e.g. a brand) is intimately tied up with other intangibles (reputation, know-how, skills, relationships). How can we define and isolate the boundaries between one class of asset and other assets for financial reporting purposes without distorting the true and fair view of accounting information?

2 Acquired vs home-grown intangibles

The arguments against the inclusion of home-grown brands in the balance sheet are 2-fold:

* it is extremely difficult to arrive at an objective valuation; and
* it contravenes SSAP22 which prohibits accounting for non-purchased goodwill.

The non-inclusion of part of one's assets contravenes the notion of faithfulness and sincerity normally attached to financial statements. If home-grown intangibles such as brands are excluded, it distorts financial information which could have grave consequences for companies who rely on internal growth (Gelle, 1990 - as quoted in Kapferer, 1992).

3 Problems associated with valuation

The balance sheet's role is to give a snapshot of the financial position of a company - the equity invested and how they are tied up. This places an emphasis on objective reporting. The value of an intangible asset lies in the future. It depends on the purpose of valuation (e.g. is it for external financial reporting, management purposes, etc.?) and the perception of future benefits. The accounting profession is quite divided on whether balance sheets should be re-defined and to include subjective elements and ipso facto become a statement of value.

At present, there is no general agreement on valuation methods. Nor can existing methods be regarded as either fully theoretically valid nor empirically verifiable. Major problems include the question of :

* asset recognition;
* separability, definition and boundaries of exactly what is being valued; and
* the estimation and valuation of future profitability.

The latter two are exacerbated by the lack of clarity over the premise of value and the on-going debate about the role, functions and objectives of the balance sheet in financial reporting. Measurement of value is a delicate problem, especially brand accounting:

* when brands are marketed under corporate names (e.g. Sony), or both corporate and individual brand names (e.g. Kellogg, Quaker), it is virtually impossible to separate the specific earnings attributable to a single brand; and
* brand values are entangled with other intangible assets (e.g. patents, trademarks, know-how, staff, franchises, market entry barriers) - thus, there is difficulty in separating that part of the profits accrued by the brand name from those contributed by other (intangible) assets.
* The valuation of intangibles calls into question the whole purpose of the balance sheet. Is it a list of balances resulting from previous transactions (as it is used to be) or is it a value statement? Should estimates of the value of difficult-to-measure intangible assets be shown in the notes rather than on the face of the balance sheet?

* Problems of the capital maintenance concept e.g. the depreciation level. ED 52 states that fixed intangible assets should have a finite useful life. But some brands have last more than a 100 years e.g. Hovis goes back to 1886 and Coca-Cola to 1887. To suggest an arbitrary life is enforced euthanasia. But to ignore depreciation may go against the concept of prudence.

At present, the balance sheet is a hotchpotch of different valuation bases e.g. a mixture of historical costs, current costs and revaluations. Valuation of assets (and liabilities) is but one aspect of the problems afflicting the balance sheet. The current argument over the valuation of intangible assets calls into question the whole purpose of the balance sheet.

The ASB's Discussion Paper *'The Role of Valuation in Financial Reporting'* (1993) reviewed the theoretical merits and demerits of various valuation methods. It believes that the present modified historical cost system involving both historical costs and irregular revaluation is unsatisfactory. However, in order to avoid disruptive changes, the Board proposes to continue with the present system, but to remove some existing anomalies by revaluing certain assets more consistently. How will this affect identifiable intangible assets?

4 Amortisation

Current accounting regulation does not provide specific guidance on the determination by a company of the useful economic life of a purchased goodwill. How is the finite life to be ascertained? Companies may tend to opt for the maximum amortisation period without assessing realistically the carrying value of the asset and its remaining economic life. *Disclosure* is needed on the *period* chosen and the *reasons* for choosing that period.

Amortisation of purchased goodwill and intangible assets would bring the UK and Ireland broadly into line with international practice, although amortisation periods in other countries vary from 5-40 years. It is argued that firms would treat amortisation and the annual review of international assets more realistically if the charges can be treated as an allowable expense for UK corporation tax purposes (as in the US). Some firms (e.g. Ladbroke) suggests that the amortisation should be charged through the statement of total recognised gains and losses and not the profit and loss account - since the purchased goodwill is related to the worth of an acquisition , not the trading results of the group.

What about 'home-grown' intangibles? It does seem that the ASB's rationale of amortisation has more to do with prudence than economic reality and this has put firms reliant on self-generated brands at a disadvantage. It is argued that amortising brands would be 'double counting of expenses to be written off because current marketing and advertising expenditure maintains the value of the brand. To justify this argument, however, the marketing expenditure must be split into investment (development) activities and maintenance expenditure or else the argument that marketing expenditure equals annual amortisation is tenuous.

5 Brand accounting: A form of creative accounting?

Frequent acquisitions by companies deplete reserves because of the accounting requirement that goodwill be written off to reserves. A successful and growing company could find the strength of its balance sheet being jeopardised. This problem highlights the attraction of capitalising 'separable and identifiable' intangible assets, particularly brands.

This is considered by some as creative accounting. Milne (1989) showed that after RHM capitalised their brands, the balance sheet was improved and their borrowing appeared to be in a proper perspective. The gearings fall from 42 to 13 per cent and the problem of writing off goodwill eased. Their shareholders' funds increased from £250m to £920m - an increase of 268 per cent.

Elliott & Elliott pointed out that the debt/equity ratio of Guinness improved dramatically after intangibles were valued in the balance sheet. An analysis of their 5-year financial summary revealed the following.

Debt/Equity	**31 Dec.**	**1990**	**1989**	**1988**	**1987**	**1986**
Including acquired brands		30%	39%	23%	35%	35%
Excluding acquired brands		68%	99%	57%	81%	81%

It is debatable whether these practices are designed to mislead the reader of financial statements or to provide useful information. Tonkin & Robertson (1991) have argued that the question of brand accounting cannot be satisfactorily resolved in terms of existing accounting regulations because this debate has 'opened the Pandora's box' - i.e. fundamental accounting issues such as separability, verifiability, information usefulness, deferred expenditure and the premise of value have been raised.

According to Wild (1995) of Touche Ross, 'there is a whole spectrum of intangibles running from the unidentifiable to the clearly identifiable and traded like any other commodity, e.g. milk quotas, and the risk of arbitrage between different accounting treatments for different things...[there appears to be lack of] consistency as you cross the line between one type [of intangible] and another.'

A major motivation for brand accounting is the undesirable consequences of SSAP 22. To mitigate these effects, companies begin to sub-divide/split the goodwill figure into different classifications so that they may not fall under SSAP 22 and that the assets may remain on the balance sheet indefinitely unless there is a permanent diminution in value. Barwise et al. (1989) of the London Business School found that a 'major aim of brand valuation has been to repair or pre-empt equity depletion caused by the UK goodwill accounting rules.'

Due to the subjective nature of brand valuation, there is a fundamental conflict between economic validity and accounting objectivity. What accountants may see as creative accounting will be to managers no more than the commercial and financial reflection of their proper responsibilities.

It must be stressed that the acceptability of a particular valuation methodologies in the treatment of intangible assets depend on their 'acceptability' and *social* characteristics of their status as measurement technologies *rather* than simply a function of the technical properties of a valuation method (Napier & Power, 1992).

Valuation principles

Definition of value

Value has many meanings. It has been described as being '....expressible in terms of a single lump sum of money considered as payable or expended at a particular point in time in exchange for property, that is, the right to receive future benefits beginning at that particular timepoint.' (Babcock).

Value is the representation of all future benefits of ownership, compressed into a single payment. Therefore, value is continually changing as those future benefits increase or decrease with the passage of time. An opinion of value can only be expressed relative to a given moment, or 'as of' a specific date and is determined largely on the *perceived* benefits of the buyer. Therefore, the future benefits of ownership cannot be quantified without defining *whose* ownership is assumed and the underlying *purpose* of the valuation.

Purpose of valuation

The valuer must understand the purpose and nature of the valuation before deciding on the premise to be used. An asset may have different values according to the purpose for which the valuation is made. There are three premises upon which valuations can be based i.e. existing use, market value and liquidation or 'break-up' value.

Intangible assets are usually valued for the following purposes:

* financial reporting
* mergers and acquisitions
* taxation
* fund raising
* brand management and licensing arrangements

When valuing intangible assets for balance sheet purposes, the aim is to obtain a (conservative) estimate of the going concern, current-use value of the intangible asset based on future earnings, cashflows or notional royalties. Thus, the liquidation value basis are rarely used in intangible asset valuations.

Valuation methodologies

It is outside the scope of this paper to explore and evaluate fully the various valuation methodologies. However, a brief review of the common valuation principles in accounting is discussed below.

In financial reporting, common valuation principles for valuing intangible assets include *cost, market value, income (economic value).* Various approaches to valuing brands concern mostly brands (European Accounting Focus, March 1989; Barwise et al 1989; Arthur Andersen, 1992; Mullen, 1993). The *Companies Act 1985 (Section 4, Part C)* permits intangibles to be recognised at *current cost,* which can be interpreted as *'value to the business'*. This is defined as the lower of its replacement cost and its recoverable cost, where the latter is the higher of net realisable value and economic value. *Chapter 5 of the Statement of Principles* proposes following major methods of current values:

* Entry values - e.g. replacement cost (RC)
* Exit values - e.g. net realisable value (NRV)
* Values in use - e.g. economic values (EV) - present values of future cashflows obtained by the asset
* 'Value to the Business' (also known as deprival value or current cost) - i.e. a combination of the above three.

It will be expensive to provide all the different methods of current value on financial statements. The ASB suggests a practical solution could be to use the 'Value to the Business' principle. This method allows the accountant to *select* which of the alternatives can be best used in the circumstances. The deprival value is expressed as the loss which would be suffered by the business if it were deprived of the use of the asset. The value is the lower of its replacement cost or recoverable amount , the latter being the higher of NRV or EV.

Difficulties arise in brand accounting. In practice, brands valuation are being carried out neither on a cost nor on a market value basis. Since it is extremely difficult or meaningless to establish a brand's replacement cost and hard to estimate its NRV, valuers tend to focus on estimating the amount recoverable from future use i.e. the economic value

Separability as a criteria

A prerequisite for intangible asset valuation is that the valuer must be able to define the boundaries of the asset in question from other assets. Studies by Barwise et al. (1989) revealed that three main approaches have been used to handle the issue of separability for brands, i.e.:

* the price premium approach,
* the royalty payments or royalty relief method and
* the brands earnings or alternative return on assets approach.

The purpose of these three methods are to separate the brand's current or base year earnings or cashflow. The subsequent valuation of the brand is then performed either via the earnings approach - by applying an earnings multiplier to the base year earnings - or by using a DCF valuation on the base year figure as a starting point.

Table 2 highlights the principal valuation methodologies available for valuing intangible assets:

TABLE 2

The food & drink industry: capitalisation of intangible assets in the balance sheet

1. COST-BASED * Historical Cost * Replacement Cost (awareness recreation method)	**2. MARKET VALUE-BASED** * Comparable Market Value (NRV) * Comparable Royalty Rate
3. BRAND CONTRIBUTION * Premium Pricing/ Premium profit * Return on Assets/Return on Capital/Utility cost * Royalty Method	**4. ECONOMIC VALUE-BASED** * Future Earnings in terms of brand contribution

A strong portfolio of brands provides the backbone for strengthening and extending market share and to facilitate globalisation, particularly in industries such as food processing and grocery retailing where saturation is imminent. Since the last decade, there as been an increasing number of takeovers in the food and drinks sector as companies attempt to achieve sufficient critical mass to compete effectively in an increasingly international marketplace (Grover, 1989; McGee and Segal-Horn, 1989, 1992). Multi-billion dollar take-overs have created new food empires, with the cigarette company Philip Morris gobbling up Kraft Foods and Jacobs Suchard, Nestle swallowing Rowntree and Perrier. Both Unilever and Nestle own a quarter of the Nielsen-Checkout Top 100 (Europe's top 100 brands)(The Times 10/11/93). A significant element influencing the bid premium which a predator might be prepared to pay is the perception of the value of the intangible asset portfolio.

In the UK, controversy has reigned ever since the food company RHM valued both their acquired *and* 'home-grown' brands in its 1988 balance sheet. Nestle's takeover of Rowntree in 1988 triggered companies to find an acceptable brand valuation methodology. Nestle paid a hefty £2.5 billion for Rowntree even though the latter's book value is only £300m and the market capitalisation was only £1 billion when the bid was first launched (Murphy, 1992).

Although British companies developed fewer global brands, their influence in food and drinks was almost unparalleled. In the 1980s, the international competitive position of Britain in consumer-packaged goods remained vibrant in an otherwise mediocre economy. Brands have long been regarded as important sources of value to companies in the food, drink, tobacco and consumer goods industries. Adding value, according to a strategist, is 'both the proper motivation of corporate activity and the measure of its achievement' (Kay, 1993).

Food and drink are industries in which companies from the West have continuing strengths. Entrepreneurs have developed a range of brands which would dominate the world industry for the rest of the century - Coca-Cola, Heinz, Campbell Soup, Quaker Oats, Kellogg, Marlboro, Guinness and Cadbury, to name but a few.

Brand accounting, was first introduced in Australia in the 1984 largely by Rupert Murdoch's News Corporation Group. Aggressive companies embroiled in the decade of corporate take-over and merger activities in the 1980s (particularly in the food, drink and media industries) capitalised various intangible assets such as newspaper titles, licences to operate TV stations and brands of beer. In UK, a series of British companies followed suit by capitalising acquired brands.

In Europe (with the exception of Germany), brand capitalisation among the food and drinks industries is spreading - increasing numbers of French, Italian and Spanish companies are including brands on their balance sheet (FEE,1992). In France, for instance, Pernod Ricard and BSN have reflected brands on the balance sheet. The latter has capitalised traditional British brands such as 'Lea & Perrins Worcestershire Sauce' (Alexander & Archer, 1992).

Brand valuation poses extreme difficulties. While few would deny the role of brands in 'adding value', existing brand valuation techniques appear less than wholly reliable. Some of the problems were highlighted by the Philip Morris decision in early 1993 to sharply reduce the price of its Marlboro cigarettes. The Marlboro brand - the product of 'one of the most successful marketing campaigns in history' (Kay 1993) had been proclaimed as the world's most valuable brand in the early 1990s. But due to competition from cheaper alternatives, it experienced rapidly falling sales.

The Marlboro price cuts led to substantial downturn in the share prices of many globally-branded, consumer-goods businesses in the short-run. The inherent volatility of brands best illustrates why accountants still remain sceptical about brand valuation.

Analysis of results

A selection of companies in the food and drink industries was taken to illustrate the problems and issues of capitalising intangible assets. These are not meant to form a representative sample, but merely to illustrate the variations in current practices. The attached tables summarise those selected companies which capitalise intangible assets in the balance sheets. The third column in Table 1 shows the percentage of intangible assets over total fixed assets. A number of companies have a percentage of less than 10% with the exception of four companies i.e. CPC (UK) Ltd., Grand Metropolitan plc, John Lusty plc, Reckitt & Colman plc. They show a proportion in excess of 40%. The entire range is from 1.1% to 62.4%. This great fluctuation makes comparisons difficult and almost impossible in determining the importance of intangible assets to different companies because of the uncertainties surrounding accounting treatments.

The fourth column in Table 2 shows the information taken from the accounts on the company's policy on capitalisation and valuation. This reflects a considerable diversity in accounting treatments, both in the nature of the item capitalised and its valuation and amortisation. The results are further examined in Tables 5 and 6.

The fifth column in Table 2 shows the gearing ratio of the 20 companies expressed as debt/equity in percentage. This information is extracted from *Financial Analysis Made Easy* (FAME) software by Jordans. Although some companies enjoy a stronger gearing ratio because of the presence of intangible assets on the balance sheet, others have high gearing ratios and fairly negligible intangible assets, e.g. Fyffes plc and Heinz Co (GB) Ltd. Although the data is fragmentary, there does not appear to be evidence of a general policy of using capitalisation of intangibles to improve gearing ratios.

The auditors expressed reservations in only 2 cases - although there is considerable uncertainty over the accounting regulations and our analysis illustrates a wide range of approaches. With Pride Foods Ltd., the goodwill had been capitalised on the balance sheet but not amortised. This is contrary to the accounting regulations in *SSAP 22 Accounting for Goodwill.* Of course, if the company had stipulated that the goodwill had been in actual fact a brand, the auditors would have had no problems as there is no requirement at present to amortise a brand. In the case of Northumbrian Fine Foods plc, the auditors pointed out the possibility of a permanent diminution in the value of the company's brands. However, no further explanation was put forward as regards to the auditors' reservations in this case.

Table 3 analyses the type of intangible assets being capitalised. A total of 8 companies (40%) capitalise goodwill and 6 companies (30%) capitalise brands. A few trends have been observed. One feature is that companies which have capitalised patents or trademarks do not capitalise brands. Table 4 analyses the frequency of classifying intangible assets in the balance sheets of the companies. It is observed that the majority of companies capitalise brands, goodwill, patents and trademarks.

Disclosure policies on valuation and amortisation methodologies are lacking and firms appear to have differing accounting treatment for similar assets. For instance, only two companies value brands at cost (ie. John Lusty and Cadbury Schweppes). The rest capitalises brands at fair value. Of the companies that capitalise brands, only one company (ie. John Lusty) depreciates brands. The remainding companies do not depreciate brands as they are deemed to have an indefinite useful life. Annual reviews are performed to detect any permanent diminution in value. Table 5 highlights the different amortisation policies (eg. on patents and trademarks) adopted by companies for similar groups intangibles. The companies which depreciate intangible assets (eg. goodwill) use a wide ranging amortisation period (ie. from 10 years to 40 years) as illustrated in Table 6.

TABLE 3
Capitalisation of different types of intangible assets

Item	Number of companies	Percentage
Goodwill	6	30
Goodwill, brands and development cost	1	5
Goodwill, trademarks and patents	1	5
Trademarks	3	15
Trademarks and patents	1	5
Trademarks, patents and development cost	1	5
Brands	5	25
Development cost	1	5
Other (milk quota)	1	5
Total	**20**	**100**

TABLE 4
Frequency of classification of intangible assets in the balance sheets

Classification	Number of occurrences
Goodwill	8
Brands	6
Patents & Trademarks	6
Development cost	3
Other (milk quota)	1
	24

TABLE 5
Amortisation of intangible assets

	Amortised	Not amortised	Not stated (annual review)	Number of occurrences
Patents & trademarks	2	1	3	6
Brands	1	5	-	6
Goodwill	7	1	-	8
Development cost	3	-	-	3
Other (milk quota)	-	1	-	1
				24

TABLE 6
Amortisation policy

	Patents & Trademarks	Brands	Goodwill	Dev cost	Other	No. of Occurrences
10 years only		1	2	1		4
10-25 years	1		2	1		4
25-40 years			1			1
40 years	1		2			3
Not stated	3			1		4
No amortisation	1	5	1		1	8

						24

Conclusions

Brands and other intangible assets are of crucial importance in corporate management in the food and drinks industries. The value and contributions of these resources have been under-estimated and there is a need for a consensus between accountants and corporate managers on key issues of accounting for the financial reporting of brands. Current financial reporting regulations are ambiguous and there is a body of opinion which considers that brands should not be shown on the balance sheet. The main arguments for this view is that it is almost impossible to separate brands from other intangible and tangible assets within the company and, therefore, they could not be disposed of without selling off the company itself. The other reason is the difficulty of valuing brands as well as the large degree of subjectivity involved.

Despite these misgivings, our analysis demonstrates that intangible assets represent a vital and valuable component of many companies' balance sheets in the food and drinks industries. Unfortunately, the uncertainty surrounding the most appropriate accounting treatment has led to a variety of approaches by firms in an attempt to account for these 'hidden' assets. This cannot be helpful to the readers of the published accounts or the managers charged with the responsibility for the assets, both tangible and intangible. Sir David Tweedie, ASB Chairman, has said that 'while we cannot hope to meet every point of every protagonist on this contentious subject....the proposals in the Working Paper should satisfy everyone.' Hopefully, the next attempt by the ASB to resolve the problem will be more sympathetic to the needs and views of those who work in industry.

References

Aaker, D.A. (1991), '*Managing Brand Equity: Capitalising on the Value of a Brand Name*', *Free Press*, New York.

Accounting Standards Board (1993) '*Goodwill & Intangible Assets*', Discussion Paper.

Accounting Standards Board (1993) '*The Role of Valuation in Financial Reporting*'.

Accounting Standards Board (1995), '*Goodwill & Intangible Assets*', Working Paper for Discussion at Public Hearing, June.

Accounting Standards Committee (1990), '*ED 52 Accounting for Intangible Assets*'.

Accounting Standards Committee (1989) SSAP 22 Accounting for Goodwill.

Alexander, D. & Archer, S. (1992), '*The European Accounting Guide*', *Academic Press*, Academic Press, London.

Allen, D. (1990), '*The Value of Brands: Wrong Figures Lead to Wrong Decisions*', *Financial Times*, 18 December, p. 12.

Arthur Andersen (1992), '*The Valuation of Intangible Assets*', Special Report, No. P254, January.

Babcock, Henry, FASA, '*Appraisal Principles & Procedures*', Washington DC: American Society of Appraisers, Chapter 6, p. 95.

Barwise et al (1989), 'Accounting for Brands', ICAEW/London Business School.

Bryant R. (1989), '*The Value of Separable Intangibles*', *Accountancy*, March , pp. 106-110.

Company Reporting (1992), '*The Carrying Value of Intangible Assets*', March, No. 21, pp. 3-8.

Coopers & Lybrand (1990), 'Intangible Assets: A survey of senior businessmen's views', March.

Damant, D (1992), '*On the Valuation of Assets*', Map Securities, 20 January.

Doyle, P (1994), '*Marketing Management & Strategy*', Prentice Hall.15. Egginton (1990), '*All Change on Goodwill, Merger and Brand Accounting*', *The Accountant's Magazine*, April, pp. 45-46.

Elliott, B. & Elliott, J. (1993), '*Financial Accounting & Reporting*', Prentice Hall.

European Accounting Focus (1989) '*Brands: Update and Methods of Valuation*', pp.14-15, March.

Federation des Experts Comptables Europeens (1992), '*FEE Analysis of European Accounting & Disclosure Practices*', Routledge, London.

Hall, R. (1989), '*The Management of Intellectual Assets: A New Corporate Perspective*' *Journal of General Management*, Autumn, Vol 15, No.1.

Hall, R. (1991), *'The Contribution of Intangible Resources to Business Success'*, *Journal of General Management*, Summer Vol 16, No. 4.
Hares, J. & Royle, D. (1994), *'Measuring the Value of Information Technology'*, John Wiley & Sons.
Hussey, R. (1994), *'Undervalued Intangibles'*, Touche Ross, London.
Irish, V. (1992), *'Legal Protection for Innovation'*, *Certified Accountant*, July pp. 18-20.
Itami, H. and Roehl, T.W. (1987), *'Mobilising Invizible Assets'*, Harvard University Press, Cambridge, Massachusetts.
Kapferer, J. N. (1992), *'Strategic Brand Management'*, Kogan Page, London.
Kay, J (1993), *'Foundations of Corporate Success'*, Oxford University Press.
McGee, J. & Segal-Horn, S. (1989), *'Changes in the European Food Industry: The Consequences of 1992'*, 8th Annual Strategic Management Conference, Armsterdam, 20 Oct. See also same authors in *'Europe & Multinationals: Issues and Responses in the 1990s'* by Young , S. & Hamill, J. (1992)
Milne, G. (1989), *'Magic Numbers in a Melting Pot,'* Accountancy Age, Jan 26, p. 18.
Moorhouse, M. (1990), *'Brands debate: Wake Up to the Real World'*, Accountancy, p. 30.
Mullen, M. (1993), *'How to Value Intangible Assets'*, Accountancy, November, pp. 92-94.
Murphy, J. (1992), *'Branding: A Key Marketing Tool'* 2nd ed., MacMillan.
Napier, C. & Power, M. (1992), *'Professional Research, Lobbying and Intangibles: A Review Essay'*, Accounting & Business Research, Vol. 23, No. 89, pp. 85-95.
Nobes, C. (1989), *'ASC outs goodwill on the balance sheets'*, Financial Times, 21 December.
Power, M. (1990), *'Brand & Goodwill Accounting Strategies'*, Woodhead Faulkner.
Rutterman, P (1990), *'Accounting for Brands and Separability'* in M. Power 's (1990), *'Brand & Goodwill Accounting Strategies'*, Woodhead Faulkner.
Tonkin, D. & Robertson, B (1991), *'Brands & Other Intangible Fixed Assets'* Financial Reporting, ICAEW 1990-91, pp. 3-28. See also *'Names in A Conceptual Framework'* Accountancy, p. 28, March 1991, by same authors.
Touche Ross (1993), *'Goodwill & Intangible Assets: The Touche Ross View'*.
Tweedie, D. & Blanchet, J. (1989), *'Brands, Goodwill & the Balance Sheet'*, Accountancy, Jan., pp. 20-22.
Tweedie, D. & Stacey, G. (1989), *'Setting a Standard for the Value of Goodwill'*, Financial Times, 7 December.
Wild, K. (1995), quoted in Fitzgerald, N. in *'Protective Thoughts'*, CA Magazines, May, pp. 38-43.

Part Four
ASPECTS OF FINANCIAL MANAGEMENT

10 Investment decisions in advanced manufacturing systems: A review and identification of research areas

Magdy G. Abdel-Kader

Introduction

Manufacturing is the most important segment in many economies. There is a clear trend towards a switch from mass production of standard products to the production of a great variety of custom-made products with shorter and amputated product life cycles, in addition to an increasing complexity and sophistication of product design. Also, consumers are demanding greater variety of products along with better quality, reliability, and lower cost (Naik & Chakravarty, 1992).

Also, rapid development in technology has made available a host of automated devices with diverse applications in manufacturing industries. Functional areas such as product design, product testing, process design, fabrication, spray painting, assembly, inspection, material handling, warehousing, and production planning and control have been dramatically impacted by automation (Huang et al., 1991). Generally, automation refers to the use of mechanical devices controlled by a host computer that can be programmed and reprogrammed to provide various operational instructions.

Arguably, manufacturing firms that desire to survive and thrive in future need to lower production costs for small batch sizes and greater product-mix complexity, while producing consistently better quality products. These firms must also develop the capabilities to introduce new products quickly, and cope with shorter delivery cycles (Naik & Chakravarty, 1992). Advanced Manufacturing Systems (AMS) such as Flexible Manufacturing Systems (FMS) and robots are able to achieve all of these.

Although the decision considering acquisition of AMS is an investment decision, these systems have special characteristics that make their justification process more complex than conventional manufacturing systems. First, these systems are much more flexible. This flexibility maintains the value of the equipment over the long run and reduced the risk of obsolescence. But the advantages of this flexibility are not easily quantified in traditional economic justification methods such as Discounted Cash Flow Methods (DCFM). Second, the synergy of these new technologies when linked together. Users consistently report qualitative benefits from such linked systems, such as speed of response to changes in customer demand, that are deemed far more important than the normal cost savings (Meredith & Suresh, 1986).

Also, these advanced systems are capital intensive. They require large investments in all stages of implementation- planning, designing, purchasing, installing and operating the system. Therefore, the investment decision for acquiring such systems needs special treatment.

An important function of management accounting systems is providing managers with models that evaluate all relevant information needed for making investment decisions (Accola, 1994). Ideally, the management accounting system must provide information and models useful for predicting the future cash flows of prospective investment alternatives and choosing among them.

The most difficult task associated with AMS investment lies in identifying and quantifying the benefits that the system will provide. Based on the difficulty of quantifying these benefits, Mensah & Miranti (1989) classified them into two categories. The first category is the primary benefits which include:(1) direct labour savings, (2) direct material savings, (3) savings from less frequent set-ups, (4) the value of higher quality output, and (5) the savings from reduced material and in process inventories. The second category is the secondary benefits which include: (1) greater manufacturing flexibility, (2) learning effects, and (3) the effects on employee morale. Because the primary benefits of automation are based on cost savings, they are easier to quantify than the secondary benefits.

However, DCF analysis is widely used to evaluate a potential investment project in practice (Somers & Gupta, 1991; Wilner et al., 1992; Primrose et al., 1985; Primrose &. Leonard, 1986; Kulatilaka, 1984). This analysis uses three estimates: (1) a forecast of annual net cash flows, (2) a discount rate (theoretically, the firm's cost of capital), and (3) an estimated life of the project (Chan & Lynn, 1993). Using DCFM, the firm should invest if the net present value of the estimated cash flows is positive or, alternatively, if the internal rate of return of the cash flows exceeds the firm's cost of capital.

Many authors have criticised applying DCFM to evaluate an investment in AMS (e.g., Medearis et al., 1990; Mensah & Miranti, 1989) because these models are biased in favour of short-term investments whose benefits are more easily quantified than longer-term projects. Consequently, several writers have concluded that DCFM should not be applied to evaluate investment in AMS

The main problem in applying DCFM for evaluating the decision to acquire AMS is the failure of these models to quantify the benefits of the acquisition of automation. DCFM focus only on future net cash savings in reduced labour costs and energy costs which are easily quantifiable and they ignore the other benefits which may not be easy to quantify such as improved product quality, greater manufacturing flexibility, learning effects, the effects on employee morale, and short lead times[1].

Although, some authors (Kulatilaka, 1984; Knott & Getto, 1982) argue that there are some benefits that can be quantified -with recognition of the difficulties to do it- such as savings resulting from: reduced inventories, higher quality output and reduction in rework costs, inspection costs and warranty costs, almost all authors in this field ascertained that traditional DCFM cannot quantify benefits such as greater manufacturing flexibility, learning effects, reduced lead times, and the effects on employee morale. These benefits are most critical in evaluating the decision of acquiring AMS.

Due to these criticisms some researchers (e.g., Medearis et al., 1990) argue to ignore financial analysis and regard the investment as a strategy that should be implemented regardless of the results of DCFM. Also, several authors suggested alternative approaches to evaluate the investment in AMS. These approaches can be either numerical or non-numerical.

The paper aims to review analytically the literature concerning evaluating investment decisions in AMS. This literature has been classified into three approaches; quantitative, qualitative, and integrated approaches. Figure (1) illustrates these approaches and the methods included in each approach.

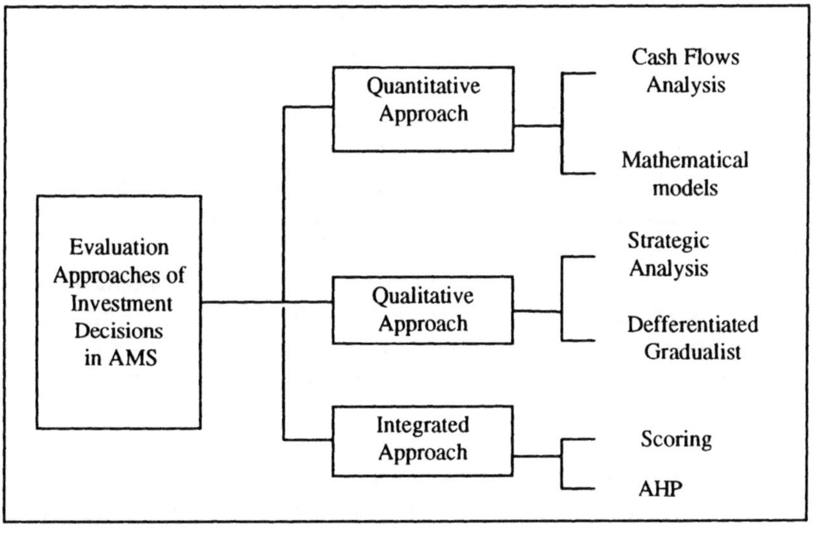

Figure 1: A classification scheme

The remainder of the paper is divided into four sections. The following three sections represent the review of each evaluation approach. The last section is a conclusion and identification of areas for future research.

The quantitative approach

This approach primarily considers the evaluation methods of investment decisions in AMS which concentrate mainly on the easily quantifiable variables, with less effort to include the qualitative variables in the decision analysis. The methods included in this approach are categorised into two groups; cash flows analysis and mathematical models.

The cash flows analysis

The most common methods which rely on cash flows analysis are payback period and DCFM, namely; NPV and IRR. These methods are usually known as economic methods[2]. The survey conducted by Klammer et al. (1991) showed that 42% of 100 large industrial firms use the payback period method as a primary or secondary technique to evaluate the high technology investment. IRR and NPV are used by 57% and 46% of firms respectively.

Payback Period method The payback period gives the time required to recover the initial investment amount. The project is acceptable if the payback period is equal or less than a predetermined payback period. The logic of this method relies on an assumption that the project of shortest recovery period provides the best return/lowest risk. The payback period method has many advantages that make it the most preferable method in practice. These advantages include; first, it is quick and simple to calculate, second, it needs minimal information for computations (Randhawa & West, 1992), third, it saves decision makers the trouble of having to forecast cash flows over the whole of a project's life since it is concerned only with the cash flows during the predetermined payback period (Lumby, 1995).

However, the payback period method has been criticised for its use in evaluation of investments in general and particularly investments in AMS. The limitations of this method are (Airey, 1983):

- Ignores cash flows after the payback point.
- Is biased against investments with the highest return in the later years of the project.
- Is inadequate for rigorous analysis of all the variables and for systematic comparison purposes.

Primrose & Leonard (1986) indicate another problem with the use of payback period method, how to determine analytically the required payback period. They also showed the relation between IRR and payback period. This relation, shown in figure (2), reveals that companies who are asking for investment with two or three years payback period are demanding an IRR of 49 and 31 %after tax respectively.

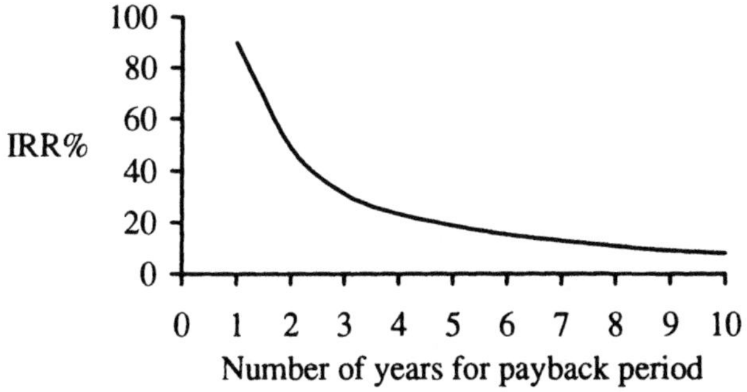

Figure 2: The relation between IRR and Payback period (Primrose and Leonard 1985, p.290)

However, this relationship is due to two reasons; first, the payback period method ignores cash flows after the payback period. Second, it does not take the time value of money into account. The latter reason can be overcome by using discounted cash flows instead of purely (non-discounted) cash flows.

Discounted Cash Flow Methods. Net Present Value (NPV) and Internal Rate of Return (IRR) are known as Discounted Cash Flows Methods (DCFM). The NPV is a figure that represents the sum of the future cash flows (positive or negative) discounted at a discount rate to time zero (equation 1). The decision rule for choosing among competitive alternatives is that the one with the greatest NPV is the most desirable. On the other hand, the IRR is a percentage figure which makes the sum of discounted future cash flows equals zero (equation 2). In equation (2), r is the IRR, usually computed through a number of trials. The decision rule for IRR is similar to that for NPV, namely, the highest alternative's IRR is the most preferable one.

$$NPV_p = \sum_{t=0}^{n} \frac{CF_t}{(1+r)^t} \qquad (1)$$

where:

NPV_p: the net present value of project p,

CF_t : the cash flows of the project in time t t = 0,1,......... n,

r: the discount rate, and

n: the life of the project in years.

$$\sum_{t=0}^{n} \frac{CF_t}{(1+r)^t} = 0 \qquad (2)$$

The DCFM are widely recommended by many authors to evaluate investment decisions in AMS.

Kulatilaka (1984) advocated the use of NPV as a technique to evaluate the investment in automation projects. Three groups of cash flows are considered in the analysis; initial costs, operating costs and benefits, and tax effects. He used the Capital Asset Pricing Model (CAPM) to arrive at a discount rate which incorporates the systematic risk (beta) associated with the different components of cash flows. His main contribution is the suggestion that the beta of a project be defined as in equation (3), then, the discount rate become as in equation (4). He, also, identified the strategic implications -such as effects due to flexibility and quality improvements- when to invest and when to abandon, and the learning value, which are considered as a subjective part of the final decision for those projects that have a positive NPV.

$$b_p = b_r [1 + (PV_{fc} / PV_p)] \qquad (3)$$

where:

b_p: the beta of the project,

b_r: the beta of revenues associated with the proposed project,

PV_{fc}: the present value of fixed costs associated with the proposed project,

PV_p: the present value of assets associated with the project.

$$r_p = r_f + b_p \qquad (4)$$

where:

r_p: risky discount rate,
r_f: risk free discount rate.

Kaplan (1986) suggested that DCF analysis might be used to evaluate the investments in CIM without considering the difficult -to- measure benefits in the analysis. If the result of the DCF analysis is positive, the investment is justified. But if the DCF is negative, then it becomes necessary to compare the difficult -to-measure benefits with the additional cash flows required to make the DCF positive. If the management is willing to pay, at least, the additional cash flows to enjoy the difficult -to- measure benefits, then the investment is justifiable and vice versa. As Naik & Chakravarty (1992) stated this comparison leaves a lot of room for inconsistency and inaccuracy. Also, this approach does not provide any means of selecting amongst the alternatives which satisfy the DCF criterion.

Refinement of this approach was introduced by Bennett & Hendricks (1987). They suggested quantifying the benefits which are not included in the first DCF analysis using a team approach and probability analysis. Then, IRR, NPV or payback period can be calculated to determine the viability of the project.

Hundy & Hamblin (1988) advocated the use of the IRR method because it has the attraction of giving a single value to the worth of the project regardless of interest rate changes. They claimed that risks inherent in a specific project can be easily modelled using spread-sheet methods. They illustrated their approach through a numerical example where a conventional machine shop and a flexible machining system are the available alternatives. Based on the pessimistic, optimistic and most likely scenarios, they concluded that the decision to install FMS facilities should be made in all scenarios.

Although, the use of DCF analysis has many advantages such as its low cost (Azzone et al., 1992), simplicity, clarity, and ease of data collection (Meredith & Suresh, 1986), there are many problems with applying it in evaluating investment decisions in AMS. Canada & Sullivan (1990) summarise these problems in three areas; arbitrary hurdle rates, comparison with the status quo, and insufficient benefits analysis.

More specifically, Canada & Sullivan (1990) indicated that firms often use an after tax hurdle rate of 20% or more. Such arbitrary high rate means that only projects having large cash flows in their early years will be regarded as feasible. Hence, the investments in AMS which tend to be more beneficial in the long-term may seem incorrectly as infeasible. The second problem in applying DCFM in evaluating investment decisions in AMS is the comparison with status quo. This means that AMS investment are being implicitly compared to 'doing nothing'. The choice of doing nothing is evaluated as if the existing process is going to continue performing as it has in the past. However, this is an unlikely scenario, a 'do nothing' firm is likely to lose market share. The last problem, insufficient benefit analysis, is due to the difficulty of quantifying the qualitative benefits of AMS investments in cash flows terms. However, qualitative and integrated approaches will address the status quo and intangible benefits problems.

Mathematical models

Miltenburg & Krinsky (1987) suggested a mathematical model to evaluate FMS utilising the DCF framework. Their suggestion was based on the application of an iterative procedure called the Decision Analysis Cycle (figure 3). The procedure is divided into three phases. In the first (deterministic) phase, the variables affecting the decision are defined, the relationships between the variables are developed, and the importance of each variable is also determined. In the second (probabilistic) phase uncertainties (i.e., probabilities) are encoded on the more important variables. Then, the associated probability distribution of the outcome variables is determined. The final (informational) phase uses the results of the first two phases to determine the economic value of eliminating uncertainty in each of the important variables. If there are profitable sources of information, then the decision should be to gather the new information and revise the original analysis. The analysis is repeated until there are no longer any profitable sources of new information. Then, from the probability distributions of the outcome variable for each alternative, the principles of stochastic dominance and risk preference are used to determine the best decision.

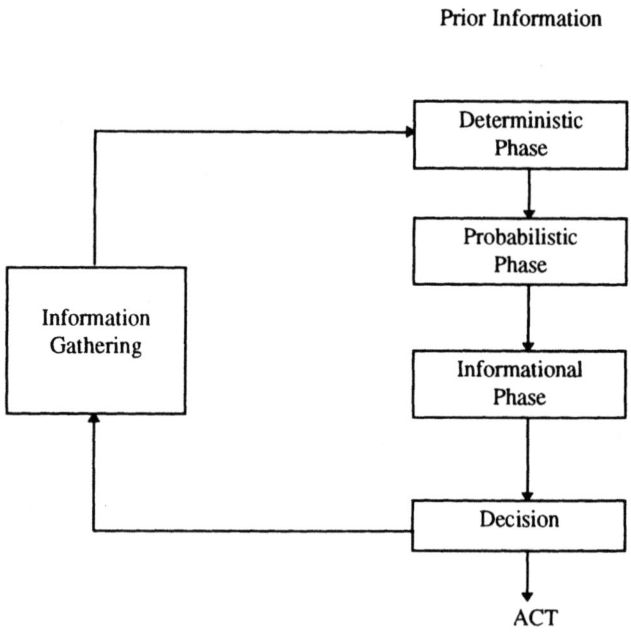

Figure 3: The decision analysis cycle (Miltenburg and Krinsky, 1987)

The most appealing feature of this model is the formal incorporation of a method for updating the state of knowledge by iteratively searching for the usefulness of new information (Mensah & Miranti, 1989). On the other hand, the model considered only the financial variables through NPV analysis.

Park & Son (1988) developed a multi-period net present value linear programming model. They proposed measurements for quality costs (prevention, appraisal, and failure costs), and flexibility (idle, set-up, waiting, and inventory costs). Also, they considered explicitly the opportunity costs in the decision model. They distinguished between capital performance (NPV1) which refers to the net present value of the initial investment, depreciation, and net salvage value, and production performance (NPV2) which refers to the net present value of benefits resulting from manufacturing and marketing, they formulated the linear programming model that maximises the NPV2 as the objective function subject to various constraints representing the limited resources and the logistic relationship between the manufacturing system and the inventory system. The model is illustrated through a case study comparing a batch shop with a proposed cellular manufacturing system.

The qualitative approach

This approach considers primarily the evaluation methods of investment decisions in AMS that concentrate mainly on the qualitative variables in the analysis. This approach includes two groups; strategic analysis and differentiated gradualist approach.

Strategic analysis

Meredith & Suresh (1986) described a strategic analysis through four concepts: (1) technical importance, (2) business objectives, (3) competitive advantage, and (4) research and development (R&D). The justification process for a project under the concept of technical importance assumes that the desired end cannot be attained unless this project is undertaken first. The same logic applies with the business objectives concept, a project is executed only if it is essential to achieve the business objectives, for example, the firm may approve implementing a project in order to give the impression to customers, vendors, and visitors, that they are progressively advanced, and up and coming organisation. Similarly, under the competitive advantage concept, the firm may invest in an automation project in order to gain a significant advantage over its competitors. Under the R&D concept, the firm treats the project as an R&D investment if it holds sufficient strategic promise to justify the investment. This concept relies on one of many such projects to eventually come through and provide returns to the firm to reimburse all the failures.

Medearis et al. (1990) introduced a framework for justifying FMS from a strategic perspective. Based on Porter's model, they argue that the forces that drive industry competition include the threat of new entrants, the bargaining power of suppliers and customers, the threat of substitute goods, and the rivalry existing among industry participants. They argue also that the profitability of a company is dependent on the strongest of these forces and a company must consider the dominant force when developing a competitive strategy. They analysed the performance of FMS with these forces and concluded that FMS offers organisations an opportunity to improve competitive positioning within an industry and even to expand the definition of the industry. Also through FMS technology, firms can improve their positioning not only in their industry but also globally.

Perhaps the most holistic attempt to develop a model for selecting an appropriate FMS from a strategic approach is the study by Elango & Meinhart (1994). This model is built on the logic that any decision with respect to the selection and implementation of an FMS should be consistent with the strategy and the environment of the firm. The analysis of the decision begins with identifying the industry and market needs using Porter's model on forces affecting industry competition, namely; industry competitors, suppliers, substitutes, buyers, and potential entrants. The strength of the five competitive forces determines the ability of the firm to earn above average profits. Once the industry and market needs have been analysed, the next step would be to develop a manufacturing strategy which takes account of the FMS strategies pursued by the dominant or majority of firms in the industry. They defined the manufacturing strategy as the amount of the strategic capability offered by the manufacturing operations of the firm to facilitate the implementation of the overall corporate and business strategy. The next step in their framework is the analysis of the strategic flexibility to determine the required amount of flexibility that should be evaluated with respect to the financial performance of this system. They advocated the use of the standard financial techniques such as return on investment, NPV, IRR, or value-based approaches for the financial evaluation of the system. The final stage of the decision analysis is to determine whether the capabilities of the organisation match the skills required to run the system effectively.

Differentiated gradualist approach

Mensah & Miranti (1989) in their review of capital expenditure analysis and automated manufacturing systems described what they called 'Differentiated Gradualist Approach' as an evaluation approach for automation projects. According to this approach, the first project is regarded as a learning experience and not subjected to rigorous DCF analysis. The evaluation of subsequent projects are modified based on the better understanding of cost patterns apparent through the review of the initial project's outcome. Then, with greater experience it is hoped that the DCF framework can be further refined.

They claimed that the merits of this approach are twofold. First, it permits a better perspective to be developed for evaluating the qualitative benefits of automation. Second, since many firms implementing automated systems undergo an extensive trial-and-error period before all bugs are worked out of the systems, this pilot approach can provide valuable information allowing management to avoid costly errors in full-scale manufacturing . Also, they mentioned that this approach is a costly approach and will be more expensive to operate (on a per unit of output basis) than full-scale manufacturing. Thus, it may be appropriate only for large firms with substantial resources who can absorb the initial strain.

Although, the qualitative approach concentrates on the qualitative variables which represent the biggest problem facing the evaluation techniques of investment in AMS, almost all the methods included in this approach are extremely judgmental in nature. They might lack adequate structures to be used with sufficient confidence as valid scientifically. Thus, these methods may be only used as secondary methods.

The integrated approach

These methods of evaluating investment decisions in AMS take into account a wider range of variables, both qualitative and quantitative, in the decision analysis. This approach includes two groups; scoring models and analytical hierarchy process.

Scoring models

The scoring models are a set of techniques which reduces a multi-attribute problem to one consisting of a single dimension (Randhawa & West, 1992). Scoring models include three basic techniques; unweighted 0-1 scoring, unweighted factor scoring and weighted factor scoring. Meredith & Suresh (1986) described the unweighted 0-1 scoring model. After selecting the relevant criteria, each alternative is rated 0 or 1 with respect to each factor depending on whether or not it satisfies this criterion. The summation of these rates for each alternative is used to rank the project.

Simplicity is the main advantage of this technique. However, this technique has two disadvantages; first, it assumes all criteria are of equal importance. Second, it does not allow for gradation of the degree to which a specific alternative meets the various criteria (Meredith & Suresh, 1986).

Nelson (1986) suggested an unweighted factor scoring model for evaluating and prioritising AMS projects. This model considers the scores of five variables; technology assessment (t), equipment evaluation (e), capacity elasticity (c), cost-budget analysis (b), and adjusted net present value (v). The total score of a project (s) can be obtained from the linear combination of these variables as in equation (5).

$$s = t + e + c + b + v \qquad (5)$$

The main advantages of Nelson's scoring model are its treatment of non-economic criteria and project interdependency. On the other hand, the disadvantages of this model are twofold. First, it considers all variables in equal weight. Second, there is duplication in two terms since the capital cost of the project is considered in calculation of cost-budget ratio score and NPV score.

Parsaei & Wilhelm (1989) proposed a weighted factor scoring model to evaluate AMS alternatives which is based on a linear additive model developed by Klee (1971). The model is divided into two stages; The first stage examines the desirability of various strategic (long-term) automation proposals available, while the second stage evaluates each tactical (short-term) alternative for implementing the strategic proposal selected as most desirable in the first stage. They proposed two sets of ordinal scale weight; one for ranking the importance of strategic and tactical alternatives and the other for evaluating the performance of each strategic and tactical alternative with respect to each alternative (table 1). These weights are then employed in the linear additive model in each stage (equation 6).

$$Max\, A_j = \sum_{i=1}^{n} W_i X_{ij} \qquad for \quad j = 1,2,.....n \qquad (6)$$

where:

A_j: the score of the alternative j,

W_i: the weight assigned to the ith attribute,

X_{ij}: the anticipated performance of the jth alternative with respect to the ith attribute.

TABLE 1
The Ordinal Scale Used in Parsaei and Wilhelm's Model

A. Ordinal scale weight for ranking the importance of the strategic and tactical alternatives	
Very important	1.00
Important	0.75
Necessary	0.50
Unimportant	0.25
B. Ordinal scale weight for evaluating the performance of each strategic and tactical alternative with respect to each attribute	
Superior	1.00
Good	0.80
Above average	0.60
Average	0.40
Below average	0.20
Poor	0.00

Source: Parsaei and Wilhelm, 1989, p.367.

This model overcomes one of the disadvantages of Nelson's scoring model; it gives weight to the considered factors. But, on the other hand, it does not consider the financial factors in the analysis.

In general, there are three reasons make that scoring models attractive; first, they provide an appropriate means to utilise management's value judgements regarding intangible factors. Second, they have the ability to incorporate management's changing priorities and objectives in the evaluation processes through changes in the weights assigned to various factors. Finally, they also permit the application of mathematical programming techniques to derive the most desirable projects which optimise the decision criteria (Mensah & Miranti, 1989). However, these models assume the linearity and independence of the criterion which may disagree with the reality. Also, there is no means to measure the consistency of decision maker's judgements data.

Analytich Hierarchy Process (AHP)

Saaty (1990) described the development of the AHP. The Technique was developed during 1970s and its theoretical treatment was set out by Saaty in 1980. The AHP enables decision makers to model the complex decisions which involve many concurrent interaction of many variables (Swann & O'Keefe, 1990; Apostolou & Hassell, 1993). The inputs of the AHP are judgements about the relative importance of each criterion and the preference on each criterion for each decision alternative. The output of the process is a prioritised ranking to denote the overall preference for each of the decision alternatives (Anderson et al., 1994).

The methodology of AHP attempts to analyse the impacts in the lowest level on the overall goal of a hierarchy (Wabalickis, 1988). To carry out the AHP, the first step is to develop a graphical representation of the problem in terms of the overall goal or focus, criteria, and decision alternatives. This graph represent the hierarchy for the problem as shown in figure (4).

The second step in the AHP is conducting pairwise comparisons to establish priority measures for both the criteria and the decision alternatives. The AHP employs a measurement scale which is shown in table (2). This step can be carried out through constructing a set of pairwise comparisons matrices. With respect to the hierarchy shown in figure (4), the priorities of both the three decision alternatives in terms of each criterion and all criteria in terms of the overall goal are determined and shown in table (3). The priority vector is computed as an average of the elements in each row of the normalised pairwise comparison matrix[3].

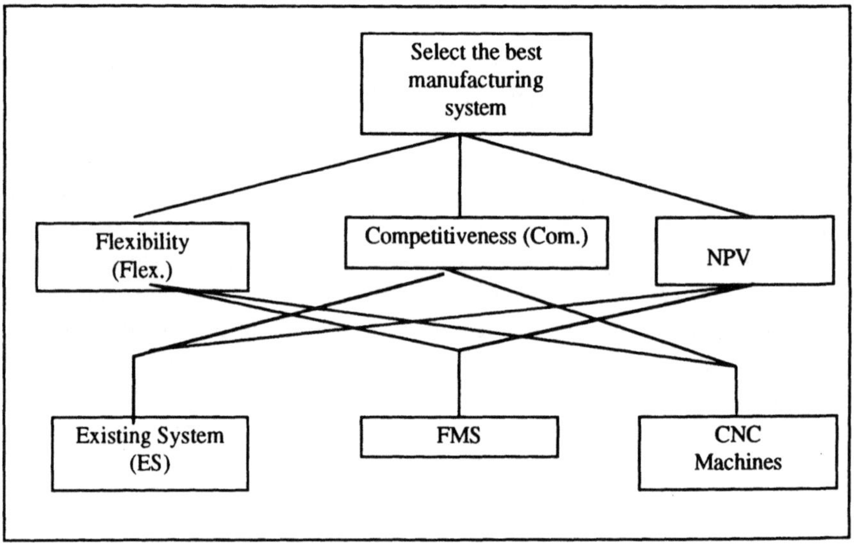

Figure 4: Developing the problem Hierarchy

TABLE 2
The measurement scale of AHP

Numerical value	Definition
1	Equal importance of both elements
3	Moderate importance of one element over another
5	Strong importance of one element over another
7	Very strong importance of one element over another
9	Extreme importance of one element over another
2,4,6,8	Intermediate values between two nearby judgements
Reciprocals	Used to reflect dominance of the second element as compared with the first

Source: Harker, 1989, p. 9.

TABLE 3
The results of pairwise comparisons

A: Pairwise comparisons of the three alternatives with respect to each criterion:					
Flexibility:					
	ES	FMS	CNC	Priority Vector	
ES	1	1/7	1/3	0.083	
FMS	7	1	5	0.723	
CNC	3	1/5	1	0.194	
					CR=0.058
Competitiveness:					
ES	1	1/4	1/3	0.118	
FMS	5	1	2	0.576	
CNC	3	1/2	1	0.306	
					CR=0.078
NPV					
ES	1	7	4	0.701	
FMS	1/7	1	1/3	0.086	
CNC	1/4	3	1	0.213	
					CR=0.028
B: Pairwise comparisons of the criteria with respect to overall goal					
	Flex.	Com.	NPV	Priority Vector	
Flex.	1	1/3	1/2	0.156	
Com.	3	1	4	0.619	
NPV	2	1/4	1	0.225	
					CR=0.095

Since the assigned weight to each decision alternative and criterion may be estimated from data or from expertise decision makers, there is a need to measure the consistency of the judgement data. The AHP provide a consistency ratio (CR) which is an indicator of the reliability of the model (Apostolou & Hassell, 1993). This ratio is designed in such a way that values of the ratio exceeding 0.10 are indicative of inconsistent judgements; in such cases, it is probably preferable to revise the original values in the pairwise comparison matrix (Anderson et al., 1994). To illustrate the computation of CR, let the pairwise comparison matrix be denoted X_1 and the priority vector be denoted X_2. Then define $X_3 = X_1 * X_2$ and $X_4 = X_3 / X_2$. These calculations in connection with the pairwise comparison matrix of the three alternatives with respect to flexibility (table 3) yield the following information.

First, X3 and X4 is determined by:

$$X_3 = \underline{\text{Pairwise comparison matrix}} \times \underline{\text{Priority vector}}$$

$$\begin{matrix} \text{ES} \\ \text{FMS} \\ \text{CNC} \end{matrix} \begin{bmatrix} 1 & 1/7 & 1/3 \\ 7 & 1 & 5 \\ 3 & 1/5 & 1 \end{bmatrix} \times \begin{bmatrix} 0.083 \\ 0.723 \\ 0.194 \end{bmatrix}$$

$$X_3 = \begin{matrix} 1 \times 0.083 + 1/7 \times 0.723 + 1/3 \times 0.194 = 0.251 \\ 7 \times 0.083 + 1 \times 0.723 + 5 \times 0.194 = 2.274 \\ 3 \times 0.083 + 1/5 \times 0.723 + 1 \times 0.194 = 0.588 \end{matrix}$$

$$X_4 = \begin{matrix} X_3 & \div & \text{Priority vector} & \\ 0.251 & \div & 0.083 & = 3.024 \\ 2.274 & \div & 0.723 & = 3.145 \\ 0.588 & \div & 0.194 & = 3.031 \end{matrix}$$

Next, the average of the elements of X_4 can be denoted as λ_{max}:

$$\lambda_{max} = \frac{3.024 + 3.145 + 3.031}{3} = 3.067$$

Then, the consistency index CI is determined by:

$$CI = \frac{\lambda_{max} - n}{n - 1} = \frac{3.067 - 3}{2} = 0.0335$$

where:

n is the number of the elements of priority vector.

Finally, the CR is determined by:

$$CR = \frac{CI}{RI} = \frac{0.0335}{0.58} = 0.058$$

where:

RI is random index computed for matrices of order n = 1 - 15 via simulation (Apostolou & Hassell, 1993).

The final step in the AHP is developing an overall priority ranking. This can be obtained by summing the products of the criterion priority times the priority of its decision alternative. In connection with the priority vector in table (3), this computation can be done as follows:

$$\underset{\text{The criterion priority}}{\begin{matrix}\text{Flex.}\\ \text{Com.}\\ \text{NPV}\end{matrix}\begin{bmatrix}0.156\\0.619\\0.225\end{bmatrix}} \times \begin{matrix}\text{ES}\\ \text{FMS}\\ \text{CNC}\end{matrix}\begin{bmatrix}0.083 & 0.118 & 0.701\\0.723 & 0.576 & 0.086\\0.194 & 0.306 & 0.213\end{bmatrix} = \underset{\text{Overall priority}}{\begin{matrix}\text{ES}\\ \text{FMS}\\ \text{CNC}\end{matrix}\begin{bmatrix}0.243\\0.489\\0.268\end{bmatrix}}$$

After obtaining the overall priority of the decision alternatives, the decision maker can choose the decision alternative which has the highest priority. In this example, the decision maker is advised to choose the FMS alternative as it has the highest overall priority (0.489).

The ability of AHP to structure a complex problem hierarchically and synthesise priorities to the decision alternatives, has attracted many researchers to apply it in the area of evaluating AMS investments. These researchers form two groups; the researchers in the first group have applied AHP to the investment evaluation in AMS directly. In other words, they formulate the problem of investment in AMS in the AHP framework and rank the decision alternatives according to the resulting priorities. The researchers in the other group have incorporated the AHP with other techniques such as simulation, the Leontief input-output model, and mixed integer programming. These two approaches will be reviewed in the following two subsections.

The direct application of AHP Wabalickis (1988) considered a hierarchy of 4 levels; overall goal, criteria, subcriteria and decision alternatives. The overall goal is to select the best manufacturing system from three alternatives; existing system, FMS, NC machines. The criteria and subcriteria are:

- Inventory costs: reduced lead time and minimise inventory,
- Sales: product mix response, profitability, and product change response,
- Operating costs: tooling , scrap and start-up costs.

Putrus (1990) treated the justification problems as a three dimensional framework of risk, benefits (tangible and intangible) and time (short, medium, and long term). He aimed to justify an AMS project based on the ratio of total benefits to total risk for different time intervals. A ratio greater than one means the benefits of the AMS project outweigh the risk of AMS for that term and vice versa. The advantage of this study is the demonstration of relationship among risk, benefit, and time in an analysis framework.

Ghosh & Wabalickis (1991) introduced an approach called comprehensive comparative analysis approach. They viewed the problem as a cost/benefit analysis. Two hierarchies have been constructed; the first one for the costs of the manufacturing systems and the other for the benefits of the manufacturing systems. The highest level of the cost hierarchy is system cost and of the benefit hierarchy is system benefit. Below this level are the major components of manufacturing which include; workforce, equipment, methods and materials, and information processing. The next lowest level are subfactors that clarify and define the factors. At the lowest level are the decision alternatives. The priority vector of qualitative factors are obtained through the pairwise comparisons while the priority vector of quantitative factors are obtained by normalising their ratio. After getting the priority vectors of both hierarchies, the cost/benefit ratio is computed for each alternative. The minimum value of the cost/benefit ratio gives the optimum manufacturing system. They demonstrated their approach through a case study. Also, sensitivity analysis was performed for the case study.

Naik & Chakravarty (1992) suggested a framework for evaluating AMS investments based on three hierarchical levels of evaluation; first, strategic level of evaluation which aims to select the best category of manufacturing system consisting of appropriate system modules at desirable levels of integration to provide desired manufacturing capabilities. This level reduced the wide range of available options. Second, an operational level of evaluation aims to identify the top two or three alternatives that have selected in the first level. This identification would be based on the received vendor quotes. The third level of evaluation is the financial evaluation level in which the detailed discounted cash flows analysis is conducted for the systems chosen at the operational level. The system with the best financial performance is selected if it meets the performance requirements of the firm. Otherwise, the evaluation process must be repeated from the strategic level.

Two studies are rather similar to Wabalickis's study. The first was introduced by Datta et al. (1992). They have included more factors than that considered in Wabalickis's study. Also, they have introduced a computer programme to ease the computational process involved in the model. The second was introduced by Mohanty & Venkataraman (1993). They have classified the factors into three groups; strategic, technological and social factors. Also, they have applied their approach to an Indian company.

O'Brien & Smith (1993) developed a strategic modelling tool which relies on the AHP to evaluate the investment in new design hardware and software technologies in electronics industries. They considered five strategies: (1) business systems strategy, (2) marketing strategy, (3) servicing strategy, (4) design and manufacturing strategy, and (5) financial control strategy. The structure of their model is a hierarchy, at the top level the objective of the company is to select the best design system, at the intermediate level the company has to define the various strategic criteria which the best design system is expected to support and to weigh the relative importance of these criteria, and at the bottom level the model requires the user to compare and score two options (new technology and present technology) as to the extent to which each option is expected to support the criteria. To assist the user in evaluating the extent to which each of the options supports the various strategies, they suggested subdividing the strategies into a number of sub-criteria.

The model is based on a two stage process. First, the relative importance of the various criteria and sub-criteria is determined by carrying out a pairwise comparison of the criteria using the scale of 1-9. Second, based on the relative weighting for the various criteria, each of the investment options is compared with each of the criteria. The final output of the strategic model is a score for each of the options which combines the assessment of the relative value of each of the options in achieving the various criteria or sub-criteria of each of the strategies with the relative weight of the associated strategies. Then, each strategy is represented by a separate hierarchy.

They claimed that this model can be used in evaluating AMS investments as a substitute of financial appraisal or /and as supporting it whether before or after analysing the financial consequences of such investments. This claim must be treated with caution because if this model is considered as a supporting tool to the financial appraisal, the strategy of financial control must be omitted from the criteria that is used in the hierarchy.

Recently, Accola (1994) has employed the AHP in a framework for evaluating the investment in AMS. In this framework, three dimensions have been considered. Two dimensions represent the quantifiable measures of financial risk and return, while the third dimension represents the non-quantifiable uncertainties which refer to the qualitative factors. The quantifiable financial measure return on investment (ROI), while quantifiable risk is represented by three measures: ruinous loss (the investment percentage of total assets), liquidity parameter (payback), and variability (standard deviation). The non-quantifiable uncertainties are represented by four qualitative factors: product reliability, product performance, flexibility, and employee benefits. In this framework, the AHP is used twice to assign values for both risk parameters and the qualitative factors.

The outputs of the framework are three groups of values for each decision alternative; return on investment, risk and non-quantifiable uncertainties. These outputs are represented in a three-dimensional graph to determine the efficient plane. However, this framework does not recommend an alternative, it merely gives the most efficient alternatives which dominate the other alternatives.

Although this framework might be considered as a generic approach because it captures the necessary factors affecting the investment decisions in AMS, it leaves the decision maker with many recommended alternatives.

To overcome this problem, it might be useful to extend this framework to include a further procedure. This procedure would consider the outputs of the framework which include the overall priority vectors of the three dimensional; risk, ROI, and non-quantifiable benefits (Non-Q), as inputs to an overall hierarchy. Then, conducting the pairwise comparisons to weigh the decision alternatives. To illustrate this procedure -using the outputs of Accola's example as in table (4). First, the two level hierarchy is constructed as in figure (5). Second, asking the decision maker to make pairwise comparisons to the three dimensions with respect to the corporate attitude of the firm. Suppose, for example, the pairwise comparisons matrix is as follows:

	Risk	ROI	Non-Q
Risk	1	7	4
ROI	1/7	1	1/3
Non-Q	1/4	3	1

TABLE 4

The outputs of Accola's Example

	Risk	ROI*	Non-Q
Project I	0.56	0.29	0.73
Project II	0.26	0.33	0.18
Project III	0.18	0.38	0.09

* Since Accola's framework used the ROI as a scale ratio, it has been normalised in order to be used as interval scale in AHP context.

Source: Accola, 1994.

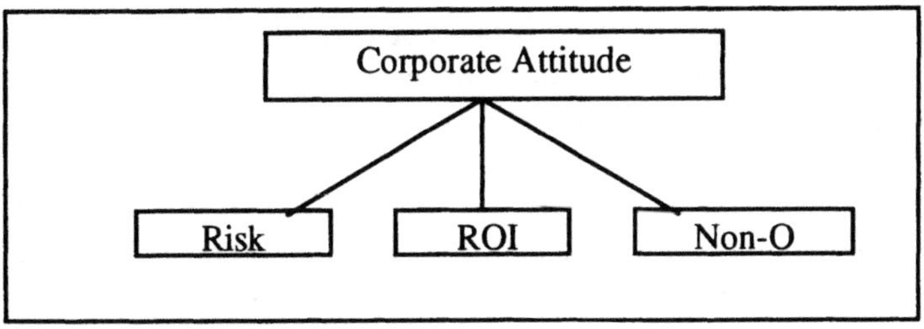

Figure 5 : The Two level hierarchy

Then, using the fundamental computations of AHP to obtain the priority vector which yield: (CR = 0.028)

$$\begin{matrix} \text{Risk} \\ \text{ROI} \\ \text{Non-Q} \end{matrix} \quad \begin{bmatrix} 0.701 \\ 0.086 \\ 0.213 \end{bmatrix}$$

Finally, the priorities of the three alternatives are determined as follows:

$$\text{Project I} = (0.56 \times 0.701) + (0.29 \times 0.086) + (0.073 \times 0.213) = 0.573$$
$$\text{Project II} = (o.26 \times 0.701) + (0.33 \times 0.086) + (0.180 \times 0.213) = 0.249$$
$$\text{Project III} = (0.18 \times 0.701) + (0.38 \times 0.086) + (0.090 \times 0.213) = 0.178$$

According to this extension, the decision maker is advised to choose project I as it has the highest priority (0.573).

Application of AHP with other techniques Srinivasan and Millen (1986) used the AHP to produce weights for the decision alternatives based on the qualitative variables which may not be reflected in the cash flow estimates. Then, these weights can be integrated with the decision alternatives' estimated cash flows. The decision alternatives can be ranked according to the relative strategic net present value (SNPV) which is computed as in equation (7). The decision alternative which has the highest SNPV is recommended.

$$SNPV_i = (PVCF_i \times W_i) - NINV_i \qquad (7)$$

where:

- $SNPV_i$: relative strategic net present value for decision alternatives i,
- $PVCF_i$: present value of the estimated cash flows for decision alternatives i,
- W_i :the priority vector of the AHP,
- $NINV_i$:net investment for decision alternative I.

Chandra & Schall (1988) used the Leontief input-output model and linear programming to set the input of AHP for evaluating two alternatives of FMS. The hierarchy has three levels; the first level represents the decision: choose the design with the minimum cost, the second level represents the attributes: capital cost, total sector multipliers, expected maximum number of finished items, and expected maximum number of scrapped items, and the last level represents the two alternatives: design I and design II.

The total sector multipliers attribute has been determined using the Leontief model whereas the expected maximum number of both finished items and scrapped items attributes have been determined using the linear programming model. The fourth attribute used in the hierarchy, capital cost, is set arbitrarily.

In the light of the output of both Leontief model, linear programming model, in addition to the judgement of the decision makers, the priorities of the two alternatives are determined. Since the focus of the hierarchy is to minimise the total cost, the design with the lowest priority should be recommended.

The advantage of this approach is that it provides more precise inputs to AHP since they are the outputs of quantitative techniques - Leontief model and linear programming model. However, the disadvantage of this approach is due to two implications; first, the linearity of the variables used in the Leontief model and the linear programming model. Second, the similarity of the benefits for all competitive alternatives as they rely only on the cost factors in selecting the best alternative. These assumptions are unrealistic.

The AHP has two major advantages which make it more preferable than scoring models. First, the decision maker compares only each pair of factors/alternatives to determine which of them is more important, without any obligation to set the absolute weight of each factor/alternative (Azzone et al., 1992). Second, it provides a means for measuring the consistency of decision maker's judgements data. This consistency measure may provide more reliability to AHP than scoring models. However, the AHP is not without its pitfalls; first, there is no theoretical framework existing for structuring the problem into a hierarchy representation (Boucher & MacStravic, 1991). The same problem may be represented in various hierarchies by different decision makers. Then, they arrive at different conclusions for the same problem. Second, the pairwise comparisons matrices might be time consuming and managers may lose interest. Finally, as Boucher & MacStravic (1991) pointed out, the nature of questions asked in making pairwise comparisons are meaningless. What does it mean to ask how strongly one prefers lead time reduction to quality improvement? For the decision maker to be able to interpret the question, it should be clear how much lead time reduction is being compared to how much quality improvement. The assumption is that the decision maker must be thinking of some average quantities when answering the question, otherwise it could not be reasonable to make a judgement.

Conclusion and identification of area for future research

The review of the literature concerning methods of evaluating investment decisions in AMS has indicated that the main difficulty facing such evaluation is how to quantify the qualitative variables and incorporate them into the decision model. To handle this difficulty, three approaches have been established in this field. The first approach advocates using the traditional cash flow analysis as a main evaluation tool with a minimum effort to include the qualitative variables in the analysis. Following this approach in evaluating AMS investments may mean that a suboptimal alternative is recommended as some relevant information has not been considered in the decision analysis.

Some authors have suggested the complete opposite of this approach recommending that the investment in AMS be regarded as a strategy that should be implemented regardless of the results of cash flows analysis. This means the evaluation method is based on analysing only the qualitative benefits which AMS projects will provide (such as greater manufacturing flexibility, learning effects, and the effect on employee morale). This approach not only neglects some important information -the financial measures- but also is extremely judgmental.

The third approach attempts to integrate the qualitative and quantitative variables in the same analysis. This integration may be made in one of three ways: (1) screening the alternatives based on their financial performance in the first instance, then choosing amongst the screened alternatives according to analysing their strategic performance, or vice versa, (2) modifying the results of DCF methods by the weight of qualitative variables and then choosing the best alternative according to the modified DCF, (3) considering the financial performance as a factor or dimension in a multi-dimension framework.

It is quite clear that the appropriate framework to evaluate investment decisions in AMS must provide a systematic consideration of qualitative variables alongside quantitative variables. Also, it is unrealistic to expect that an evaluation method is applicable without considering the cash flows analysis.

The previous discussion may support the use of AHP as a flexible method which could properly treat both quantitative and qualitative variables. Accola's model may provide a good way to employ AHP. However, some refinements to this model may be needed such as considering a discounted cash flow method -NPV or IRR- instead of ROI which has been criticised as a measure of projects' viability. Also, sensitivity analysis may provide the decision maker with useful information about the critical factors that affect the decision. Finally, the applicability of this model needs to be examined through an empirical study. These refinements may suggest areas for future research.

All methods presented above have been subjected to two assumptions. First, the decision of acquiring an AMS is considered as a replacement decision. The consideration of this decision in case of a new firm willing to acquire an AMS may suggest an area for future research. Second, it has been assumed that all parts of AMS are acquired at the same time. The consideration of the project as a sequential investment project may suggest another area for future research.

Notes

1. This problem is stressed in almost all relevant literature available on the topic of justification of AMS (e.g., Accola, 1994; Cheung, 1993; Lavelle & Liggett, 1992; Naik & Chakravarty, 1992; Srinivasan & Millen, 1986; Park & Son, 1988; Azzone et al., 1992; Rayburn, 1989; Kaplan, 1986).
2. All of these methods are well documented in almost all text books available on the topic of Management Accounting or Engineering Economic (e.g., Lumby, 1995; Garrison, 1991; Hilton, 1991; Stevens, 1979; Riggs & West, 1986).
3. To obtain the normalised pairwise comparison matrix, first sum the values in each column in the pairwise comparison matrix, then divide each element in the column by its column total.

References

Accola, W.L. (1994). 'Assessing risk and uncertainty in new technology investments', *Accounting Horizons*, Vol. 8, No.3, September, pp. 19-35.

Airey, J. & Young, C. (1983). 'Economic justification-counting the strategic benefits' In K. Rathmill (ed.), *Proceedings of 2nd International Conference on Flexible Manufacturing Systems*, London, October.

Anderson, D.R., Sweeney, D.J. & William, T.A. (1994)..*An Introduction To Management Science: Quantitative Approaches To Decision Making*, West Publishing Company, NY.

Apostolou, B. & Hassell, J.M. (1993). 'An overview of the analytic hierarchy process and its use in accounting research', *Journal of Accounting Literature*, Vol. 12, pp. 1-28.

Azzone, G., Bertele, U. & Masella, C. (1992). 'Selecting techniques for the financial justification of advanced manufacturing technologies: contingent approach' In H.R. Parsaei, et al.(eds.), *Economic and financial Justification of Advanced Manufacturing Technologies*, pp. 19-35, Amsterdam, Elsevier Science Publishers.

Bennett, R.E. & Hendricks, J.A. (1987). 'Justifying the acquisition of automated equipment', *Management Accounting*, Vol. 67, July, pp. 39-46.

Boucher, T.O. &. MacStravic, E.L. (1991). 'Multiattribute evaluation within a present value framework and its relation to the analytic hierarchy process', *The Engineering Economist*, Vol. 37, No. 1, Fall, 1991, pp. 1-32.

Canada, J.R. & Sullivan, W.G. (1990). 'Persistent pitfalls and applicable approaches for justification of advanced manufacturing systems', *Engineering Costs and Production Economics*, Vol. 18, pp. 247-253.

Chan, Y.L. & Lynn, B.E. (1993). 'Hierarchical analysis as a means of evaluating tangibles and intangibles of capital investments', *The Mid-Atlantic Journal of Business*, Vol. 29, No. 1, March, pp. 59-74.

Chandra, J. & Schall, S.O. (1988). 'Economic justification of flexible manufacturing systems using the Leontief input-output model', *The Engineering Economist*, Vol. 34, No. 1, Fall, pp. 27-50.

Charles Stark Draper Laboratory (1984). *Flexible Manufacturing System Handbook*, Noyes Publications, New Jersey.

Cheung, J.K. (1993). 'Managerial flexibility in capital investment decisions literature', *Journal of Accounting Literature*, Vol. 12, pp. 29-66.

Datta, V., Sambasivarao, K.V., Kodali, R. & Deshmukh, S.G. (1992). 'Multi-attribute decision model using the analytic hierarchy process for the justification of manufacturing systems', *International Journal of Production Economics*, Vol. 28, pp. 227-234.

Elango, B. & Meinhart, W.A. (1994). 'Selecting a flexible manufacturing system - a strategic approach', *Long Range Planning*, Vol. 27, No. 3, June, pp. 118-126.

Garrison, R.H. (1991). *Managerial Accounting: Concepts For Planning, Control, Decision Making*, 6th. ed., Boston, IRWIN.

Ghosh, B.K. & Wabalickis, R.N. (1991). 'A Comparative analysis for the justification of future manufacturing systems', *International Journal of Operations & Production Management*, Vol. 9, pp. 4-23.

Hilton, R.W. (1991). *Managerial Accounting*, New York, McGraw-Hill, Inc

Huang, P.Y., Moore, L.J. & Shin, S. (1991). 'World-class manufacturing in the 1990s: integrated TQC, JIT, FA, and TPM with worker participation', *Manufacturing Review*, Vol. 4, No. 2, June, pp. 87-95.

Hundy B.B. & Hamblin, D.J. (1988). 'Risk and assessment of investment in new technology', *International Journal of Production Research*, Vol. 26, No. 11, November, pp. 1799-1810.

Kaplan, R.S. (1986). 'Must CIM be justify by faith alone?', *Harvard Business Review*, March-April, pp. 87-93.

Klammer, T., Koch, B. & Wilner, N. (1991). 'Capital budgeting practices- a survey of corporate use', *Journal of Management Accounting Research*, American Accounting Association, Vol. 3, Fall, pp. 113-130.

Klee, A.S. (1971). 'The role of decision models in the evaluation of competing environmental health alternatives', *Management Science*, Vol. 18, No. 2, October, pp. B-52- B-67.

Knott, K. & Getto, R.D. (1982). 'A model for evaluating alternative robot systems under uncertainty', *International Journal of Production Research*, Vol. 20, pp. 155-165.

Kulatilaka, N. (1984). 'Financial, economic and strategic issues concerning the decision to invest in advanced automation', *International Journal of Production Research*, Vol. 22, No.6,pp. 949-968.

Lavelle, J.P. & Liggett, H.R. (1992). 'Economic methods for evaluating investments in advanced manufacturing technologies' In H.R. Parsaei, et al.(eds.), *Economic and financial Justification of Advanced Manufacturing Technologies*, pp. 119-139, Amsterdam, Elsevier Science Publishers.

Lumby, S. (1995). *Investment Appraisal and Financial Decisions*, London, Champman & Hall.

Medearis, H.D., Helms, M.M. & Ettkin, L.P. (1990). 'Justifying flexible manufacturing systems (FMS) from a strategic perspective', *Manufacturing Review*, Vol. 3, No. 4, December, pp. 219-223.

Mensah, Y.M. & Miranti, P.J. (1989). 'Capital expenditure analysis and automated manufacturing systems: a review and synthesis', *Journal of Accounting Literature*, Vol. 8, pp. 181-207.

Meredith, J. R. & Suresh, N.C. (1986). 'Justification techniques for advanced manufacturing technologies', *International Journal of Production Research*, Vol. 24, No. 5, Sept./Oct., pp. 1043-1057.

Miltenburg, G.J. & Krinsky, I. (1987). 'Evaluating flexible manufacturing', *IIE Transactions*, Vol. 19, No. 2, June, pp. 222-233.

Mohanty, R.P., & Venkatarman, S. (1993). 'Use of the analytic hierarchy process for selecting automated manufacturing systems', *International Journal of Operations & Production Management*, Vol. 13, No. 8, pp. 45-57.

Naik, B. & Chakravarty, A.K. (1992). 'Strategic acquisition of new manufacturing technology', *International Journal of Production Research*, Vol. 30, No. 7, July, pp. 1575-1601.

Nelson, C.A. (1986). 'A Scoring model for flexible manufacturing systems project selection', *European Journal of Operational Research*, Vol. 24, pp. 346-359.

O'Brien, C. & Smith, S.J. (1993). 'Design of the decision process for strategic investment in advanced manufacturing systems', *International Journal of Production Economics*, Vol. 30-31, pp. 309-322.

Park, C.S. & Son, Y.K. (1988). 'An economic evaluation model for advanced manufacturing systems', *The Engineering Economist*, Vol. 34, No. 1, Fall, pp. 1-26.

Parsaei, H.R. & Wilhelm, M.R. (1989). 'A justification methodology for automated manufacturing technologies', *Computers and Industrial Engineering*, Vol. 16, No. 3, pp. 363-373.

Primrose, P.L., Creamer, G.D. & Leonard, R. (1985). 'Identifying and quantifying the company-wide benefits of cad within the structure of a comprehensive investment program', *Computer Aided Design*, Vol. 17, No. 1, Jan./Feb., pp.3-8.

Primrose, P.L. & Leonard, R. (1985). 'Evaluating the "intangible" benefits of flexible manufacturing systems by use of discounted cash flow algorithms within a comprehensive computer program' In F. Choobineh & R. Suri (eds.), *Flexible Manufacturing Systems: Current Issues and Models*, pp. 289-294, Atlanta, Industrial Engineering and Management Press.

Putrus, R. (1990). 'Accounting for intangible in integrated manufacturing', *Information Strategy: The Executives Journal*, Vol. 6, No. 4, Summer, pp. 25-30.

Randhawa, S.U. & West, T.M. (1992). 'Evaluating automated manufacturing technologies: part i- concepts and literature review', *Computer- Integrated Manufacturing Systems*, Vol. 5, No. 3, August, pp. 208-218.

Rayburn, L.G. (1989). *Principles of Cost Accounting Using a Cost Management Approach*, 4th. ed., Boston, IRWIN.

Riggs, J.L. & West, T.M. (1986). *Engineering Economics*, McGraw-Hill Book Company, New York.

Saaty, T.L. (1990). *The Analytic Hierarchy Process: Priority Setting, Resource Allocation (Multicriteria Decision Making)*, Vol. 1, RWS Publications, Pittsburgh, USA.

__________ (1980). *The Analytic Hierarchy Process*, McGraw Hill, New York.

Somers, T. & Gupta, Y.P. (1991). 'Factory automation: U. S. versus Japanese experiences', *Manufacturing Review*, Vol. 4, No. 3, September, pp. 157-167.

Srinivasan, V. & Millen, R.A. (1986). 'Evaluating flexible manufacturing systems as a strategic investment', In K. E Stecke & R. Suri (eds.), *Proceedings of the Second ORSA/TIMS Conference on Flexible Manufacturing Systems: Operations Research Models and Applications*, pp. 83- 93, Amsterdam, Elsevier Science Publishers.

Stevens, G.T., Jr. (1979). *Economic and Financial Analysis of Capital Investments*, New York, John Wiley & Sons.

Swann, K. & O'Keefe, W.D. (1990). 'Advanced manufacturing technology: investment decision process. Part 1', *Management Decision*, Vol. 28, No.1, pp. 20-31.

Wabalickis, R.N. (1988). 'Justification of FMS with the analytic hierarchy', *Journal of Manufacturing Systems*, Vol. 7, No. 3, pp. 175-182.

Wilner, N., Koch, B. & Klammer, T. (1992). 'Justification of high technologycapital investment- An empirical study', *The Engineering Economist*, Vol. 37, No. 4, Summer, pp. 341-353.

11 Facts and fallacies about the determinants of the beta

Abimbola Adedeji

Introduction

Beaver, Kettler and Scholes (1970) suggested that there is a relationship between market beta[1] and the conventional accounting/financial measures of risk, such as financial leverage, dividend payout ratio, growth, liquidity, size and variability of earnings/cyclicality. This suggestion is reexamined in this paper for two main reasons. One of them is that questions have been raised about the validity of the suggestion. For instance, Bowman (1979, 1981) disagrees with the view that market beta is theoretically related to variability of earnings/cyclicality, size, growth and/or dividend payout ratio, but agrees with the view that financial leverage is a theoretical determinant of market beta. He also indicates that corporation tax rate is a theoretical determinant of market beta, whereas Beaver, Kettler and Scholes did not suggest this.

The other reason for undertaking this study is that little research evidence is available in the literature at this moment about the relationship between market beta and the other variables referred to above in the UK. The main empirical studies that have been reported are based on data of firms in the USA. Given the difference between the taxation systems in the UK and USA, investors in the UK may react differently from their counterparts in the USA to changes in the values of some of the variables referred to above. For this reason, the relationship between market beta and the other variables referred to above in the UK may not be exactly the same as in the USA.

Thus, an attempt is made in this study to test the two contradictory suggestions stated above on data of non-financial firms in the UK. The results obtained support the view that financial leverage, operating leverage, size and variability of earnings/cyclicality are empirical determinants of market beta, but contradict the suggestion that liquidity, growth, payout ratio and tax rate are reliable determinants of the beta. The results, therefore, shed some light on the variables that are relevant to the process(es) generating market beta and values of firms in the UK. The results are useful for teaching purposes because they have direct practical implications for corporate financing, investment and portfolio management decisions in the UK.

The rest of this paper is divided into four sections. In the next section, a brief review of the previous studies is presented. This is followed by the description of the sample, variables and data used in the study. The results obtained are discussed in the penultimate section and the study is concluded in the final section.

Previous studies

The main empirical studies that have been reported are Beaver, Kettler and Scholes (1970), Hamada (1972), Gonedes (1973), Lev (1974), Beaver and Manegold (1975), Bildersee (1975) and Mandelker and Rhee (1984). Evidence reported by Beaver, Kettler and Scholes (1970) indicates that, empirically, market beta has a significant positive relationship with variability of earnings and growth, and a significant negative relationship with the payout ratio. The evidence also indicates that market beta has no significant empirical relationship with financial leverage, liquidity and size.

However, contrary to the observation of Beaver, Kettler and Scholes referred to above, Hamada (1972) and Mandelker and Rhee (1984) observe that market beta has a positive empirical relationship with financial leverage. Similarly, Lev (1974) observes that market beta has a positive empirical relationship with operating leverage, and the evidence reported by Mandelker and Rhee (1984) supports this observation. Also, Chan and Chen (1988) reported some evidence which indicate that there is an almost perfect inverse relationship between market beta and size in the US, and contradicts the suggestion of Beaver, Kettler and Scholes that there is no significant empirical relationship between the two variables.

A major inadequacy of these studies is that most of them have a narrow focus. With the exception of Beaver, Kettler and Scholes (1970) which examined the effects of financial leverage, dividend payout, growth, liquidity, size and variability of earnings on market beta, only one other study (Hamada [1972]) considered the empirical effect of financial leverage (alone) on market beta. Similarly, only one other study, Lev (1974), considered the empirical effect of operating leverage (alone) on market beta. Mandelker and Rhee (1984) examined the empirical effects of both operating leverage and financial leverage on market beta, but they did not consider the relationship of the beta with the other variables referred to above. The studies by Gonedes (1973), Beaver and Manegold (1975) and Bildersee (1975) focused mainly on the association between market beta and accounting beta. Therefore, they do not provide a direct evidence that can be used to determine whether the variables stated above are empirical determinants of market beta or not.

In summary, it is difficult to say which of the contradictory views stated above is valid empirically, because the results of the few previous studies that tested them are not wholly in agreement with one another. Thus, there is still an important gap in the empirical literature about the relationship between market beta and the other variables referred to above. The purpose of this study is to bridge part of the gap by adding the UK evidence to the literature.

Data and measurment of variables

The proposition tested in this paper is that financial leverage, operating leverage, payout ratio, expected growth, liquidity, corporation tax rate, size and variability of earnings/cyclicality are determinants of market beta. All the data used for the test were obtained from Datastream.

Market Beta (β) is represented by the beta estimate in Datastream, i.e. -

β_{jt} = estimate of market beta of ordinary shares of firm j at time t in Datastream.

Financial Leverage (FL): Financial leverage is represented by the borrowing ratio measured in market value. It is defined as follows:-

$$FL_{jt} = \frac{BORG_{jt} - STI_{jt}}{MVE_{jt} + BORG_{jt}}$$

where:

FL_{jt} = financial leverage of firm j at time t;
$BORG_{jt}$ = borrowing (i.e. the sum of the book values of long term loans, short term loans and overdrafts) of firm j in year t;
STI_{jt} = book value of short term investments of firm j in year t; and
MVE_{jt} = estimate of the market value of equity of firm j at time t.

Liquidity (LQ) is defined as -

$$LQ_{jt} = \frac{CA_{jt}}{CL_{jt}}$$

where:

LQ_{jt} = liquidity of firm j in year t;
CA_{jt} = book value of current assets of firm j in year t; and

CL_{jt} = book value of current liabilities of firm j in year t.

Operating Leverage (OL) is represented by -

$$OL_{jt} = \frac{NFA_{jt}}{TA_{jt}}$$

where:

OL_{jt} = operating leverage of firm j in year t;
NFA_{jt} = book value of net fixed assets of firm j in year t; and
Ta_{jt} = book value of total assets of firm j in year t.

Expected Growth (PE) is represented by the price-earnings ratio.

It is measured by -

$$PE_{jt} = \frac{P_{jt}}{EPS_{jt}},$$

where:

PE_{jt} = price-earnings ratio of firm j at time t;
P_{jt} = share price of firm j at time t; and
EPS_{jt} = earnings per share of firm j in year t.

The *Payout Ratio* (PR) is defined as -

$$PR_{jt} = \frac{DIV_{jt}}{DE_{jt}},$$

where:

PR_{jt} = payout ratio of firm j in year t;
DIV_{jt} = dividends to ordinary shareholders of firm j in year t; and
DE_{jt} = distributable earnings to ordinary shareholders of firm j in year t.

Size (SZ) is represented by -

SZ_{jt} = Market value of equity (in £ millions) of firm j at time t.

Tax rate (TR) is represented by -

$$TR_{jt} = \frac{TAX_{jt}}{PBT_{jt}},$$

where:

TR_{jt} = tax rate of firm j in year t;
TAX_{jt} = tax charge in the account of firm j in year t; and
PBT_{jt} = profit before tax of firm j in year t.

Variability of earnings/cyclicality (IND)

Variability of earnings/cyclicality is represented by -

IND_{jt} = the London Stock Exchange industry classification code of firm j in year t in Datastream.

The measures of market beta (β), liquidity (LQ), payout ratio (PR) and size (SZ) stated above are similar to the ones used by Beaver, Kettler and Scholes (1970). There are different suggestions in the literature about how market beta should be measured in order to minimise measurement error which may be caused by infrequent or thin trading, or the lack of synchroneity in returns data [Vasicek (1973), Dimson (1979), Dimson and Marsh (1983) and Ball and Kothari (1989)]. The market beta values used in this study, obtained from Datastream, are calculated by using the procedure suggested by Vasicek (1973). The procedure uses the Bayesian method to estimate market beta values and corrects for the measurement errors that may be caused by some of the problems referred to above. An important reason for using the beta values in Datastream is that they are widely available to managers and investors in the market. Therefore, they are more likely to be used for decision making than any other beta values that may be obtained from other source(s).

However, the measures of financial leverage (FL), expected growth (PE) and variability of earnings/cyclicality (IND) stated above are different from those used by Beaver, Kettler and Scholes. Beaver, Kettler and Scholes used the total debt ratio[2] to represent financial leverage. They also used average annual growth rate of the book value of total assets over ten years to represent growth, and measured variability of earnings/cyclicality by the standard deviation of profit after tax over ten years. They had no measure of operating leverage, because their study did not consider the effect of operating leverage on market beta.

The reason for using the borrowing ratio to represent financial leverage (FL) in this study is that the ratio contains only interest bearing debts. Non-interest bearing debts, such as trade credits, do not normally generate obligations to firms to make regular fixed payments over time. Therefore, such debt items will not increase the variability of the earnings stream to shareholders. Hence, they are not quite relevant to the predicted relationship between financial leverage and market beta.

The borrowing ratio is measured in market value. The advantage of this measure is that it is consistent with the prediction that is being tested which assumes that financial leverage (FL) is measured in market value. The market value of a firm is measured by the sum of the market value of its equity and the book values of its long term loans, short term loans and overdrafts. The book values of long term loans, short term loans and overdrafts are used in the estimation of the market values of firms because the market values of these items are not available in Datastream for many firms. The book values of long term loans and short term loans used include the capitalised value of finance leases. Finance leases are included because, like debt, they generate obligations to firms to make regular fixed payments over time. Similarly, short term loans and overdrafts are included because some firms may use them as long term debt by simply rolling them over. Then, in determining the net borrowing of firms, the book value of their short term investments is deducted from the book value of the total amount they have borrowed (i.e. long term loans, short term loans and overdrafts) in order to ensure that firms which borrow some money and invest it in short term assets show up as not owing.

There are two main reasons for representing expected growth (PE) and variability of earnings/cyclicality (IND) by variables which are different from the measures used by Beaver, Kettler and Scholes, described above. One of the reasons is that Datastream does not have the necessary data (total assets and profits after tax) for long periods of time for many firms. Therefore, if expected growth and variability of earnings are measured in the same way that Beaver, Kettler and Scholes did, many observations will be lost, and this will result in a relatively small sample.

The second reason is that there are alternative variables that can be used as proxies for expected growth and variability of earnings/cyclicality which are, perhaps, more widely recognised and more consistent with the predictions being tested than the variables used by Beaver, Kettler and Scholes. Thus, the PE ratio is used to represent expected growth, because it is widely referred to in the literature as a good proxy for expected growth (see Brealey and Myers, 1991, p. 61; Haugen, 1993, p. 604; and Levy and Sarnat, 1994, p. 523-5, among others). Similarly, variability of earnings/cyclicality (IND) is represented by industry classification of firms because of the suggestion often made in the literature that industry classification of firms is a good surrogate for the variability of their earnings/cyclicality and an important determinant of market beta[3].

Also, the variable used as proxy for operating leverage (OL) in this study, described above, is different from the measures used by Lev (1974) and Mandelker and Rhee (1984)[4] for a number of reasons. One of them is insufficient data. A good estimate of any of the measures used in the two previous studies requires relevant data for a long period, which, as stated earlier, are not available in Datastream. Another reason is that there is an alternative measure of operating leverage which appears not to have been tried by any previous study. Given that operating leverage is usually defined in corporate finance textbooks as the proportion of fixed costs in the total operating costs[5], the variable used as a proxy for operating leverage (OL) in this study, described above, is appropriate, because it is a good indicator of the proportion of fixed costs that a firm has. The variable is particularly useful for a direct test of the prediction that the proportion of fixed costs in the total operating costs is positively related to market beta (β).

The study covered the period 1990-94. The reason for choosing 1990 as the starting date is that some of the data needed for the study are not available in Datastream for a large number of firms prior to this date. Therefore, sample size would have reduced considerably if an earlier date had been chosen. However, 1994 is chosen as the end of the study period because it is the latest year for which the relevant financial data is available in Datastream for a reasonable number of firms at the time of this study.

Two main criteria are used to select the study sample. One of them is that any firm which is included in the sample must have all the relevant data for years 1990-94. The second criteria is that firms that are selected must belong to a large industry with at least ten useful observations. This criteria is imposed to ensure that some industries in the sample would have sufficient number of observations for the test of their influence on beta values. Application of these criteria resulted in the exclusion of a large number of firms and produced a sample of about 375 observations each year. The summary statistics of the sample are stated in Table 1 below.

The statistics in Table 1 show that the average value of market beta (β) is about 0.84 and that this value is less than a standard deviation away from the theoretical value of the beta (β), which is one[6]. The statistics also show that the average value of financial leverage (FL) is between 10%-12%. The minimum value of this variable is negative in every year covered by the study because of the deduction of the book value of short term investments from the book value of the total amount borrowed. The negative value indicates that some firms in the sample are net lenders, rather than net borrowers, in the sense that the book value of their short term investments exceed the book value of the total amount they have borrowed. Anyway, such firms are few in the sample[7]. Some other interesting indications of the statistics in Table 1 are that the mean value of operating leverage (OL) is generally about 38%, the average value of the payout ratio (PR) is about 45%, the average size (SZ) of the firms in the sample is over £640 million and the average tax rate (TR) of the firms is about 33%.

TABLE 1.
Sample Summary Statistics

Variables		1990	1991	1992	1993	1994
β:	Mean	0.8292	0.8468	0.8490	0.8356	0.8590
	Std. dev.	0.3142	0.3107	0.3235	0.2964	0.3098
	Minimum	0.0280	0.0280	0.0280	0.0220	0.0600
	Maximum	1.668	1.591	1.729	1.6520	1.8040
FL:	Mean	0.1150	0.1200	0.1078	0.1018	0.1083
	Std. dev.	0.1187	0.1109	0.1086	0.1168	0.1130
	Minimum	-0.5238	-0.3805	-0.4867	-0.5735	-0.4583
	Maximum	0.4155	0.4298	0.4387	0.4755	0.4280
LQ:	Mean	1.7291	1.6940	1.6664	1.6853	1.6580
	Std. dev.	0.9989	1.0672	1.0148	0.9296	0.7984
	Minimum	0.2425	0.2913	0.1606	0.1593	0.1788
	Maximum	10.48	13.68	13.13	7.635	5.598
OL:	Mean	0.3729	0.3861	0.3914	0.3848	0.3813
	Std. dev.	0.2072	0.2118	0.2110	0.2205	0.2229
	Minimum	0.0009	0.0024	0.0020	0.0017	0.0017
	Maximum	0.9475	0.9391	0.9386	0.9538	0.9540
PE:	Mean	11.982	15.056	17.090	24.650	22.064
	Std. dev.	12.144	10.056	9.9324	66.999	56.121
	Minimum	3.800	3.500	3.100	3.900	2.500
	Maximum	181.8	145.5	111.9	1285.0	920.2
PR:	Mean	0.3929	0.4470	0.4621	0.4551	0.4399
	Std. dev.	0.1615	0.1881	0.1979	0.1941	0.1891
	Minimum	0.0000	0.0000	0.0000	0.0000	0.0000
	Maximum	0.9847	1.0000	1.0000	1.0000	0.9621
SZ:	(£ 'm)					
	Mean	487.20	516.47	679.25	749.16	787.30
	Std. dev.	1,586.8	1,740.30	2,113.8	2248.7	2473.30
	Minimum	1.100	1.300	1.110	1.600	1.360
	Maximum	17,920	25,620	23,980	22,060	23,400
TR:	Mean	0.3462	0.3316	0.3249	0.3220	0.3157
	Std. dev.	0.0400	0.0439	0.0459	0.0559	0.0681
	Minimum	0.0000	0.0000	0.0000	0.0000	0.0000
	Maximum	0.4346	0.4233	0.4675	0.4812	0.4817
Number of observations		344	382	378	378	394

Notes: β = market beta estimate in Datastream.
FL = financial leverage. It is represented by the borrowing

ratio, measured by net borrowing (as defined below)/(Market value of equity plus borrowing).
Borrowing = the sum of the book values of long term loans, short term loans and overdrafts.
Net borrowing = borrowing less the book value of short term investments. Market value of equity is represented by share price multiplied by the number of shares outstanding.
LQ = liquidity, measured by current assets/current liabilities.
OL = operating leverage, measured by the book value of net fixed assets divided by total assets.
PE = the PE ratio, measured by share price divided by earnings per share.
PR = payout ratio, measured by dividends to ordinary shareholders divided by distributable earnings to ordinary shareholders.
SZ = size, represented by the market value of equity (measured in £' millions).
TR = tax rate, measured by tax charge for the current year divided by profit before tax for the year.

All the data used were obtained from Datastream. The estimates reported in this Appendix were obtained with the descriptive statistics procedure in LIMDEP (version 6.0).

Analyses and results

The first analysis carried out is the calculation of Spearman's moment correlation coefficient for all the variables in Table 1 above. The correlation estimates obtained are summarised in Appendices A(i) - (ii). Given the predictions stated earlier, (β) is expected to correlate positively with (FL), (OL) and (PE), and correlate negatively with (LQ), (PR), (ln(SZ)) and (TR).

However, the correlation estimates in Appendices A(i)-(ii) indicate that although (β) has the expected positive and significant correlation with (FL), its correlation with (OL) and (PE) is generally negative and insignificant. The estimates also indicate that (LQ) and (TR) have a generally negative and insignificant correlation with (β), but the (PR) and (ln(SZ)) have a generally positive and significant correlation with the (β). These results seem to support only the suggestion that (FL) is a positive determinant of (β). The indication of the results that the (PR), and (ln(SZ)) in particular, are positive, rather than negative, determinants of (β) is against expectation, and, therefore, requires further investigation to ascertain its reliability.

The OLS regression technique is used next to test the relationship between market beta and the other variables referred to above. (LQ) is excluded from the variables tested, because the correlation estimates reported in Appendices A(i)-(ii) above indicate that the variable has a large and significant negative correlation with (FL) and, especially, (OL). This implies that there is likely to be multicollinearity if the three variables are used together as regressors in the same OLS regression equation. If there is multicollinearity, the estimate of the t-statistic that will be obtained in an OLS regression may be biased downward considerably. This may lead to the mistaken conclusion that some of the variables affected are not significant determinants of market beta, when, in fact, they are.

It is felt that the exclusion of (LQ) at this stage from the list of variables that will be tested will not bias the regression results that will be obtained or lead to a wrong conclusion. The basis for this feeling is that the correlation estimates in Appendices A(i)-(ii) indicate that (LQ) has a generally low and insignificant correlation with (β) in all the years covered by this study. This implies that (LQ) is unlikely to be a significant determinant of (β) in an OLS regression test. Therefore, it seems reasonable to expect that its exclusion from the test will not have any significant adverse effect on the result of the test.

The effect of variability of earnings/cyclicality on market beta is tested by examining whether industry classification of firms (IND) affects their market (β) values. For the purpose of the test, firms in the sample are classified into industries, using the London Stock Exchance industry classification codes in Datastream. Application of this classification procedure results in identification of seventeen industries in the sub-sample for each year. The industries are divided into two groups, namely, the *test group* and the *control group*. The test group consists of ten industries which are used to test industry influence. The control group consists of the remaining seven industries which are used to form a benchmark for assessing the (β) values of the industries in the test group.

The sample is divided into the control group and the test group in order to ensure that the test of industry influence that is carried out is appropriate. The average beta value of the control group will take the place of the constant in the OLS regression. Therefore, in the regression test, the average value of (β) of the control group is compared with the average value of (β) of each of the other industries (i.e. the industries in the test group) for the purpose of establishing whether there is industry influence or not. Although one industry can be used to form the control group, this is not done in this test, because the aim of the test is to compare the average value of (β) of each industry in the test group with the overall average of the beta for the UK. Thus, the reason why seven industries are put in the control group used in this test is to try and make the group to be as large as possible so that it can provide a reliable estimate of the overall average of the market beta of firms in the UK. The implication of this is that if the result of the OLS regression test is significant for any industry in the test group, it should be interpreted as indicating that the average value of market beta of the industry concerned is significantly different from the average value of market beta of the other firms in the UK.

As stated earlier, there are ten industries in the test group. They are building, brewery, chemicals, electronics, engineering, leisure, retail, services, textiles and utilities. The criteria used to select these industries is that it is relatively easy to predict whether their (β) values should be greater or less than the (β) values of the other industries (i.e. the industries in the control group). For instance, it is often suggested that firms in the building trade, leisure business, service industries and capital intensive/manufacturing industries usually experience relatively greater variability of earnings/cyclicality than firms in other industries. Therefore, if this suggestion is supported by the sample observed in this study, the average value of market beta of firms in these industries should be significantly greater than the corresponding value for the firms in the control group. Another view which is often expressed is that firms in the brewery, retail and, especially, utilities industries usually experience relatively less variability of earnings/cyclicality than other firms. If this suggestion is consistent with the behaviour of firms in the UK during the period covered by this study, then, the average value of market beta of firms in these industries should be less than the corresponding value for the firms in the control group. The names of the industries in the sub-sample for each year, the number of firms in each of them, as well as the industries that are included in the control group and the test group respectively are indicated in Appendix B.

Each industry in the test group is represented by a dummy variable, thereby giving a total of ten dummy variables. The OLS regression equation estimated to test the various suggestions stated above is as follows:-

$$\beta = \alpha_0 + \alpha_1(FL) + \alpha_2(OL) + \alpha_3(PE) + \alpha_4(PR) + \alpha_5(\ln(SZ)) + \alpha_6(TR) + \sum_{i=1}^{10} \alpha_{i+6} IND_i + \varepsilon \qquad (1)$$

Estimates of this equation, summarised in Table 2 below, indicate that the coefficients of (FL) and (ln(SZ)) are positive and significant, and the coefficient of (OL) is generally negative and significant, in all the cross-sectional estimates. The results in the Table also indicate that the coefficients of (PE), the (PR) and (TR) are either generally insignificant or have inconsistent signs.

Another important indication of the results in Table 2 is that industry classification of firms (IND) is a determinant of (β). The results show that the values of (β) of firms in the building industry are generally greater than the values of (β) of firms in the control group, and the values of (β) of firms in the brewery industry are generally less than the values of (β) of firms in the control group. It is also interesting to note that, apart from the building and brewery industries, no other industry in the test group has a market beta value that is significantly greater or less than the average (β) value of the industries in the control group from year to year. This implies that the effect of industry classification on (β) is narrow rather than pervasive. But despite this implication, the results in Table 2 support the view, among others, that variability of earnings/cyclicality (IND) is a positive (β) determinant[8,9].

TABLE 2
OLS regression estimates of the following equation

$$\beta = \alpha_0 + \alpha_1(FL) + \alpha_2(OL) + \alpha_3(PE) + \alpha_4(PR) + \alpha_5(\ln(SZ)) + \alpha_6(TR) + \sum_{i=1}^{10} \alpha_{6+i}(IND)_i + \epsilon$$

Variables	Coefficients	1990	1991	1992	1993	1994
Constant	α_0	0.1332 (0.997)	0.3207 (2.240)*	0.4127 (3.052)*	0.4596 (5.486)*	0.6638 (8.012)*
FL	α_1	0.5429 (4.390)*		0.5826 (3.981)*	0.5537 (4.265)*	0.6159 (5.106)*
OL	α_2	-0.0268 (-0.296)	-0.0891 (-1.175)	-0.1560 (-1.859)*	-0.1623 (-2.098)*	-0.2448 (-3.220)*
PE	α_3	-0.0017 (-0.773)	-0.0013 (-1.138)	0.0032 (2.050)*	-0.0003 (-5.062)*	-0.0005 (-2.869)*
PR	α_4	0.1001 (1.138)	0.2008 (3.099)*	0.2427 (3.116)*	-0.0262 (-0.410)	-0.0205 (-0.265)
ln(SZ)	α_5	0.0809 (8.295)*	0.0998 (10.113)*	0.0840 (8.184)*	0.0832 (8.880)*	0.0794 (8.490)*
TR	α_6	0.8034 (2.569)*	-0.1078 (-0.281)	-0.4112 (-1.110)	0.0269 (0.117)	-0.4423 (-1.864)*

Building	α_7	0.2336 (2.070)*	0.3013 (3.384)*	0.2864 (2.961)*	0.3142 (4.238)*	0.2510 (3.178)*
Brewery	α_8	-0.1915 (-2.358)*	-0.1824 (-2.420)*	-0.1776 (-2.107)*	-0.1844 (-2.772)*	-0.1215 (-1.601)
Chemicals	α_9	0.0046 (0.058)	0.0035 (0.055)	-0.0065 (-0.099)	0.0052 (0.083)	0.0493 (0.741)
Electronics	α_{10}	-0.0122 (-0.229)	0.0313 (0.618)	-0.0370 (-0.661)	0.0253 (0.529)	-0.0171 (-0.382)
Engineering	α_{11}	0.0255 (0.601)	0.0438 (0.985)	0.0313 (0.680)	-0.0959 (-2.368)*	-0.0608 (-1.411)
Leisure	α_{12}	-0.0050 (-0.054)	0.0588 (0.846)	0.0655 (0.728)	-0.0910 (-1.380)	-0.0113 (-0.142)
Retail	α_{13}	-0.0017 (-0.036)	0.0240 (0.458)	-0.0284 (-0.536)	-0.0067 (-0.124)	-0.0436 (-0.842)
Services	α_{14}	-0.0455 (-0.859)	-0.0119 (-0.267)	-0.0273 (-0.501)	-0.0040 (-0.082)	0.0131 (0.260)
Textiles	α_{15}	-0.0239 (-0.452)	0.0045 (0.099)	0.0200 (0.382)	-0.0329 (-0.534)	-0.0223 (-0.407)
Utilities	α_{16}	-0.0062 (-0.091)	-0.0566 (-1.128)	-0.0724 (-1.254)	-0.0549 (-1.176)	-0.0607 (-1.285)
Adj. R^2		0.3143	0.3574	0.3007	0.3424	0.3098
F-statistic		10.826*	14.242*	11.132*	13.267*	12.026*
No. of obs.		344	382	378	378	394

Notes:

1. T-values are in parentheses. They are corrected for heteroscedasticity.
2. * indicates values that are significant at the 5% or higher levels.
3. β = market beta estimate in Datastream. FL = financial leverage. It is represented by the borrowing ratio, measured by net borrowing (as defined below)/(Market value of equity plus borrowing). Borrowing = the sum of the book values of long term loans, short term loans and overdrafts. Net borrowing = borrowing less the book value of short term investments. Market value of equity is represented by share price multiplied by the number of shares outstanding. LQ = liquidity, measured by current assets/current liabilities. OL = operating leverage, measured by the book value of net fixed assets divided by total assets. PE = the PE ratio, measured by share price divided by earnings per share. PR = payout ratio, measured by dividends to ordinary shareholders divided by distributable earnings to ordinary shareholders. SZ = size, represented by the market value of equity (measured in £' millions).TR = tax rate, measured by tax charge for the current year divided by profit before tax for the year. All the data used were obtained from

Datastream. The estimates reported in this Appendix were obtained with the regression procedure in LIMDEP (version 6.0).

Conclusions

The results of this study support the contentions of both Beaver, Kettler and Scholes (1970) and Bowman (1979) half-half. On the one hand, the results support the contention of Beaver, Kettler and Scholes that (FL), (ln(SZ)) and variability of earnings/cyclicality (IND) are determinants of (β), but contradict their suggestion that (PE), (LQ) and (PR) are also determinants of market (β). On the other hand, while the results support the contention of Bowman (1979) that (PE) and (PR) are not determinants of (β), they (i.e. the results) contradict his suggestion that (TR) is a (β) determinant. The results also do not support his contention that (ln(SZ)) and variability of earnings/cyclicality (IND) are not (β) determinants.

It is observed in this study that (OL) is a negative, and (ln(SZ)) a positive, empirical determinant of (β) in the UK. The observation that (β) and (OL) are negatively related is contradictory to the existing theory and the results of previous studies by Lev (1974) and Mandelker and Rhee (1984). However, as explained in note (4) above, the measures of (OL) used in the two previous studies are different from the variable used in this study. This probably explains why their results are different from the results of this study. The measures of (OL) used by them, referred to above, are not used in this study because of data problems.

However, the variable used as a proxy for (OL) in this study (i.e. the ratio of the book value of net fixed assets to total assets) is consistent with the theoretical definition of operating leverage that is often stated in corporate finance textbooks. The observation of this study that market lot of investment in fixed assets tend to have relatively low volatility of earnings/cyclicality and (β) values, and vice versa. This is what should be expected, if managers of firms are supposed to predict the variability of the earnings of their firms (and finance theory suggests that they will) before deciding how much of their firms' costs should be fixed and how much should be variable.

Similarly, the observation that (β) has a positive relationship with (ln(SZ)) is against the theory as well as the evidence reported for the USA which indicates an almost perfect negative relationship between (β) and (ln(SZ))[10]. The difference in the pattern of empirical relationship between market beta (β) and (ln(SZ)) in the UK and USA is probably an indication that firms in the USA generally employ more efficient diversification strategies to increase their sizes than firms in the UK.

More research is necessary to further investigate whether (OL) is a positive or negative empirical determinant of (β). Moreover, since not many previous studies have conducted a rigorous test of the effects of (ln(SZ)) and variability of earnings/cyclicality (IND) on (β), further studies of the empirical relationships among these variables will be useful. Finally, more research is needed to assess the observation of this study that (PE), (PR) and (TR) are not reliable empirical determinants of (β).

Notes

1. This term refers to the β in the capital asset pricing model (CAPM) stated below:

$$E(R_j) = r_f + \left[E(R_m) - r_f\right]\beta_j$$

where:

$E(R_j)$ and $E(R_m)$	= expected returns on security j and the market portfolio respectively;
r_f	= the risk free rate; and
β_j	= market beta of security j.

Market beta is sometimes called other names in the literature, such as market risk (see Beaver, Kettler and Scholes , 1970) or market β (see Fama and French, 1992). It is sometimes referred to as the beta in this paper. Some previous studies have suggested that market beta values are non-stationary (e.g. Vasicek, 1973; Blume, 1975; Dimson, 1979; Dimson and Marsh, 1983; and Ball and Kothari, 1989, among others). The results of these studies provide an important justification for the research into the variables which drive or determine the values of market beta.

2. This variable was measured as follows:-

$$\text{Total debt ratio} = \left(\sum_{t=1}^{T} \frac{\textit{Total senior securities, year t}}{\textit{Total assets, year t}}\right) \Big/ T$$

Senior securities were defined as all (presumably debt) securities which give their holders priority of claims to the assets of firms before equityholders. The British equivalent of such debt securities are long term loans or debentures and current liabilities. The T refers to the number of years in each sub-period used in the study. The study covered a total period of nineteen years (i.e. 1947-65), but this was divided into two sub-periods of ten years (i.e. 1947-56) and nine years (i.e. 1957-65). Thus, the value of T was 10 and 9 for the first and second sub-periods of the study respectively [Beaver, Kettler and Scholes (1970, pp. 661 and 666)].

3. Again, see Brealey and Myers (1991, pp. 199-200), Lumby (1994, p. 273) and Weston and Copeland (1992, pp. 417-420), among others.
4. Lev (1974) represented operating leverage (OL) by the estimate of variable cost per unit obtained from a regression of total operating costs on output i.e.

$$TC_{jt} = a_j + v_j Q_{jt} + u_{jt},$$

where:

TC_{jt} = Total operating costs of firm j in year t;
Q_{jt} = Output of firm j in year t (substituted with sales volume whenever physical output data was not available); and a_j and v_j = estimates of fixed and variable costs per unit respectively of firm j.

A time-series estimate of the equation above was obtained for each firm in a sample of 122 firms over a twenty year period (i.e. 1949-68). Lev then suggested that, if operating leverage and market beta are positively related, the estimates of variable costs per unit (v_j) and market beta used in the study should be negatively related. The tests results he obtained supported this suggestion [Lev (1974, pp. 633-638)]. However, the measure of (OL) used by Mandelker and Rhee (1984) is different from that of Lev (1974) described above. Mandelker and Rhee represented (OL) by percentage change in profit before interest and taxes per unit of sales/output. The following equation was used to estimate the variable:-

$$Ln\tilde{X}_{jt} = a_j + c_j Ln\tilde{S}_{jt} + \tilde{u}_{jt}, \qquad j = 1-255$$
$$t = 1957 - 1976\ (i.e.\ 20\ years)$$

where:

$\tilde{X}_{jt}$ = profit before interest and taxes of firm j in year t;
$\tilde{S}_{jt}$ = sales/output of firm j in year t; and
c_j = estimate of operating leverage (i.e. estimate of profit before interest and taxes per unit of sales) of firm j.

The 255 US firms used in the study are grouped into 51 portfolios of five firms each, after which a test of the relationship between market beta and the estimate of (OL) obtained indicated a significant positive relationship between the measure of (OL) and the beta estimate used in the study (Mandelker and Rhee (1984, pp. 50-53)).

5. For support on this, see Brealey and Myers (1991, pp. 199-200), Lev (1974, p. 627), Lumby (1994, p. 273), Ross, Westerfield and Jordan (1995, p. 283-285) among others.
6. This therefore implies that the average value of (β) obtained for each year is not significantly different from 1.
7. The number of firms with negative values of financial leverage (i.e. borrowing ratio) is 20 in the data for 1990, 19 in the data for 1991, 20 in the data for1992, 19 in the data for 1993 and 20 again in the data for 1994.
8. An attempt is made to determine whether (LQ) would have been a significant determinant of (β) if it had been included in equation (1) above. This is done by adding (LQ) to the equation and re-estimating it. (LQ) is not significant in all the cross sectional estimates obtained. These results provide a convincing evidence that (LQ) is not a determinant of (β) in the UK during 1990-94. However, the results are not reported here due to insufficient space.
9. An attempt is also made to determine whether a different measure of (FL) would have had a different relationship with (β). Hence, three other measures of financial leverage are substituted for the estimate of the borrowing ratio in equation (1) above and the equation is then reestimated. The three other measures used are the book value of the borrowing ratio (i.e. the book value of equity is substituted for its market value) and two estimates of the total debt ratio (i.e. the book value and market value estimates of the ratio). All the results obtained are similar to those reported in Table 2 above. Again, the results are not reported here because of space limitation, but any reader who is interested can have them on request to the author.
10. Please refer to Chan and Chen (1988, p. 317) for this evidence.

Appendix A(i)
Correlation matrices

1990

	β	FL	LQ	OL	PE	PR	ln(SZ)
FL	0.2797*						
LQ	-0.0802	-0.3441*					
OL	0.0388	0.1634*	-0.3893*				
PE	-0.0885	-0.0576	0.0389	0.0787			
PR	0.1519*	0.1459*	-0.0542	0.0843	-0.1552*		
ln(SZ)	0.4936*	0.1755*	-0.2040*	0.2569*	0.0105	0.0996	
TR	0.0800	-0.0405	-0.1210*	-0.1697*	-0.0057	-0.1558*	-0.0585

Number of observations = 344. * indicates values that are significant at the 5% or higher levels.

1991

	β	FL	LQ	OL	PE	PR	ln(SZ)
FL	0.2099*						
LQ	-0.0572	-0.2530*					
OL	-0.0198	0.2223*	-0.3865*				
PE	-0.0301	-0.0177	-0.0463	0.0007			
PR	0.1699*	0.1988*	0.0089	-0.0698	-0.0430		
ln(SZ)	0.5190*	0.1145*	-0.2136*	0.2180*	0.0454	-0.0119	
TR	0.0316	-0.0529	-0.0177	-0.1105*	0.0336	0.0929	0.0366

Number of observations = 382. * indicates values that are significant at the 5% or higher levels.

1992

	β	FL	LQ	OL	PE	PR	ln(SZ)
FL	0.2034*						
LQ	-0.0595	-0.3576*					
OL	-0.0603	0.2911*	-0.3668*				
PE	0.1304*	-0.0961	0.0410	-0.0488			
PR	0.2129*	0.1680*	0.0547	-0.0555	-0.0641		
ln(SZ)	0.4423*	0.0973	-0.2106*	0.1813*	0.1412*	0.0456	
TR	0.0198	-0.1014*	0.0343	-0.1185*	0.0588	0.0935	0.1211*

Number of observations = 378. * indicates values that are significant at the 5% or higher levels.

Notes:

β = market beta estimate in Datastream. FL = financial leverage. It is represented by the borrowing ratio, measured by net borrowing (as defined below)/(Market value of equity plus borrowing). Borrowing = the sum of the book values of long term loans, short term loans and overdrafts. Net borrowing = borrowing less the book value of short term investments.

Market value of equity is represented by share price multiplied by the number of shares outstanding. LQ = liquidity, measured by current assets/current liabilities. OL = operating leverage, measured by the book value of net fixed assets divided by total assets. PE = the PE ratio, measured by share price divided by earnings per share. PR = payout ratio, measured by dividends to ordinary shareholders divided by distributable earnings to ordinary shareholders. SZ = size, represented by the market value of equity (measured in £' millions). TR = tax rate, measured by tax charge for the current year divided by profit before tax for the year. All the data used were obtained from Datastream. The estimates reported in this Appendix were obtained with the correlation procedure in SPSS.

Appendix A(ii)
Correlation matrices

1993

	β	FL	LQ	OL	PE	PR	ln(SZ)
FL	0.1402*						
LQ	-0.0318	-0.2478*					
OL	-0.0937	0.2795*	-0.3910*				
PE	-0.0794	0.1324*	-0.0395	0.0941			
PR	0.0271	-0.0155	-0.0953	-0.0262	-0.0292		
ln(SZ)	0.4663*	-0.0068	-0.1248*	0.2048*	-0.0530	0.0588	
TR	-0.0458	-0.0794	-0.0851	-0.1143*	0.0114	0.1878*	0.1123*

Number of observations = 378. * indicates values that are significant at the 5% or higher levels.

1994

	β	FL	LQ	OL	PE	PR	ln(SZ)
FL	0.1933*						
LQ	-0.0044	-0.2889*					
OL	-0.1363*	0.2391*	-0.4840*				
PE	-0.1004*	0.1184*	-0.0147	0.0551			
PR	0.0124	0.0546	-0.0480	0.0044	-0.0756		
ln(SZ)	0.3964*	0.0398*	-0.1995*	0.2135*	-0.0620	0.1132*	
TR	-0.1057*	-0.1237*	-0.1104*	0.1149*	0.0042	0.2843*	0.2021*

Number of observations = 394. * indicates values that are significant at the 5% or higher levels.

Notes:

β = market beta estimate in Datastream. FL = financial leverage. It is represented by the borrowing ratio, measured by net borrowing (as defined below)/(Market value of equity plus borrowing).

Borrowing = the sum of the book values of long term loans, short term loans and overdrafts. Net borrowing = borrowing less the book value of

Borrowing = the sum of the book values of long term loans, short term loans and overdrafts. Net borrowing = borrowing less the book value of short term investments. Market value of equity is represented by share price multiplied by the number of shares outstanding. LQ = liquidity, measured by current assets/current liabilities. OL = operating leverage, measured by the book value of net fixed assets divided by total assets. PE = the PE ratio, measured by share price divided by earnings per share. PR = payout ratio, measured by dividends to ordinary shareholders divided by distributable earnings to ordinary shareholders. SZ = size, represented by the market value of equity (measured in £' millions). TR = tax rate, measured by tax charge for the current year divided by profit before tax for the year. All the data used wereobtained from Datastream. The estimates reported in this Appendix were obtained with the correlation procedure in SPSS.

Appendix B
Result of the T-test of industry influence on the beta values

	1990		1991		1992		1993		1994	
Industries	Obs.	Av. beta	Obs	Av. beta	Obs.	Av. beta	Obs	Av. beta	Obs.	Av beta
Control group:										
Distribution	17	0.8779	20	0.8737	24	0.8937	28	0.8879	26	0.8321
Industrials	12	1.0092	13	0.9872	13	1.0795	13	1.0662	17	1.1085
Food mfg.	13	0.8152	18	0.7755	15	0.6986	0	-	0	-
Health	16	0.8441	21	0.8401	21	0.8470	20	0.7556	19	0.8045
H'sehld. gds.	15	0.7085	17	0.7336	15	0.7196	15	0.6853	15	0.7061
Oil	11	0.8330	10	0.7260	9	0.7113	11	0.8465	9	0.8942
Prtg. & Pkg.	17	0.9301	21	0.9548	24	0.9484	28	0.8861	31	0.8821
Group Average	101	0.8591	120	0.8474	121	0.8568	115	0.8542	117	0.8696
Test group:										
Building	13	1.0188 (1.82)*	15	1.0905 (3.02)*	13	1.0928 (2.48) *	19	1.1697 (4.48)*	25	1.1554 (4.28)*
Brewery	14	0.7164 (-1.88)*	14	0.7164 (-1.67)*	13	0.7221 (-1.50)	14	0.7124 (-1.89)*	14	0.7612 (-1.37)
Chemicals	16	0.8971 (0.51)	19	0.9392 (1.36)	17	0.9013 (0.56)	17	0.8979 (0.63)	19	0.9611 (1.32)
Electronics	22	0.7802 (-1.29)	23	0.8065 (-0.65)	24	0.7826 (-1.10)	30	0.8184 (-0.66)	29	0.8140 (-1.00)
Engineering	61	0.8192 (-0.87)	51	0.8381 (-0.19)	53	0.8786 (0.42)	43	0.7252 (-2.77)*	43	0.7747 (-1.98)*
Leisure	15	0.8419 (-0.21)	19	0.8938 (0.64)	15	0.8970 (0.46)	18	0.7252 (-1.79)*	18	0.7990 (-0.95)
Retail	30	0.8545 (-0.08)	29	0.8872 (0.70)	30	0.8227 (-0.54)	35	0.8507 (-0.06)	38	0.8220 (-0.87)

Services	32	0.7357 (-2.27)*	32	0.7384 (-2.02)*	29	0.7737 (-1.33)	36	0.7937 (-1.21)	35	0.8434 (-0.50)
Textiles	27	0.7113 (-2.55)*	30	0.7441 (-1.81)*	27	0.7916 (-1.00)	16	0.7077 (-2.11)*	20	0.7703 (-1.51)
Utilities	13	0.9788 (1.64)	30	0.9186 (1.31)	36	0.8625 (0.10)	35	0.9020 (0.96)	36	0.8738 (0.08)
Group Average	243	0.8169 (-1.13)	262	0.8465 (-0.03)	257	0.8454 (-0.32)	263	0.8274 (-0.81)	277	0.8546 (-0.44)
Total	344	0.8292	382	0.8468	378	0.8490	378	0.8356	394	0.8590

Notes:

1. T-values are in parentheses.
2. * indicates values that are significant at the 5%or higher levels.
3. Obs. = Number of firms in the industry/group.
4. Av. beta = Average value of market beta of firms in the industry/group.
5. All the data used were obtained from Datastream. The grouping of firms into industries reported in this Appendix is based on the London Stock Exchange industry classification codes in Datastream. The grouping was performed by using the frequency procedure in SPSS. The t-test results were obtained with the T-test procedure in SPSS.

References

Ball, R. and Kothari, S. P. (1989) 'Risk Shifts and Serial Correlation in Returns', *Journal of Financial Economics*, 25, 51-74.

Beaver, W. H., Kettler, P. and Scholes, M. (1970) 'The Association between Market-Determined and Accounting-Determined Risk Measures', *Accounting Review*, 45, October, 654-682.

------------------ and Manegold, J. (1975) 'The Association between Market-Determined and Accounting-Determined Measures of Systematic Risk: Some Further Evidence', *Journal of Financial and Quantitative Analysis*, 10, June, 231-284.

Bildersee, J. S. (1975) 'The Association between a Market-Determined Measure of Risk and Alternative Measures of Risk', *Accounting Review*, January, 81-98.

Blume, M. E. (1975) 'Betas and Their Regression Tendencies', *Journal of Finance*, June, 785-795.

Bowman, R. G. (1979) 'The Theoretical Relationship Between Systematic Risk and Financial (Accounting) Variables', *Journal of Finance*, XXXIV, No. 3, June, 617-630.

-------------------- (1981) 'The Theoretical Relationship Between Systematic Risk and Financial (Accounting) Variables: Reply', *Journal of Finance*, June, 749-750.

Brealey, R. A. and Myers, S. C. (1991) *Principles of Corporate Finance, 4th edition*, McGraw Hill, London.

Chan, K. C. and Chen, N. (1988) 'An unconditional asset-pricing test and the role of firm size as an instrumental variable for risk', *Journal of Finance*, 43, 309-325.

Conine, T. E. (1982) 'On the Theoretical Relationship Between Business Risk and Systematic Risk', *Journal of Business Finance and Accounting*, Summer, 199-205.

Dimson, E. (1979) 'Risk measurement when shares are subject to infrequent trading', *Journal of Financial Economics*, 7 197-226.

-------------- and Marsh, P. R. (1983) 'The Stability of UK Risk Measures and the Problem of Thin Trading', *Journal of Finance*,XXXVIII, No. 3, June, 753-783.

Fama, E. F. and French, K. R. (1992) 'The cross-section of expected stock returns', *Journal of Finance*, 47, 427-465.

Gahlon, J. M. and Gentry, J. A. (1982) 'On the Relationship Between Systematic Risk and the Degree of Operating and Financial Leverage', *Financial Management*, 11, Summer, 15-23.

Gonedes, N. J. (1973) 'Evidence on the Information Content to Accounting Numbers: Accounting-Based and Market-Based Estimates of Systematic Risk', *Journal of Financial and Quantitative Analysis*, 8, June, 407-444.

Hamada, R. S. (1972) 'The Effects of the Firm's Capital Structure on the Systematic Risk of Common Stocks', *Journal of Finance*, 27, May, 435-452.

Haugen, R. A. (1993) *Modern Investment Theory, 3rd edition*, Prentice Hall International, London.

Lev, B. (1974) 'On the Association between Operating Leverage and Risk', *Journal of Financial and Quantitative Analysis*, 9, September, 627-641.

Levy, H. and Sarnat, M. (1994) *Capital Investment and Financial Decisions, 5th edition*, Prentice Hall International, London.

Lumby, S. (1994) *Investment Appraisal and Financial Decisions, 5th edition*, Chapman & Hall, London.

Mandelker, G. N. and Rhee, S. G. (1984) 'The Impact of the Degrees of Operating and Financial Leverage on Systematic Risk of Common Stock', *Journal of Financial and Quantitative Analysis*, 19, No. 1, March, 45-57.

Miller, M. and Modigliani, F. (1961) 'Dividend Policy, Growth and the Valuation of Shares', *Journal of Business*, October, 411-433.

Ross, S. A., Westerfield, R. W. and Jordan, B. D. (1995) *Fundamentals of Corporate Finance, 3rd edition*, Irwin, London.

Vasicek, O. A. (1973) 'A Note on using cross-sectional information in Bayesian Estimation of Security Betas', *Journal of Finance*, 28, December, 1233-9.

Weston, J. F. and Copeland, T. E. (1992) *Managerial Finance, 9th edition*, Dryden Press, London.

12 An international study of dividend policy: Some preliminary results

Fiona Dalton and John Pointon

Introduction

Dividend policy is important for an understanding of share valuation and the cost of capital to industry and commerce, which in turn has significant ramifications for capital investment and economic growth. Also, with the increasing internationalization of investment and finance, variations in dividend policy across countries demand scrutiny.

There have been many studies which have sought to identify the determinants of corporate dividend policy. We shall briefly review the significance of stability, growth, financial risk, capital investment needs, frictional costs, liquidity, signalling, agency costs, taxation and cultural effects. Research to date suggests that there has been little attempt to identify factors which might be specific to individual countries. In this study we examine several of these key factors, using both univariate and multivariate linear regression techniques, in order to gain an insight into their relative importance for individual countries. Dividend stability and the signalling of future earnings are found to have universal importance, whereas capital investment needs and liquidity can have varying degrees of significance for different countries. We also provide some evidence on cultural differences, which appear to warrant future research.

Background

The role of dividend policy has been a contentious issue in corporate finance, especially since the well-known Miller and Modigliani (1961) proposition that it ought to be irrelevant to share valuation in a perfect tax-free capital market. The firm can substitute new issues of equity for retentions and so shareholders should find reduced capital gains compensated by increased current dividends.

Even if the firm increases retentions, shareholders can create their own 'dividends' by selling part of their holdings. Whether capital needs are met by new issues of equity or retentions should make no difference to the overall shareholder wealth. We shall now turn to several factors, which may be important in an imperfect real-world environment.

Stability

Managers tend to prefer stable dividends and avoid risking an increase in dividends, that may have to be reduced in future years. This view was supported in an old US study by Lintner (1956) but is still important to modern financial executives, including those in the UK (Rutterford, 1994, who cites Gill and Green, 1993).

Growth

A steady growth trend in dividends is believed by managers to be important for shareholders (Rutterford, 1994). Whether expected returns are affected is difficult to test (Black and Scholes, 1974). Also increased dividends result in a reduction in funds available to creditors which in extreme circumstances could affect credit terms (Black, 1976).

Financial risk

Shareholders in more highly geared firms may demand higher dividends as a compensation for the level of financial risk. Chang and Rhee (1990) found this to be the case for 508 firms.

Capital investment needs

Capital investment needs are likely to put restraints on dividends. Indeed, Bond and Meghir (1994) found that, for 626 large UK firms, financing constraints on capital investment from 1971 - 1986 were consistent with a hierarchy of finance model, i.e. 'cheaper' internal funds are preferred to external share issues and borrowing. Olson and McCann (1994) found that US firms, that pursued a residual dividend policy, had a higher growth of asset turnover, and had a lower growth of revenues.

Frictional costs

Capital markets are not frictionless. Investors can incur transaction costs when selling shares. Thus, when firms reduce dividends and investors want to sell fractional holdings to rectify deficiencies in income, the frictional transactions costs involved would tend to limit such activities. Alternatively, when firms pay dividends at such a level that insufficient is retained to meet capital investment requirements, seeking external finance through the capital markets has associated costs, which for unlisted securities can vary with the method of issue (Buckland and Davis, 1989). The transactions costs at the investor level and the issue costs at the corporate level have opposite influences on dividend policy. However, the transactions costs to investors are avoidable by holding shares instead, whereas the issue costs to firms when raising external finance are unavoidable.

Liquidity

Dividend cuts may reflect low liquidity. However, it has been suggested that, in the UK, dividend payments have been excessive at least in relation to cash flows (Lawson and Stark, 1981). However, this may have been a reflection of inflationary effects and the influence of historic cost profits (Theobald, 1978).

Signalling

In a world of uncertainty, there may be a positive role for the determination of dividends as a signalling device, conveying information from the directors of a company to its shareholders. So, deviations from an established target payout ratio may be interpreted as a change in the future earnings anticipated by the directors (Miller and Modigliani, 1961). Adjustments in dividends as a signal of expected future earnings were supported in a UK regression study by Edwards, Mayer, Pasherdes and Poterba (1985). As to the US, Olson and McCann (1994) found that firms which followed a signalling dividend policy, similarly to those which adopted a residuals policy, tended to have a higher growth of asset turnover, but a lower growth of revenues. However, the revenues of the signalling firms were more variable.

The role of signalling in dividend policy was also consistent with a study by Asquith and Mullins (1983) of firms that paid their first dividends or resumed payments after a break of at least ten years. Excess returns were discovered.

Agency costs

To assure shareholders that directors are managing corporate affairs in their best interests (Jensen and Meckling, 1976), dividend payments may be one way of indicating this, thus reducing the availability of cash for non-essential activities. Easterbrook (1984) suggested that if firms pay dividends at such a level that they need to raise external finance, then managers are driven to reduce agency costs and transmit new financial information to investors.

This theory has been supported by empirical evidence (Moh'd, Perry and Rimbey, 1995). Firms which have lower payout ratios have been found to have fewer insiders holding shares (Rozeff, 1982). However, Schooley and Barney (1994) found that, when the level of share ownership by chief executive officers is less than about 15 percent, the dividend yield falls as ownership increases, whereas above this level the dividend yield increases with ownership.

Taxation

When the assumption of a tax-free environment is relaxed, the dividend irrelevancy proposition can be questioned. In most countries there is a differential tax treatment of dividends and capital gains, induced by retentions. The Miller-Modigliani (1961) suggestion that individuals would reduce shareholdings to convert gains into income is challenged by fiscal incentives in some countries to lengthen the period of share ownership. For example, in Germany long-term capital gains are exempt from taxation and in Japan only fifty percent is taxable (Price Waterhouse, 1995). In the UK and Australia acquisition costs are indexed linked so that real gains are taxable. In a number of countries, including the UK, even though gains are taxed at income tax rates, exemption threshold levels reduce the effective tax rates on chargeable gains.

At the corporate level there can be a differential tax rate on distributions, for example in Germany. Also degrees of imputation can vary between twenty percent of the gross equivalent of the dividend, as in the UK, to the full corporate rate in France and Germany. Elsewhere, classical systems can operate, as in the US. Some countries have applied an imputation system for many years, for example the UK; others such as Australia have adopted such a system more recently, whilst Japan has in the past moved away from an imputation system. A classification of systems is provided in Table 1. Changes in systems at both the personal and corporate level can provide a fruitful study for empirical research. In the UK, although Menyah (1993) did not find support for the tax-induced dividend clientele hypothesis in his study of the ex-dividend pricing of equities from 1955 to 1984, Chui, Strong and Cadle (1992) discovered for 1955 to 1983, that when companies which suffered from advance corporation tax setoff exhaustion were excluded, the hypothesis that tax coefficients were the same across three different tax regimes was rejected. That UK tax clienteles exist has also been supported by Crossland, Dempsey and Moizer (1991), although Black (1976) has argued that if certain shares are avoided for tax reasons, investors would not be able to construct a well-diversified portfolio.

Cultural effects

Country influence has been found to be a significant determinant of the capital structure of firms with headquarters in different countries (Stonehill and Stitzel, 1969; Collins and Sekely, 1983). One explanation given for this is that there are different cultural factors which influence corporate capital structure (Sekely and Collins, 1988). Cultural factors cover a wide range from social norms to a society's economic structure. There has been much debate as to the definition of culture but most definitions 'include the following elements: social institutions, belief systems, aesthetics, language and material culture' (Sekely and Collins, 1988).

In order to identify cultural influences it is first necessary to classify countries according to certain criteria. Broek and Webb (1973) identified seven culture realms each of which can be sub-divided into smaller areas of cultural influence. Sekely and Collins (1987) felt that these particular classifications have 'fundamental unity of composition, arrangement and integration of significant traits which distinguish them from other realms'. They adapted these seven culture realms for the specific countries in their study. Significant differences in capital structure were evident.

Of the countries considered in this study there are four clear culture realms according to the Broek model as adapted by Sekely and Collins. These are:

a) Anglo-American - Australia, United Kingdom and United States
b) West Central Europe - Germany
c) Mediterranean Europe - France
d) East Asian - Japan

These represent a mixture of social structures, economic structures and technological capabilities.

Countries which are security based will be more sensitive to stock-market changes than those which are bank oriented. This is one of the primary reasons for inter-country differences in dividend policy. In this study the UK, France and the US are classified as security based systems (Coates, Davies, Reeves and Zafar, 1995; Buckland, 1989; Van Ees and Garretsen, 1994). Germany is a bank oriented system whilst Japan has characteristics of both systems (Coates et al, 1995; Allen 1992).

It is possible to make some preliminary assessments as to the importance of the factors affecting dividend policy for each of the countries included in the study.

1 Germany

Banks play a significant role in the provision of debt to German firms. German banks will also help by channelling equity to German firms. These firms therefore have a far closer relationship with banks and corporate clients than their UK and US compatriots. German firms can easily improve liquidity by approaching the savings banks (Coates et al, 1995).

There is a marked contrast between UK and German firms in terms of dividend payout levels and changes. Mayer (1994) points to the lack of flexibility in UK dividend policy in stark contrast to German firms that regularly cut or waive dividends where necessary.

This leads to the initial conclusion that liquidity, stability, growth and gearing are not factors which will be critically important in determining corporate dividend policy in Germany.

2 The UK, France and the US

These countries have strong, influential stock exchanges. The sensitivity of these stock markets to changes in dividends and the potential impact on the firm's share price can help to explain the reluctance of UK or US firms to cut dividends (Coates et al, 1995). The existence of asymmetric information, a result of the diverse ownership and relative autonomy of managers in the UK and the US, supports the need for a signalling device and a way of monitoring management performance.

An initial conclusion, therefore, would be that both signalling and growth would be important determinants of dividend policy in the UK and the US. Liquidity and capital investment factors are likely to be of less importance.

3 Japan

Japanese companies follow the practice of paying dividends at a constant percentage of par value (usually 10%), which makes it seem unlikely that dividends act as a signalling device (Allen, 1992). This is supported by the fact that '...the system of cross-shareholdings or 'mochiai' which is dominant in Japan...and the close relationship between group companies mean that direct channels of information between group company management and *some* shareholders are prevalent in Japan' (Allen, 1992). A large proportion of external finance is provided by bank funding, the vast majority of which consists of short-term borrowing. The reason for this is partly historic in that '...Japanese government security market regulations used to restrict both the supply and demand for corporate debt.' (Allen, 1992).

Initial conclusions would suggest that signalling, growth, and liquidity would not be critically important determinants of dividend policy in Japan.

Summary

The theoretical and empirical literature suggests a range of variables which should explain much of the variation in corporate dividend policy across firms and across countries. It should be noted that most of the studies are based upon the analysis of UK and US firms. This further reinforces the need to examine dividend policy in other countries, where the culture effects may be different and where conventional explanations may not be valid.

Hypotheses

The literature examined so far suggests that, at least in some countries, the dividend policy of a firm is determined by the desire for stability and growth, the need for capital investment, the degree of liquidity and the financial risk experienced by the firm. The following hypotheses are proposed:

H1: Firms follow a stable dividend policy.
H2: There will be a steady growth rate in dividend payouts.
H3: An increase in capital investment will result in a higher retention of earnings.
H4: Firms with low liquidity are likely to cut dividends.
H5: Shareholders in firms which are highly geared are likely to demand higher dividends.
H6: A firm's dividend policy is likely to be explained by a combination of these factors.
H7: For different cultures there will be different explanations of dividend policy.

Data

The data set analysed consists of accounting data drawn from the Datastream financial database. Data for 50 companies from each of six countries were identified. The countries were chosen to try and achieve a cross section of cultures. The data were chosen to satisfy the following criteria: (i) no missing values were found for any of the specified variables; and (ii) firms paid a dividend for either the base year or the previous year.

The base year is 1994 which is represented as time t.

Methodology

In this initial study the strength of the determinant factors of dividend policy will be tested. The factors will include stability, growth, signalling, liquidity, capital investment and financial risk. In order to understand the impact of these factors both individually and collectively univariate and multivariate linear regression techniques are used to construct models from which a better understanding of the impact of these variables may be achieved.

Variable definition

In this study a model is constructed using proxies for the factors discussed above. The dependent variable for all regressions is 'ordinary dividends paid in time t' (Ord Divi [T]), the independent variables tested are 'ordinary dividends paid in time t-1' (Ord Divi [T-1]), 'post taxation earnings in time t+1' (Earnings [T+1]), the 'liquidity of the company as measured by the current ratio in time t' (Liquidity), the 'level of capital investment by the company in time t as measured by the change in capital expenditure between time t and t-1'(Change in FA) and the 'level of gearing in the company as measured by the company's gearing ratio in time t' (Gearing).

A significant t-statistic for the variables Earnings (T+1) and Ord Divi (T-1), would indicate, respectively, that current dividends are a signal for future earnings and that there is evidence of stability in corporate dividend payments. A regression coefficient for Ord Divi (T-1) greater than 1, would support H2, that there is growth in dividend payments.

The resultant models are of the form:

(i) for a univariate model:

$$\text{Ord Divi (T)} = \alpha + \gamma_1 X + \varepsilon$$

(ii) for a multivariate model:

$$\text{Ord Divi (T)} = \alpha + \gamma_1 X + \gamma_2 X + \ldots + \gamma_n X + \varepsilon$$

The results

Summary of univariate regression results

Table 2 shows the simple regression results for each of the countries in the study. The t statistic was used to determine the significance of the independent variables. The results of this test indicate that prior year dividends and current earnings are significant beyond the 99% level for all countries. Thus H1 and H2 are accepted for all countries, consistency of dividend policy being important to firms in all countries tested as well as short term future earnings. From the results achieved in this study both of these factors are of most importance to the UK and consistency of dividend policy is of least importance in the USA, whilst short term future earnings is of least importance in Japan

The results of the students t-test for the capital investment, liquidity and gearing variables are more varied between countries. The test for capital investment, for example, was significant at the 99.9% level in Australia, at the 99% level in the US and at the 95% level in Japan. H3 is accepted for these countries, that is a change in the level of capital investment is likely to be reflected in a change in retained earnings. The test was not significant for the UK, Germany or France.

When testing for the significance of liquidity the results show that in France and the US the test was not significant, so for these countries H4 is rejected. There is no evidence to suggest that firms in Australia and the US cut dividends when they are experiencing poor liquidity. The liquidity variable is significant at the 80% level which may indicate some support for H4 in the remaining countries.

A growth pattern of dividend payments over the two years selected was only evident in the UK and France.

Summary of multivariate regression results

Comparing the multiple regression results in Table 3, for the countries under study, we can conclude that in all of the countries the most important influence on dividend policy would appear to be the level of dividends in the previous year. In the UK, however, there is no multiple regression equation which produces a better explanation than the simple regression model of Ord Divi [T] and Ord Divi [T-1].

In Germany and France, however, the best explanation of dividend policy comes from a consideration of both last year's dividend payment and the signalling effect of future earnings. In France the company's liquidity position is also of importance to the dividend decision.

In both the USA, Japan and Australia the level of capital investment is an important explanatory variable as well as the previous year's dividend payment. In the USA the level of future earnings in determining dividend policy should be included. Multicollinearity is a problem in both the Australian and Japanese regression results.

Summary of cultural differences

Some initial conclusions about the relevance of cultural influences in the determination of dividend policy can be drawn from these preliminary results.

The results do not reflect the culture realms proposed by Sekely and Collins (1988) or Broek (1973). The results would suggest that there are country differences and a possible cultural effect if a different classification is used. A suggested classification is given in Table 4.

There is some evidence that countries with similar tax regimes have similar determinant factors of dividend policy. This is an area where future research is needed.

Conclusion

In conclusion it can be seen from the results that a number of influences impact on a corporation's dividend policy. These will also vary between countries. The key factors for all countries are dividend stability and signalling of future earnings. Capital investment needs and liquidity are of minimal importance in the European countries, but are in some cases very significant in the US, Australia and Japan.

These results give some evidence that cultural differences do provide some explanation of the varying importance of factors for different countries. This influence of culture supports the call by Sekely and Collins (1988) for future research to examine the effects of different social and legal structures on corporate decision making processes.

References

Allen, D.E. (1992), 'Some Features of Dividend Policy In Japan' *Managerial Finance*, 18, 1,49-69.

Asquith, P. and Mullins Jnr., D.W. (1983), 'The Impact of Initiating Dividend Payments on Shareholders' Wealth', *Journal of Business*, 56, 1, 77-96.

Black, F. (1976), 'The Dividend Puzzle', *The Journal of Portfolio Management*, Winter, 5-8.

Black, F. and Scholes, M. (1974), 'The Effects of Dividend Yield and Dividend Policy on Common Stock Prices and Returns', *Journal of Financial Economics*, 1, 1, May, 1-22.

Bond, S. and Meghir, C. (1994), 'Financial Constraints and Company Investment' *Fiscal Studies*, 15, 2, 1-18.

Broek, J.O.M. and Webb, J.W. (1973), 'Culture Realms', *A Geography of Mankind*, New York, McGraw Hill, 179-203.

Buckland, R. (1989), 'Second-Tier Equity Markets in the UK and France', *British Accounting Review*, 21, 3-22.

Buckland, R. and Davis, E.W. (1989), *The Unlisted Securities Market*, Oxford: Clarendon Press.

Coates, J.B., Davies, E.W., Reeves, N.B.R. and Zafar, A.(1995), 'The Role of Corporate Measurement Systems in the UK and Germany: Challenging Short-Terminism?', CIMA Progress Report.

Collins, J.M. and Sekely, W.S. (1983), 'The Relationship of Headquarters, Country and Industry Classification to Financial Structure', *Financial Management*, Autumn: 45-51.

Chang, R. P. and Rhee, S.G. (1990), 'The Impact of Personal Taxes on Corporate Dividend Policy and Capital Structure Decisions' *Financial Management,* Summer, 21-31.

Chui, A., Strong N. and Cadle, J. (1992), 'The Empirical Significance of Tax Effects on the Valuation of Dividends: the UK evidence', *Journal of Business Finance and Accounting*, June, 515-532.

Crossland, M., Dempsey M. and Moizer, P. (1991), The Effect of Cum-to Ex-Dividend Changes on UK share prices', *Accounting and Business Research,* Winter, 47-50.

Easterbrook, F.H. (1984), 'Two Agency-Cost Explanations of Dividends', *American Economic Review*, 74, September, 650-659.

Edwards, J., Mayer, C., Pasherdes, P., and Poterba, J. (1985), 'The Effects of Taxation on Corporate Dividend Distributions' Institute for Fiscal Studies Working Paper No. 78, June.

Gill, J. and Green, J.P. (1993), 'Dividend Policy and its Relationship to Investment and Financing Policies: UK Empirical Evidence', University of Ulster Working Paper.

Jensen, M.C. and Meckling, W.H. (1976), 'Theory of the Firm: Managerial Behaviour, Agency Costs and Ownership Structure', *Journal of Financial Economics,* October, 305-60.

Lawson, G.H. and Stark, A.W. (1981), 'Equity Values and Inflation:Dividends and Debt Financing' *Lloyds Bank Review*, 139, January.

Lintner, J. (1956), 'Distribution of Incomes and Dividends Among Corporations, Retained Earnings and Taxes', *American Economic Review,* 46, 2, May, 97-113.

Mayer, C. (1994), 'Stock-Markets, Financial Institutions and Corporate Performance'. In: Dimsdale, N. and Prevezer, M, *Capital Markets and Corporate Governance*, Oxford: Oxford University Press.

Menyah, K. (1993), 'Ex-Dividend Equity Pricing under UK Tax Regimes' *Journal of Business Finance and Accounting*, January, 61-81.

Miller, M.H. and Modigliani, F. (1961), 'Dividend Policy, Growth and the Valuation of Shares', *Journal of Business,* October, 411-33.

Moh'd, M.A., Perry, L.G. and Rimbey, J.N. (1995), 'An Investigation of the Dynamic Relationship between Agency Theory and Dividend Policy', *Financial Review*, 30, 2, May, 367-385.

Olson, G.T. and McCann, P.D. (1994), 'The Linkages between Dividends and Earnings', *Financial Review*, 29, 1, February, 1-22.

Price Waterhouse, (1995), *Individual Taxes: A Worldwide Survey*, London: Price Waterhouse.

Rozeff, M.S. (1982), 'Growth, Beta and Agency Costs as Determinants of Dividend Payout Ratios', *Journal of Financial Research*, 5, Fall, 249-259.

Rutterford, J. (1994), 'The Dividend Puzzle', *Technical Focus,* Institute of Chartered Accountants in England and Wales, February.

Schooley, D.K. (1994), 'Using Dividend Policy and Managerial Ownership to Reduce Agency Costs', 17, 3, 363-373.

Sekely, W.S. and Collins, J.M. (1988), 'Cultural Influences on International Capital Structure', *Journal of International Business Studies*, Spring, 1988, 87-100.

Stonehill, A and Stitzel, T (1969), 'Financial Structure and Multinational Corporations', *California Management Review*, Fall: 91-96.

Theobald, M. (1978), 'Intertemporal Dividend Models - An Empirical Analysis Using Recent UK Data' *Journal of Business Finance and Accounting*, 5, 1, Spring, 123-135.

Van Ees, H. and Garretsen, H. (1994), 'Liquidity and Business Investment: Evidence from Dutch Panel Data', *Journal of Macroeconomics*, Fall, 613-627.

TABLE 1

A Classification of Tax Systems

Classical Systems	• Japan • US
Imputation Systems	• Australia • France • Germany • UK

TABLE 2 Summary of Univariate Regression Results

Country		UK	France	Germany	USA	Australia	Japan
No. of firms		**44**	**32**	**27**	**25**	**31**	**34**
Divi (T-1)	**R-Sq**	0.929	0.894	0.893	0.816	0.867	0.934
	t-statistic	23.491	15.903	14.438	10.102	13.727	21.617
	Regression coefficient	1.104	1.030	0.895	0.832	0.916	0.981
Earn (T+1)	**R-Sq**	0.857	0.759	0.851	0.757	0.460	0.440
	t-statistic	15.652	9.553	11.934	8.460	4.968	5.192
	Regression coefficient	0.445	0.223	0.339	0.442	0.269	0.266
Liquidity (T)	**R-Sq**	0.048	0.072	0.010	0.018	0.105	0.051
	t-statistic	**1.433**	**1.501**	**0.496**	**-0.624**	-1.845*	**-1.666**
	Regression coefficient	108,244	386,197	28,977	458,323	-86,858	-11,344,399
Capital Inv (T)	**R-Sq**	0.000	0.005	-	0.287	0.299	0.158
	t-statistic	**-0.016**	**-0.378**	-	3.045	3.517	*2.684*
	Regression coefficient	-0.001	-0.029	-	0.262	0.099	0.078
Gearing	**R-Sq**	0.003	0.006	0.025	0.047	0.008	-
	t-statistic	**0.327**	**0.149**	**-0.804**	**-1.093**	**0.475**	-
	Regression coefficient	**0.017**	**0.5820**	**-0.046**	**-0.022**	**-0.06**	-

Emboldened figures indicate that the t-statistic is *not* significant, figures in *italics* indicates that the figure is significant at the 95% level, * this figure is significant at the 90% level. All other figures are significant at the 99% level.

TABLE 3 Summary of Multivariate Regression Results

			Divi (T-1)		Earnings (T+1)		Capital Investment	
Country	F-statistic (t-test)	Adjusted R-squared	Correlation Coefficient	Regression coefficient	Correlation Coefficient	Regression coefficient	Correlation Coefficient	Regression coefficient
UK	(23.49)	0.929	0.964	1.104	-	-	-	-
France	139.33	0.931	0.945	0.957	0.871	0.066	-	-
Germany	239.55	0.948	0.945	0.547	0.922	0.162	-	-
USA	64.89	0.897	0.903	0.533	0.870	0.151	0.536	0.110
Australia	165.97	0.917	0.931	1.183	-	-	0.547	-0.065
Japan	147.5	0.947	0.967	1.020	-	-	0.429	-0.022

TABLE 4 Suggested classification of countries

Culture Realm	Countries	System of Taxation	Determinants of Dividend Policy
Northern European	UK France	Imputation Imputation	Stability, signalling, growth
West Central Europe	Germany	Imputation	Stability, signalling
American	US	Classic	Stability, signalling, capital investment
Pacific	Australia Japan	Imputation Classic	Stability, capital investment, some liquidity

13 A model for evaluating lease/purchase decisions in capital investment

Sue Farrar

Introduction

In the first section of this paper, the current UK treatment of finance leases is discussed, and relevant aspects of the literature concerning the valuation of debt interest tax shields is reviewed in the context of the UK tax system. A number of authors have recognised that tax-induced interactions between investment and financing require a simultaneous approach to these decisions, and mathematical programming models have been developed to address the problem. However, conventional lease evaluation methods do not take into account the tax effects of interactions between the cash flows of the project and those of the firm's other investment and financing activities, while mathematical programming models of lease evaluation have assumed that the scale of the lease is a continuous variable, which may be unrealistic.

The second section describes a mathematical programming model which aims to evaluate the lease/purchase decision simultaneously as part of the firm's overall optimal investment, financing and investment strategy. Via an iterative process using the Capital Asset Pricing Model, a discount rate is obtained which takes into account the effect of taxes on the returns to shareholders. The process also enables the model to accommodate a constant gearing ratio constraint. The firm's revised debt and equity financing includes the effect on the value of equity of incremental projects, which itself is determined on the assumption that the optimal tax strategy is followed at the same time. It may be assumed that leasing displaces debt for the purpose of calculating debt interest payments, or alternatively that lease finance does not affect the cost of debt. Examples of the model's output are presented and discussed.

I Debt, taxes and finance leasing

The UK treatment of finance leases

In a leasing contract, the lessor buys the item of capital equipment and claims the tax benefits of the capital allowances available. Some of the tax benefits may be shared with the lessee by reducing the lease payments. The rental payments compensate the lessor for the capital cost, the time value of money and the risk of default by the lessee.

In April 1991, the Inland Revenue issued a statement of tax practice, SP 3/91, to the effect that the tax treatment for lessees would thereafter follow Statement of Standard Accounting Practice No. 21 (SSAP 21), *Accounting for leases and hire purchase contracts*. Under SSAP 21 assets are treated as if they are owned by the lessee. This approach is consistent with the view that a lease is essentially a financing arrangement, since the lessee carries both the risks and rewards of ownership and the operational responsibilities. The provisions of SSAP 21 are that assets leased for their useful life are capitalised on the balance sheet, and depreciation is charged. The present value of the future rentals, taking the implicit rate of interest in the lease as the discount rate, is shown as a liability in the balance sheet. The finance charge component of the lease payment is the interest on the present value of the future rentals, charged at the implicit rate. This is added to the liability account and charged to the profit and loss account as an expense of the period. The lessee's accounting profit is therefore reduced by the depreciation charge and finance charge, which together form the lessee's 'tax shield'. The lessor pays taxes on the full rentals, but claims the capital allowances on the leased asset.

UK taxes and capital project financing

Modigliani and Miller (MM) (1963) demonstrated that under certain assumptions, the value of the geared firm is equal to the value of the equivalent ungeared firm plus the tax shield resulting from debt interest deductibility. The MM model assumes that the firm's debt generates a perpetual, level and certain stream of interest 'tax shields', implying that the firm will always be in a position to obtain the benefit of the interest deductions and that the tax rate will remain constant. If these conditions apply then it is appropriate to value the debt interest 'tax shields' at the debt interest rate. But if these assumptions are relaxed, the benefit of debt interest deductibility is less certain. In an asymmetrical tax system which does not provide immediate and costless relief for tax losses, the effective tax value of the debt 'tax shield' will be reduced. An optimal capital structure may therefore exist for each individual firm (DeAngelo and Masulis, 1980; Mayer, 1986). Under the UK tax system, negative taxable capacity may occur as a result of substitute tax shields such as capital allowances, or losses brought forward or claimed from other companies in a group structure. These are all deducted before debt interest in determining taxable profit. Tax exhaustion has been prevalent in the UK during periods of recession and/or the availability of generous capital allowances (Young, 1992).

Although the carry forward provisions allow excess debt tax shields to be set against future income if the firm has insufficient profits to utilise them fully, their present value will be reduced because of the time value of money and the uncertainty over the timing of the eventual setoff. The timing of setoff and the rate at which it occurs will be partly determined by the existence of other tax shields such as capital allowances, so that the investment and financing decisions interact. Where tax rates are not constant but are determined by the level of taxable profits and other tax deductible allowances, there is additional uncertainty over the eventual value of the debt interest tax shield in future periods. The value of the debt interest tax shield therefore depends on the firm's present and future investment and financing decisions, but optimal investment and financing decisions can only be made with a knowledge of the tax effects of those decisions. A suitable technique for optimal investment and financing decisions under taxation should be capable of considering these decisions simultaneously. As Cooper and Franks (1983) commented:

> The effective tax rate for the firm with tax losses will be less than the full tax rate and is endogenous to the firm's current and future set of real assets and financial transactions; the latter include financial leasing, acquisitions and lending decisions. As a result, the value of any asset can only be calculated simultaneously with the firm's optimal choice of both real assets and financial transactions.

Further, the UK imputation tax system creates interdependencies between personal taxes and optimal financing (for instance, King, 1977; Ashton, 1989a, 1989b). The relative advantage of debt financing under the imputation system is less than it would be under the corresponding classical system. Ashton (1991) concluded that the tax advantage to debt in the UK is quite small (about 7.5 per cent of its market value under 1994 tax rates). Where the firm is not perpetually in a full taxpaying position, the relationship between optimal financing and the imputation system becomes complex. Surplus ACT will increase the effective cost of paying a dividend, reducing the attractiveness of equity financing. On the other hand, the after tax cost of debt will be increased, since the present value of the tax savings from interest deductibility will be reduced as the unrelieved interest is carried forward. The firm's ability to set off its ACT may be affected by the level of debt interest payments, which reduces the mainstream corporation tax liability. Restricted setoff of ACT therefore creates an interaction between the investment, financing and dividend decisions, so that a complex relationship exists between the value of the geared and ungeared firms under the imputation system (Pointon, 1981a).

The simultaneous nature of the investment and financing decision under taxation may be accommodated using mathematical programming models to select the optimal combination of investment and financing decisions and tax strategy. With this aim, aspects of the UK tax system have been incorporated into this type of model in varying degrees of complexity (Berry and Dyson, 1979; Pointon, 1981b, 1991; Ashford, Berry and Dyson, 1986).

Leasing and UK taxes

Miller and Upton (1976) showed that in a perfect capital market where the lessor and lessee have symmetrical tax positions, the after tax present value to the lessor of the leasing rental income is the same as the discounted after tax cost to the lessee of the rental costs. In equilibrium, there is no advantage to leasing. Excess returns would be eliminated by competition between lessors, up to the point where the present value to the lessor of the asset's leasing rentals after tax would equal its discounted after tax purchase cost and disposal proceeds.

However, the tax position of the lessee and lessor may differ: the lessee's profits, including the cash flows of the lease itself, may fall within the limit for the small companies' rate or into the band where the higher marginal rate applies, or there may be a tax loss so that the lessee is temporarily tax exhausted. Since the patterns of tax-deductible items are different for the lease or buy decision, the timing of the setoff of the firm's debt interest and ACT may be affected. Under these circumstances the cash flows from leasing and purchasing of an asset may be significantly different. Also, if lenders do not have perfect knowledge of a firm's leasing commitments, the lessee and lessor may face differing costs of debt so that leasing and purchasing are no longer financially equivalent.

The literature concerned with the analysis of the tax benefits of leasing, as compared to asset purchase, has focused mainly on the contractual nature of lease payments and therefore on their similarity to debt obligations. Leasing may therefore be regarded as displacing debt, and will affect the financial risk characteristics and debt capacity of the firm as a whole. As a result of this, allocating funds to a leased project may affect the financing of subsequent projects leading to arbitrary decisions on project acceptance.

For this reason, Drury (1989) argues that the firm's weighted average cost of capital (or WACC) should be used to evaluate specific projects before the financing stage is considered. But there are drawbacks to this approach. It is inappropriate to use the overall WACC where the project's risk differs significantly from the average risk of the firm's existing assets, or where the existing debt-equity ratio may not be constant before and after project acceptance. Also, the WACC cannot be used easily in a situation where the company is temporarily not paying taxes and tax relief on debt interest is delayed because the after-tax cost of debt will then be different in each period.

Assuming that the firm does not have limitless debt capacity and given the similarities in the contractual nature of both debt and leasing cash flows, leasing may be regarded as displacing debt. But if leasing displaces borrowing capacity, a further complication is that the amount of debt displaced depends on the value of the lease, but the value of the lease depends on the debt displaced. The need for an approach which can deal with these aspects simultaneously was recognised early in the development of the leasing literature. As Fawthrop and Terry (1976) pointed out:

> A decision to lease cannot be taken in isolation from the decision to acquire the asset. Given that a decision to acquire the asset must review, inter alia, taxation costs and benefits; and given that these differ when leasing is used as compared with ownership financing; then the investment appraisal becomes dependent on the financing decision. The decision to lease, therefore, is unquestionably a simultaneous investment and financing decision and, as such, any attendant technique must adequately recognise and engage this notoriously complex area of capital budgeting.

Assuming an MM world of debt and taxes, Myers, Dill and Bautista (1976) (MDB) applied the 'adjusted present value' methodology developed by Myers (1974) to derive a lease valuation formula which solves simultaneously for the value of the lease contract and the value of the equivalent loan, that is, the value of the debt displaced by the lease. MDB modelled the situation where lease rental payments are allowable in full against tax, as in the US and formerly in the UK, as:

$$B_0 = \sum_{t=0}^{H} \frac{P_t(1-T)+b_t T}{(1+r^*)^t}$$

where:

P_t = lease payment in t per £1 of leased asset
T = the marginal corporate tax rate
b_t = depreciation allowance in t per £1 of the leased asset's value
r^* = the firm's after tax borrowing rate
H = the final period of the lease.

Since the cash flows in all future periods are assumed to be identical, the net advantage of leasing is the difference between B_0, the amount borrowed, and the purchase cost. The lost interest tax shields of displaced debt are implicitly recognised in the adjusted discount rate r^*. Franks and Hodges (1978) showed an alternative derivation of the same formula.

The assumptions of this approach are:

(i) Debt is valuable, in the MM sense;
(ii) dividend policy is irrelevant;
(iii) in the absence of leasing, the firm borrows an 'optimal amount' which depends on the value and business risk characteristics of the firm's assets, and the value of tax shields generated by depreciation and interest;
(iv) the tax shields generated by the lease payments are treated in the same way as the shields generated by depreciation and interest.

These assumptions are questionable in the UK context, since the tax shields from leasing, depreciation and interest are not treated in the same way. Tax shields from leasing or depreciation may lead to a trading loss which may be carried back as well as forward, but excess charges on interest cannot. Under the imputation system the treatment of ACT may be affected by the level of debt interest payments, which reduces the mainstream corporation tax liability, and so dividend policy is not independent of the lease/purchase decision where the firm is ACT exhausted.

Also, in order to use the formula in project appraisal, it is necessary to know:

(i) the schedule of lease payments;
(ii) the asset's tax depreciation schedule;
(iii) the firm's cost of borrowing;
(iv) the firm's marginal tax rate.

The last three of these should be derived endogenously by the overall activities of the firm, including the leased project. If the project is appraised separately, as in the example above, incorrect assumptions may be made about the appropriate values of the cost of debt and the relevant marginal tax rate. The tax effects of the capital allowances available if the asset is purchased rather than leased will similarly depend on the interactions between the cash flows of the project and those of the firm's existing activities and debt commitments.

Although for the firm which is temporarily non taxpaying, the valuation method may be modified by adjusting the after tax cost of debt to take account of the time lag in obtaining tax relief, the future tax paying date is treated as certain and exogenous to the acceptance of the project, whereas the project's cash flows and tax effects and the firm's future tax situation will be interdependent. Acceptance of the project may even alter the firm's pattern of tax relief on the interest relating to existing debt commitments, so that the after tax cost of that debt will also be distorted.

The effect of any incremental project, and its financing, on the amount and timing of the firm's cash flows should ideally be assessed simultaneously in an overall tax context. In order to take complex tax effects fully into account, lease evaluation should take place in the context of the firm as a whole rather than in isolation. This may be achieved by the use of a mathematical programming model to incorporate all the relevant cash flows for both the leasing and purchasing alternatives. Fawthrop and Terry (1976) recognised that a mathematical programming model could provide a suitable lease valuation technique, but did not attempt to develop a model of this type. An attempt to analyse the reasons for leasing in a mathematical programming framework was made by Ashton (1978). Ashton formulated the investment policy and financing policy of the firm as a problem in constrained optimisation, determining the contribution made by a lease using Kuhn-Tucker optimality conditions. The analysis assumes that any lease decision is made such that the subsequent rearrangement of debt and equity is optimal, with the appropriate discount rate arising from within the solution framework rather than being specified exogenously. By assuming that the debt capacity and the scale of the lease undertaken are continuous variables, the conditions for optimality when applied to the leasing variable may be derived. In this way values may be obtained for the marginal increase in the value of the firm associated with leasing and the opportunity cost of capital. A difficulty with this approach in the context of project appraisal is that a lease is generally a fairly large, discrete block of finance which is not continuously divisible. As a result, the linear programme and the shadow prices which arise out of it cannot be applied to determine whether the lease or purchase alternative is preferable. Similarly, Cooper and Franks (1983) assessed the leasing and purchasing alternatives in a linear programming context, arguing that the timing of the tax effects of projects may be taken into account through the 'effective' tax rates which arise as shadow prices in the solution. This model allows for the possible carry forward of tax shields to future periods, so allowing for the impact of this on the effective tax rate. Franks and Hodges (1978) proposed a simple linear programming model which optimises the lessee's schedule of payments by setting the lessor's net present value at zero. The linear program maximises the initial cash flow for the buy and borrow alternative, subject to constraints which equate the future cash flows to those for leasing. The amounts borrowed and repaid are included as decision variables and additional equations calculate the loan balance each period. Franks and Hodges suggested that the approach could be extended from the simple situation where tax losses carried forward are subsequently absorbed in full in a single year, to a more complex scenario where absorption occurs over a number of years and the tax savings produced are limited by the company's stream of taxable income. There do not appear to have been any attempts in the literature to develop a mathematical programming model for lease evaluation in complex tax situations where a number of alternative tax strategies exist.

II The mathematical programming model

The model developed by Farrar (1995) aims to maximise shareholder wealth, subject to a number of constraints representing the logic of the relevant tax rules and other externally or internally imposed restrictions on the firm's behaviour. Within the bounds imposed by the constraints, all possible combinations of investment, financing and tax strategies are assessed simultaneously in the solution process and the optimal solution is determined.

The main tax areas incorporated in the model are: the offset rules and the carry back/carry forward provisions relating to the treatment of trading losses, ACT and debenture interest, including the possibility of group relief, and the provisions relating to finance leasing as an alternative to capital asset purchase. Constraints ensure that the net cash flows from projects, dividend payments, lending less borrowing costs, equity issues and tax payments, are sufficient to maintain the firm's liquidity. Short term lending and borrowing are permitted. A target debt/equity ratio may be imposed, or alternatively the model may be given a free choice of funding policy. The firm's cost of debt is assumed to be determined by its debt/equity ratio, so that it faces an increasing interest rate on incremental debt as the ratio rises. Alternative forms of horizon valuation may be used, depending on the assumptions made about the fate of the firm and its dividend policy beyond the horizon.

The final version of the model maximises the returns to shareholders, taking into account dividend payments and new equity issues. The returns are derived as a residual, after deduction of all contractual payments such as debenture interest and other cash outflows. Dividends may be constrained according to some given stable growth requirement, or the model may be allowed to choose a pattern of dividend payments which maximises shareholder wealth. The returns to shareholders are discounted at the cost of equity, which is determined by an iterative method using a CAPM spreadsheet model in conjunction with the optimisation model.

The assumptions of the model are:

(i) there is no capital rationing;
(ii) the horizon date is set beyond the completion of all the projects under consideration;
(iii) the firm expects to have sufficient profits in the year after the horizon date to absorb any amount of losses and ACT carried forward from the horizon;
(iv) assets are purchased at the start of the year;
(v) the firm's non-trading income is unaffected by project acceptance;
(vi) dividends and debt interest payments occur at the year end;
(vii) lease rental payments are made at the beginning of each year;
(viii) any timing differences between the tax year and the firm's own accounting period are ignored;
(ix) any interim dividend payments are ignored;
(x) markets are assumed to be efficient, so that the firm's current market value must incorporate the present value of its expected future cash flows including those arising from future investment opportunities.

The commercial mathematical programming package XPRESS-MP was selected to create an operational version of the model. The final model was developed in a number of stages, with successive refinements and extensions being made at each stage using the XPRESS-MP language directly. A number of features were also developed and incorporated to assist the solution process and make it as efficient as possible. Some of these are implicit in the model structure, while others are concerned with control of the actual solution process. Data inputs were imported from tables generated from external sources, thus enabling the data to be changed easily without having to alter the actual model file. In each run, the current data in the specified sources were taken to create the model matrix. The external data sources used were ASCII (text) files and the spreadsheet package QUATTRO-PRO, which conforms to the Lotus 1-2-3 format.

Leased assets

It is assumed that the first rental payment occurs at the beginning of the period in which the lease commences and that the payments are equal. The rental payments are calculated within the spreadsheet file from which the model takes its data inputs, so that for instance for a three year project the rental payment R is determined given the purchase cost C and the implicit rate of interest i from

$$C = R + R/(1+i) + R/(1+i)^2$$

$$R = C/\left[1 + 1/(1+i) + 1/(1+i)^2\right]$$

The finance charge is determined within the optimisation model itself, using the data tables of rental payments, implicit interest rates and the purchase cost of the asset.

The charge in year 1 of the leased asset's life will be:

$$F_{t=1} = i(C - R) \quad \text{(i)}$$

In year 2:

$$F_{t=2} = i\left[(C - R)(1+i) - R\right]$$

and in year 3:

$$F_{t=3} = i\left\{\left[(C - R)(1+i) - R\right](1+i) - R\right\}$$

so that in general, the finance charge in each year after year 1 will be:

$$F_t = \left[(F_{t-1} / i)(1+i) - R\right]i$$

$$= F_{t-1}(1+i) - Ri. \quad \text{(ii)}$$

This approach is used in the model to calculate the finance charge for a leased project in a particular time period. It is necessary for the model to be able to distinguish between the first, subsequent, and final periods of the lease. This is achieved by conditional generation of the appropriate statements, utilising the data given in the tables for lease rentals, purchase cost of the asset and implicit rate of interest. If the rental payments are zero in the previous year but greater than zero in both the current and the next year, then the necessary conditions for the first year of the lease are present and the finance charge is calculated accordingly from (i). If the rental payment is greater than zero in the previous year and in the next year, then the finance charge is calculated from (ii) above. In all other conditions the finance charge will be zero.

Depreciation is assumed to be taken on the straight-line basis. For any asset which may be either leased or purchased, a decision to accept at most one of these alternatives in the optimal solution is enforced by a mutual exclusivity constraint.

The model has been applied to a variety of situations, arising from different assumptions about the firm's structure, existing activities and tax situation, and policies regarding dividend payments and capital structure. It is assumed in the following examples that the firm faces three possible future scenarios or states of nature, referred to as Outcome X, Y or Z, with different cash flows in each. To be consistent with an objective of maximising shareholder wealth, project appraisal should incorporate all the relevant cash flows, including taxes, and the tax cash flows used should take into account the optimal tax strategy of the firm as a whole if the project is accepted. The outcome of this appraisal should be compared with the firm's optimal situation after tax without the additional investment.

Example 1: The 'base case' scenario

This situation considers the ongoing activities only of a single firm without any possible selection of additional projects. The cash flows that will occur in each outcome, and their probabilities, are presented in Table 1 with the most likely outcome, Y, having the same cash flows as the example in the previous section. The optimisation model was run under each of the three possible outcomes with an initial required rate of return of 15 per cent, assuming a beta value of 1.0 (see Table 2). The returns to shareholders, in the form of gross dividends, and the expected values of equity in each period, formed the input to the spreadsheet CAPM model. The required rates of return determined by the spreadsheet model formed the input for the next iteration of the optimisation model under each of the three possible outcomes. The expected objective function value was also an input to the next iteration, as the opening value of equity. This input is needed by the model in order to calculate the debt interest payments, which vary according to the gearing ratio. The new output values from the next iteration again formed the input to the spreadsheet CAPM model and required rates of return were determined. The process was repeated until, on comparison of two successive iterations, all the following conditions were satisfied:

(i) the selected strategy of tax treatment remained stable;
(ii) the required rates of return determined were stable to four decimal places;
(ii) the change in the expected objective function value was less than £5,000 (approximately 0.055 per cent in this instance).

The most important of the model's output variables under each outcome are presented in Tables 3a to 3c. Table 3d shows the final objective function values, beta characteristics and rates of return determined by the optimisation model in conjunction with the spreadsheet model. In this case the expected rates of return are all greater than the CAPM required rate.

The expected value of equity at the start of the model's initial period, corresponding to the expected objective function value, was unaltered over the time span considered since the model chose to make no retentions. Although constraints to enforce a target gearing ratio were not included in this model the debt/equity ratio also remained unaltered, since no debt repayments were made.

Under the 'pessimistic' outcome X, a trading loss of £100,000 arises which the model chooses to set against other profits of the same period. An excess of debt interest charges then results, which is carried forward until it may be set against future trading profits in periods 3 and 4.

The full dividend payout, combined with low taxable profits as a result of the firm's capital allowances, results in surplus ACT which is carried forward since there is no remaining ACT offset capacity in earlier years. A large amount of surplus ACT exists at the horizon period which is valued, according to the assumptions of the model, by discounting back to the horizon at the average required rate of return. This presents a difficulty, since the surplus ACT at the horizon may not be recoverable.

The model was therefore run again under each set of outcome assumptions, with the horizon value constraint adjusted so that surplus ACT at the horizon had no value. The decision to make a full dividend payout was unaltered, although the horizon value and therefore the objective function value were reduced by the appropriately discounted value of the surplus ACT at the horizon date. Also, the data input value of the firm's assets at the horizon date may be regarded as incorporating the expectation that some of the ACT may be irrecoverable. For these reasons the horizon valuation of surplus ACT was retained in the model.

Example 2: The lease/purchase decision, with maintenance of existing debt/equity ratio

It is assumed that the firm's present activities are the same as in Example 1, and that it is considering a single lease/purchase project shown in Table 4. The implicit rate of interest on the lease is 8.5 per cent, the same as the firm's lowest rate of interest on debt finance. A mutual exclusivity constraint was included in the model to ensure that either project option, or neither, may be accepted but not both.

In the first iteration the discount rates used were those derived from the 'base case' and so was the opening value of equity, that is, £9.06m. The model chose to accept the purchased version of the project in each state of nature. The additional funding of £1m was selected by the model in the approximate ratio of 52:48 debt:equity, taking the debt level to its maximum limit of 22.5 per cent of total financing. However, the first iteration gave an expected objective function value of £9.369m. On the second iteration this value was used as the opening value of equity, which enabled the model to increase the amount of debt finance used to fund the project. The iterative process ultimately converged to give a funding ratio of approximately 63:37 debt:equity. The final solution therefore represents a value of equity which incorporates the new project, financed in such a way that the firm's target gearing ratio is maintained.

The solution output (Tables 5a to 5d) shows that in outcome X, there is a trading loss in period 1 of £264,600 which is set firstly against other profits of the period and then carried forward rather than back. Although the firm has profits in earlier periods against which the loss could be set, this strategy would result in the displacement of ACT set off in those earlier periods which would then be carried forward to the horizon since there is no capacity to set it off before the horizon.

Example 3: Leasing displaces debt

Here no target gearing ratio is imposed, and the outstanding capital on the lease is assumed to have the same impact as other forms of debt on the firm's cost of incremental debt, so that leasing finance has the effect of displacing debt on a 1:1 basis. The model is constrained to accept only the leased project, ignoring the purchase option. The constraints relating to the calculation of debt interest are modified to include additional variables for the amount of debt commitment represented by the lease at the start of *t*. The firm faces an increasing cost of debt as its debt commitments increase, and so the cost of the firm's debt interest payments in the solution output reflects the lease finance commitment, which declines over the life of the lease. A feature of the solution output (Tables 6a to 6d) is that the expected rate of return in period 1 is actually lower than the required rate, although acceptance of the leased project would significantly increase shareholder wealth.

Example 4: Leasing does not displace debt

By comparison, this represents the situation where leasing does not displace debt for the purposes of calculating the appropriate debt interest rate (Tables 7a to 7d). In outcome X, where there is a trading loss in period 7, the model chooses to carry the whole amount of the loss forward, so that full use is not made of the available setoff against other profits of the period. It would have been possible, for instance, in outcome X to set the loss of £265,147 against the other income for the period of £200,000, with the remainder of £65,147 being carried forward along with the £191,250 debt interest charge which could not then be set off. The total loss carried forward would then be only £256,397 and the tax for period 1 would be nil. However, the optimal chosen strategy maximises the relief at the 35 per cent marginal tax rate in period 3.

Conclusion

The system of corporate taxation in the UK can create interdependencies between capital investment projects and the associated financing decision, and between ongoing and additional projects being considered; and the tax rules themselves interact, creating particularly complex situations where the firm has no taxable profits or where there is surplus ACT. Conventional methods of valuing debt interest tax shields and the value of lease contracts require as inputs the relevant tax rates and timing of cash flows, although these will in fact be endogenous to the firm's overall set of activities including the project(s) currently being evaluated. The computerised mathematical programming model described in this paper is able to decide the optimal combination of investment decisions, financing decisions and tax strategy simultaneously in the context of the firm's overall activities and tax situation. Operational experience of the model reveals that its decisions may be significantly different from those indicated by conventional NPV analysis of individual projects.

With regard to practical applications, the firm would need to identify the likely investment opportunities that will arise over the period between the present time and the horizon, and estimate their values at the horizon. If the model is unaware of these opportunities it chooses to make a full dividend payout, and this choice will determine its optimal tax strategy. Since the model's output and the required rate of return are sensitive to the input horizon value of the firm's assets, exclusive of tax effects, the appropriate value of this input would need to be considered carefully in any practical situation. Although the optimisation model itself is essentially a 'black box' which gives as output a single optimal solution, the solution process is sufficiently fast for the model to be run repeatedly under sensitivity analysis.

References

Ashford, R., Berry, R. and Dyson, R. (1986), 'Taxation Induced Interactions in Capital Budgeting', *Warwick Papers in Management,* No. 8, November.

Ashton, D.J. (1978), 'The Reasons for Leasing - A Mathematical Programming Framework', *Journal of Business Finance and Accounting,* Vol. 5, no. 2.

Ashton, D.J. (1989a), 'The Cost of Capital and the Imputation System', *Journal of Business Finance and Accounting,* Vol. 16, pp. 75-88.

Ashton, D.J. (1989b), 'Textbook Formulae and UK Taxation: Modigliani and Miller Revisited', *Accounting and Business Research,* Vol. 19, pp. 207-212.

Ashton, D.J. (1991), 'Corporate Financial Policy: American Analytics and UK Taxation', *Journal of Business Finance and Accounting*, Vol. 18, pp. 465-482.

Berry, R.H. and Dyson, R.G. (1979) 'A Mathematical Programming Approach to Taxation Induced Interdependencies in Investment Appraisal', *Journal of Business Finance and Accounting*, Vol. 6, No. 4.

Cooper, I., and Franks, J.R. (1983), 'The Interaction of Financial and Investment Decisions When the Firm has Unused Tax Credits,' *Journal of Finance,* Vol. 38, pp. 571-584.

DeAngelo, H. and Masulis, R.W. (1980), 'Optimal Capital Structure under Corporate and Personal Taxation', Journal of Financial Economics, Vol. 8, pp. 3-30.

Drury, C. (1989), 'Evaluating the Lease or Purchase Decision', *Managerial Finance*, Vol. 15, no. 1/2.

Drury, C. and Braund, S.L. (1990), 'A Survey Of UK Leasing Practice', *Management Accounting*, April.

Farrar, S.V. (1995), *Optimisation Models for Corporate Taxation in Capital Budgeting*, PhD thesis, University of Plymouth, 1995.

Fawthrop, R.A. and Terry, B. (1976), 'The Evaluation of an Integrated Investment and Financing Decision', *Journal of Business Finance and Accounting*, Vol. 3, pp. 79-111.

Franks, J.R. and Hodges, S.D. (1978), 'Valuation of Financial Lease Contracts: A Note', *Journal of Finance*, Vol. 30, no. 2.

King, M.A. (1977), *Public Policy and the Corporation*, London: Chapman and Hall.

Mayer, C.P. (1986), 'Corporation Tax, Finance and the Cost of Capital', Review of Economic Studies, Vol. 53. pp. 93-112.

Miller, M.H. and Upton, C.W. (1976), 'Leasing, Buying and the Cost of Capital Services', *Journal of Finance*, Vol. 31, no. 3.

Modigliani, F., and Miller, M.H., (1963), 'Corporate Income Taxes and the Cost of Capital: A Correction', *American Economic Review*, Vol. 53, no. 3

Myers, S.C., Dill, D.A. and Bautista, A.J. (1976), 'Valuation of Financial Lease Contracts', *Journal of Finance,* Vol.31, no. 3.

Pointon, J. (1981a), 'Optimal Capital Structure under the Imputation System', *Accounting and Business Research,* Summer.

Pointon, J. (1981b), *Investment and Financing Decision Models Under the Imputation Tax System*, PhD Thesis, University of Warwick, 1981.

Pointon, J. (1991), *Programming for the Tax Interactivities of Capital Investment and Financing Decisions,* Research Paper, Business Taxation Research Unit, Polytechnic South West.

Young, G. (1992), 'A New Approach to Modelling Corporation Tax', *National Institute Economic Review*, May, pp. 98-105.

14 Stochastic modelling and financial shocks

John Pointon

Introduction

Risk factors are common to most financial management problems, whether they relate to exchange risks, bankruptcies, technological obsolescence, takeovers or fiscal shifts. However, although financial models need to reflect such aspects, these are different characteristics of risk. It is emphasised here that there is a distinction between a dramatic shock and less dramatic variations. A dramatic shock, for example, may be the sudden expropriation of an overseas asset, a sudden change in management resulting from a takeover or a sudden appointment of a liquidator. By contrast a less dramatic variation may be a change in the exchange rate under a floating rate system or a change in wage rates. As far as fiscal policy is concerned a shock would be the complete withdrawal of a tax, whereas a less dramatic variation would be the change in the rate of an existing tax.

Of course, there have been various ways of dealing with risk. Simulations provide one way of assessing its impact. For diversified portfolios the capital asset pricing model (Sharpe, 1964) is a neat way of pricing the impact of an additional security, although it is also applied to capital investments. As well as through diversification, frequently firms seek to eliminate risk through hedging, particularly with regard to currency transactions (Collier et al, 1990). The principle of hedging is also at the heart of option pricing (Black and Scholes, 1973) and can be extended to real options (Trigeorgis, 1993; Busby and Pitts, 1996). But each method has its drawbacks. Simulations do not necessarily indicate the most effective and efficient course of action. Beta risk is inadequate in representing the risk to the firm of a large scale corporate investment or failure (Grinyer, 1986), because it emphasises small investments in relation to a widely diversified portfolio. Hedging breaks down if there is no matching of assets or liabilities available and if forward contracts do not extend sufficiently far into the future.

In this paper the modelling will focus on the impact of a sudden financial shock, in particular a bankruptcy or takeover, on the price of a security, whose returns are also subjected to the less dramatic vagaries of its financial environment. In the next session there will be a brief discussion of bankruptcies and takeovers. This is followed by an explanation of the methodology used in combining different risk attributes and devising an overall valuation. Finally, the quantitative model is presented.

Bankruptcies and takeovers

When a takeover or bankruptcy takes place there is likely to be a sudden shift in the price of a security. In the first case it is generally favourable. If the performance of a company is unsatisfactory then it may become a target for a takeover. In a UK study Limmack (1991) demonstrated that there were wealth increases to the shareholders of victim companies during the period 1977-86, although the opposite was true for the bidding firms. Cheung and Shum (1993) found that shareholders of victim firms obtained large positive abnormal returns around the announcement dates of takeovers in Hong Kong between 1986-91. Speculation before a takeover announcement can lead to a positive impact on share prices. Indeed Franks and Harris (1989) found abnormal returns. However, in one Australian study (Aitken and Czernkowski, 1992) the impact of the press was demonstrated to have explained at least most of the unexpected returns. Target firms may adopt defensive strategies to fend off an unwelcome takeover (Sudarsanam, 1995). Where the strategy is successful, the shareholders of the victim companies can make significant gains (Parkinson and Dobbin, 1993). A number of researchers have attempted to predict which firms are likely to be taken over (for example: Barnes, 1990; Keasey and McGuinness, 1990).

Predictive methods, particularly multiple discriminant analysis, have more frequently been used in studies into corporate failure. For example, Altman (1968) and Taffler (1982, 1983) are noted for their US and UK studies, respectively. In a study of voluntary liquidations in the US, Ghosh et al (1991) isolated the associated features, which included declining growth. They noted that these voluntary liquidations generally follow unsolicited takeover attempts. Thus, there is a link between models of takeovers and bankruptcies. The particular methodology chosen for the model in this paper is explained in the next section.

Brownian motion and Poisson jumps

Economics researchers have frequently applied models that were originally designed for the natural sciences. Geometric Brownian motions have been used to model interest rates, exchange rates and inflation rates, as well as underlying cash flows in options valuations (Black and Scholes, 1973). The motion itself, which first related to movements of microscopic particles in liquid, can be traced back to Robert Brown, Norbert Wiener and Albert Einstein (Kendall, 1988). But this is also well suited to share price behaviour. In particular the process possesses the Markov property. It is rather like the absent-minded reader in business finance, who sits at the terminal in the library ready to use the LIBERTAS system, and forgets all previous events, including the name of the required journal. So, the share price stands at a certain level. The previous prices are irrelevant. On the basis of market efficiency all relevant information is fully and immediately absorbed into the share price. Under the semi-strong form of the efficient markets theory only all publicly available information is included. Furthermore a number of studies have found that share prices follow a random walk (see the review by Firth, 1986). The current price reflects the current financial position of the firm and expectations of the future. Increments follow a stochastic process. If there is no perceived trend, the price at the next moment in time is expected to be the same as at the moment. However, in this research paper variations are assumed to be normally distributed.

Random shocks can be represented by a Poisson jump. A friend once remarked that this is rather like a salmon leaping! The event is random in that at most only one 'arrival' can occur within a 'small' moment of time. The number of arrivals would depend upon the length of the time interval. The time between events is represented by a negative exponential distribution, the mean time being $1/\lambda$, where λ is the Poisson arrival rate. The relationship between these is succinctly described by Wagner (1975, p 860).

Now, a geometric Brownian motion can be combined with a Poisson jump. One application in multinational capital budgeting (Pointon and Hooper, 1995) is to treat an expropriation risk as a Poisson jump (a financial shock) and exchange rate movements as a geometric Brownian motion (a less dramatic variation). The basic methodology of this type of analysis is explained by Dixit and Pindyck (1994). There are six stages in deriving such a model. First, the underlying flows are identified before any Poisson event is taken into account. Second, a growth trend can be introduced. In the case of the takeover-bankruptcy model this will be a declining trend. Third, an incremental change in flows is modelled by a standard normal distribution. Fourth, the Poisson event is introduced, which changes the financial position. Fifth, a valuation process is established. This step is basically a discounted cash flow approach, with a few modifications to deal with the risk. Account is taken of: the flow during a small period of time; an exogenous end of period expected value, given no Poisson event; a corresponding value with a Poisson event and the discount rate. Sixth, the value is determined by solving a differential equation. For economic problems of this nature, Dixit and Pindyck (1994) demonstrate that the general solution of the homogenous version of the differential equation leads to either an economic interpretation that does not make sense or a purely speculative component. Hence, any particular solution of the non-homogeneous version solves the problem. In the next section these fundamental principles are applied to the share price of a company that is identified as susceptible to either a potential takeover or bankruptcy. These alternatives are assumed to be mutually exclusive.

A Stochastic model for a takeover or bankruptcy

In the model that follows dividends will be treated as an explanatory variable of price. Now, in practice, dividends tend to exhibit an element of stability (Rutterford, 1994; Dalton and Pointon, 1995). However when the rate of return on new assets equals the marginal discount rate a share price can be stated in terms of earnings or dividends (Solomon, 1969; Karathanassis, 1983). Of course, the daily pattern of earnings is more variable than reported annual earnings figures would suggest. In this stochastic model although dividends are assumed to follow a geometric Brownian motion, the rationale is that essentially it is the cash equivalent of the continuous underlying earnings that are assumed to exhibit such behaviour. Also, on this occasion tax implications will be ignored. Assume the firm pays dividends D at a declining expected rate of f. The standard deviation parameter of the dividends is σ. Increments are standard normally distributed, where N represents the standard normal variate. Under the geometric Brownian motion:

$$dD = -fDdt + \sigma DN\sqrt{dt} \tag{1}$$

A financial shock is expected to occur with a mean time of $1/\lambda$. Hence λ represents the Poisson 'arrival' rate of the event. Here a single Poisson jump occurs after which no other shock is expected. The event is consistent with a Poisson distribution. It may occur at any time, but the probability within a small period of time dt is simply λdt.

The share price P is given by:

$$P = Ddt + E(P_{NS})(1-\lambda dt)/(1+kdt) + E(P_{FS})\lambda dt/(1+kdt) \tag{2}$$

The rationale for this is that during dt dividends of D are paid. The expected price at the end of the period is either P_{NS}, the price with no financial shock, or P_{FS}, the price with a financial shock. Using Itô's lemma (Itô, 1965), following a Taylor series expansion and a normally distributed Wiener process, for a geometric Brownian motion the expected change in price is a function of first and second derivatives of the price with respect to dividends:

$$E(dP) = -\frac{dP}{dD} fDdt + \frac{1}{2}\frac{d^2P}{dD^2}\sigma^2 D^2 dt \tag{3}$$

But:

$$E(P_{NS}) = P + E(dP) \tag{4}$$

i.e. the expected price, given no financial shock, is simply the current price plus the expected increase which has been evaluated.

Therefore:

$$P = Ddt + \left(P - \frac{dP}{dD} fDdt + \frac{1}{2}\frac{d^2P}{dD^2}\sigma^2 D^2 dt\right)\left(\frac{1-\lambda dt}{1+kdt}\right)$$
$$+E(P_{FS})\lambda dt / (1+kdt) \tag{5}$$

Now ignoring terms in $(dt)^2$, $1/(1+kdt)$ is equal to $1-kdt$. This can be derived either by using a binomial expansion for $(1+kdt)^{-1}$ or by multiplying $1/(1+kdt)$ by $(1-kdt)/(1-kdt)$ and simplifying. Hence from equation (4) and still ignoring terms in $(dt)^2$, it follows that:

$$\frac{1}{2}\sigma^2 D^2 \frac{d^2P}{dD^2} - fD\frac{dP}{dD} - (\lambda + k)P$$
$$= -\lambda P_{FS} - D \tag{6}$$

dropping the expectations operator for the price with a financial shock.

Now P_{FS} is a linear function of D. Let:

$$P_{FS} = hD \tag{7}$$

Given the linearity in D on the right-hand side the trial function, i.e. the function which is used to try to find a particular solution to the inhomogeneous equation, is:

$P = mD$ $\quad\quad\quad\quad$ m constant

$$P = mD \qquad m \text{ constant}$$

(8)

Therefore, using equations (6) and (7) and given that:
$dP / dD = m$ and $d^2P / dD^2 = 0$:

$$0 - fDm - (\lambda + k)(mD + c) = -\lambda hD - D$$

(9)

Hence one particular solution is:

$$m = (1 + \lambda h)/(f + \lambda + k)$$

(10)

By substituting into equation (8), the share price is given by:

$$P = \frac{D(1 + \lambda h)}{f + \lambda + k}$$

(11)

For example dividends are 10 pence per share, declining at 5 per cent. The cost of capital is 12 per cent and the mean time to a bankruptcy is 4 years. Hence under the bankruptcy model, with a price on bankruptcy at zero, the current share would be worth:

$$P = \frac{£0.40}{0.05 + 0.25 + 0.12} = £0.95$$

This assumes that there is no liquidating distribution and no possible takeover. In the event of a takeover, suppose there would be a new growth rate in dividends denoted g. Hence, based on a dividend of D

$$P_{FS} = D/(k - g) = hD$$

(12)

If, following a takeover, the dividend rate were declining at only 3 per cent and the mean time to the takeover was 2 years, then the share price would be:

$$P = \frac{£0.40(1 + 0.5/(0.12 + 0.03))}{0.05 + 0.5 + 0.12}$$
$$= £2.59.$$

This assumes no possibility of a bankruptcy.
However, given no takeover or bankruptcy possibilities, the share price would be:

$$P = \frac{£0.40}{0.12 + 0.05} = £2.35,$$

with a 5 per cent declining trend, and:

$$P = \frac{£0.40}{0.12 + 0.03} = £2.67,$$

with a 3 per cent declining trend.

Conclusion

A distinction has been made between dramatic financial shocks and less dramatic variations in financial returns. Examples of takeovers and bankruptcies have been used to illustrate financial shocks resulting in positive and negative effects on share values respectively. A geometric Brownian motion, to model less dramatic variations, has been combined with a Poisson jump. By solving a second-order linear ordinary differential equation, a share valuation model has been derived that can be applied either to shares subject to takeover threats or to significant bankruptcy risks.

References

Aitken, M. and Czernkowski, R. (1992), 'Information Leakage Prior to Takeover Announcements: the Effect of Media Reports' *Accounting and Business Research,* Vol. 23, No. 89, pp. 3-20.

Altman, E.I. (1968), 'Financial Ratios, Discriminant Analysis and the Prediction of Corporate Bankruptcy', *Journal of Finance,* Vol. 23, No. 4, pp. 589-609.

Barnes, P.A. (1990), 'The Prediction of Takeover Targets in the UK by Means of Multiple Discriminant Analysis', *Journal of Business Finance and Accounting*, Vol. 17, No. 1, pp.73-84.

Black, F. and Scholes, M.J. (1973), 'The Pricing of Options and Corporate Liabilities', *Journal of Political Economy*, Vol. 81, pp. 637-54.

Busby, J.S. and Pitts, C.G.C. (1996), 'Real Options in Practice: An Exploratory Survey of How Decision Makers in Industry Think About Flexibility', Warwick Business School Research Bureau, No. 210.

Cheung, Y.L. and Shum, C.K. (1993), 'Corporate Takeover and Shareholders' Wealth in Hong Kong', *British Accounting Review*, Vol. 25, No. 3, pp. 213-26.

Dalton, F. and Pointon, J. (1995), 'An International Study of Dividend Policy: Some Preliminary Results', British Accounting Association Conference Paper, University of Plymouth, reprinted in this volume.

Dixit, A. and Pindyck, R. (1994), *Investment Under Uncertainty*, Princeton University Press: Princeton, Illinois.

Firth, M. (1986), 'The Efficient Markets Theory', In: M. Firth and S.M. Keane, *Issues in Finance*, Philip Allan: Oxford.

Franks, J.R. and Harris, R.S. (1989), 'Shareholder Wealth Effects of Corporate Takeovers: the UK Experience 1955-1985' *Journal of Financial Economics*, Vol. 23, pp. 225-49.

Ghosh, C., Owers, J.E. and Rogers, R.C. (1991), 'The Financial Characteristics Associated with Voluntary Liquidations', *Journal of Business Finance and Accounting*, Vol. 18, No. 6, pp. 773-89.

Grinyer, J.R. (1986), 'An Alternative to Maximisation of Shareholders' Wealth in Capital Budgeting Decisions', *Accounting and Business Research*, Vol. 16, No. 64, pp. 319-26.

Itô, K. (1965), 'On Stochastic Differential Equations', *Memoirs of the American Mathematical Society*, No. 4, pp. 1-51.

Karathanassis, G. (1983), 'Empirical Valuation Models: How Useful Have They Been?' *Accounting and Business Research*. Vol. 13, No. 52, pp. 289-291.

Keasey, K. and McGuinness, P. (1990), 'The Failure of UK Industrial Firms 1976-1984: Logistic Analysis and Entropy Measures', *Journal of Business Finance and Accounting*, Vol. 17, No. 1, pp. 119-135.

Kendall, W. (1988) *M343: Applications of Probability*, Open University Press: Milton Keynes.

Limmack, R.J. (1991), 'Corporate Mergers and Shareholder Wealth Effects: 1977-1986', *Accounting and Business Research*, Vol. 21, No. 83, pp. 239-51.

Parkinson, C. and Dobbins, R. (1993), 'Returns to Shareholders in Successfully Defended Takeover Bids: UK Evidence 1975-1984', *Journal of Business Finance and Accounting*, Vol. 20, No. 4, pp. 501-520.

Pointon, J. and Hooper V. (1995), 'Exchange Rate and Expropriation Risk in Multinational Capital Budgeting', *International Journal of Business Studies*, Vol. 3, No. 2, pp.81 - 88.

Rutterford, J. (1994), 'The Dividend Puzzle', *Technical Focus*, Institute of Chartered Accountants in England and Wales, February.

Sharpe, W.F. (1964), 'Capital Asset Prices: A Theory of Market Equilibrium Under Conditions of Risk', *Journal of Finance*, Vol. 19, No. 3, pp. 425-42.

Solomon, E. (1969), *The Theory of Financial Management*, Columbia University Press: New York.

Sudarsanam, P.S. (1995), 'The Role of Defensive Strategies and Ownership Structure of Target Firms: Evidence from UK Hostile Takeover Bids', *European Financial Management*, Vol. 1, No. 3, pp. 223-40.

Taffler, R.J. (1982), 'Forecasting Company Failure in the UK Using Discriminant Analysis and Financial Ratio Data', *Journal of the Royal Statistical Society*, Series A (General), Vol. 145, Part 3, pp. 342-58.

Taffler, R.J. (1983), 'The Assessment of Company Solvency and Performance Using a Statistical Model', *Accounting and Business Research*, Vol. 13, No. 52, pp. 295-307.

Trigeorgis, L. (1993), 'Real Options and Interactions with Financial Flexibility', *Financial Management*, Autumn, pp. 202-24.

Wagner, H.M. (1975), *Principles of Operations Research: with Applications to Managerial Decisions*, Prentice-Hall: London.

15 The impact of the macroeconomic environment upon the European corporate capital structure

Jonathan Tucker

Introduction

Whilst research into the nature of the determinants of the corporate capital structure has progressed markedly in certain areas, in particular with respect to the influence of taxation, various corporate environment influences, agency factors, and information asymmetry factors, the precise nature of the influence of the macroeconomic environment upon the corporate capital structure appears somewhat under-researched. Indeed, in theoretical models of corporate capital structure determination, macroeconomic factors often implicitly constitute the *ceteris paribus* assumptions underpinning the model. Furthermore, in time series empirical models, authors generally ignore the influence of the macroeconomy, except where it impinges upon the direct costs of external finance. Moreover, where the literature *does* consider the influence of the macroeconomy, it is generally from the narrow perspective of the US and UK economies alone.

Yet further shortcomings of the existing literature may be identified when considering the influence of individual potential macroeconomic environment determinants of the capital structure. The literature appears to give rise to numerous theories of the influence of inflation upon the corporate capital structure, many of which are competing and are thus not readily reconciled. Additionally, authors generally do not explore the effect of the term length of interest rates upon the debt decision. Finally, the influence of macroeconomic activity, measured by the growth of GDP and the growth of aggregate investment, appears to be almost entirely unresearched.

An important question to be considered before conducting any new research in this area is why should the macroeconomic environment influence the corporate capital structure of the firm at all? In response it might be argued that the macroeconomic environment within which the firm is positioned should exert a significant influence upon all of the financial and investment decisions that the finance manager makes as it constitutes the monetary and real market framework within which firms operate.

The apparent inadequacy of the literature in addressing the influence of the macroeconomic environment upon the corporate capital structure thus demands a structured theoretical and empirical analysis, to produce a more comprehensive framework within which to consider the role of the macroeconomy in corporate capital structure determination. This paper examines the existing theoretical and empirical literature which explores the influence of the macroeconomy upon the corporate capital structure. Hypotheses specifying the influence of the macroeconomic environment factors upon the corporate capital structure are derived from the existing literature, as well as theoretical discussion of the potential influence of each factor. The data set analysed is drawn from the Datastream financial database, and consists of quoted firm capital structure data and macroeconomic data for the UK, the Netherlands, Germany and France for the period 1968 to 1993. The empirical analysis comprises the construction and estimation of bivariate time series regression models in first differences form, as well as the application of the Engle and Granger (1987) cointegration methodology. The results from the analysis are drawn together and developed towards addressing the central hypothesis that macroeconomic environment factors significantly influence the European corporate capital structure. The objective of the paper, therefore, is to determine the impact of the macroeconomic environment upon the European corporate capital structure, both in the short-run and the long-run.

Literature review

The theoretical and empirical literature underpinning the influence of inflation, the performance of stock markets, debt interest rates, the growth of GDP, and the growth of aggregate investment upon the corporate capital structure are examined in this section, as a basis for the development of the hypotheses to follow.

The literature identifies three possible causes of a positive relationship between corporate gearing and inflation. Firstly, Franks and Broyles (1979), and the authors of many other standard finance texts, argue that the relationship between gearing and inflation depends on the extent to which expectations are reflected in interest rates. If inflation exceeds that expected then firms will gain at the expense of investors whereas if inflation is less than expected then investors will gain at the expense of firms. Intuitively, if inflation exceeds expectations then the firm gains as it is essentially repaying 'cheaper' pounds to investors whilst not compensating them fully through adequate interest rate increases. However, following this line of argument, a positive relationship can only exist in the long-run if investors may be consistently fooled with respect to interest rate expectations. There are two reasons why the argument may be unrealistic: investors are generally assumed in financial economics to be rational economic agents who may not be fooled consistently through time as they learn from their mistakes, and additionally, investors, particularly those in European countries such as the UK, are predominantly institutional in nature anyway and thus are unlikely to be so naive as to be consistently fooled. Secondly, authors such as Corcoran (1977) argued that any relationship between gearing and inflation depends on the extent to which inflation and interest rates rise together. If they rise equally then the cost of debt finance will fall approximately by the amount of the increased tax deductions. Thus, a positive relationship may arise because higher inflation causes higher interest rates and higher tax-deductions on corporate debt interest. Thirdly, authors such as DeAngelo and Masulis (1980) argued that inflation decreases the real value of investment allowances, thus reducing the 'crowding out' of debt tax-deductions by such investment allowances, in turn encouraging corporate gearing.

Most other authors, such as Zwick (1977) and Modigliani (1982), also suggest a positive relationship between corporate gearing and inflation, arising from theoretical propositions which are largely variants of those identified above. A notable exception to this is the research of Schall (1984), who suggests a negative relationship whereby in inflationary conditions, investors sell debt in exchange for equity as the real after-tax return on equity becomes relatively higher than the return on debt, while the net return on both declines. However, Kim and Wu (1988) explained Schall's alternative theoretical result by suggesting that inflation decreases the demand for debt if the debt yield becomes relatively lower than the equity yield, but the supply of debt will increase if the tax-deductibility effect related to debt exceeds the tax-deductibility effect related to inflation. Therefore, overall, there is overwhelming theoretical support for a positive relationship between corporate gearing and inflation. Furthermore, empirical evidence appears to support such a relationship. Zwick (1977) found that the higher inflation experienced between 1968 and 1974 caused US firms to significantly increase their debt-equity ratios. Corcoran (1977) studied US non-financial firms and found that the debt-to-debt-plus-equity ratios of such firms increased from 22 per cent to 42 per cent over the 1965 to 1974 period, paralleling the acceleration of inflation. Holland and Myers (1977) discovered a similar relationship for US firms. Rudolph (1978) studied the effect of inflation on the entire balance sheet of 311 US manufacturing firms over the period 1964 to 1974 and found that long-term-debt-to-total-assets increased with increases in the rate of inflation. Kim and Wu (1988) studied 1,092 US firms over the period 1953 to 1980 and determined from their regression model that a 1 per cent rise in inflation leads to a 0.7 per cent rise in the corporate debt ratio. Therefore, the theoretical and empirical literature clearly supports a positive relationship between corporate gearing and inflation, although it is noted that the empirics focus on the behaviour of US firms alone.

It is intuitive that financial market conditions, which encompass the performance of equity markets (the cost of equity capital) and the debt interest rate, will influence the corporate capital structure decision of the firm as it is essential for the finance manager to gauge the strength of demand for new debt and equity claims on the firm before issuing the form of external financial instrument most favourable to the firm. Authors generally agree that the finance manager would be more likely to issue equity than debt when the stock market is performing strongly. Indeed, Martin and Scott (1974) argued that equity issues are more likely when equity prices are buoyant and price-earnings ratios are thus high. King (1977) and Marsh (1982) argued that managers are more likely to issue equity after periods of strong equity market performance. Martin and Scott found evidence to support this relationship in their multiple discriminant analysis of 112 US firms issuing securities during 1971, finding that the price-earnings ratio was a very significant differentiating factor between debt and equity-issuing firms and that lower price-earnings ratios were associated with debt-issuing firms. Marsh conducted a logit analysis of the choice between equity and long-term debt for 748 security issues by UK companies during the period 1959 to 1970, and found that market conditions and the past history of security prices were very strong determinants of the debt-equity choice of the firm. However, King found no relationship between stock market performance and the capital structure decision in his analysis of UK companies over the period 1950 to 1971. Therefore, on balance, there is theoretical and empirical support for a negative relationship between stock market performance and corporate gearing as finance managers are unwilling to issue equity when its price is depressed.

Similarly, authors such as Marsh (1982) argued that the level of debt issuance is related to the performance of bond markets such that finance managers are more likely to issue debt when interest rates are low or are expected to rise, finding evidence in his empirical study of UK firms over the period 1959 to 1970 to support this proposition. Alternatively, a positive relationship may exist between gearing and interest rates due to the proposition of authors such as Corcoran (1977), discussed earlier when examining the potential influence of inflation. Part of this inflation transmission mechanism argument states that higher interest rates may give rise to higher debt interest tax deductions, encouraging greater gearing. Therefore, there could exist either a negative or a positive relationship between gearing and the level of interest rates. In addition to these arguments, it is unclear which term of interest rate influences the corporate capital structure decision most significantly. It is proposed that the finance manager is more likely to adjust the long-run external funding stock to changes in longer-term interest rates as he or she will largely ignore fluctuations in interest rates, particularly those embodied in shorter-term rates. Thus, it is clear that conditions in debt and equity markets are capable of exerting a significant influence upon the corporate capital structure decision as such conditions impinge upon the direct costs of external finance borne by the firm.

It is argued that the economic cycle should exert some influence upon the corporate capital structure decision. Perhaps the best proxies to the economic cycle are GDP growth and the growth of aggregate investment and it is thus necessary to briefly consider their likely influence upon the gearing decision of the firm. Rudolph (1978) constructed a theoretical model of the effect of the economic environment on balance sheet items, predicting that as an economy moves from recession to recovery, firms should raise their gearing ratios. The argument underpinning this states that as the economy improves, especially if firms are investing in fixed assets, then increasing emphasis should be placed on longer-term financing. However, he found no evidence to support this proposition in his study of 311 US manufacturing firms for the period 1964 to 1974. Although there is no apparent empirical support for a positive relationship, on an intuitive level it is likely that firms will greatly increase their long-term debt financing towards the perceived end of a recession to finance investments in order to cope with the increased demand associated with eventual recovery. When emerging from a recession, debt financing may be preferred to equity financing as firms may be unwilling at that stage to issue equity until prices are more buoyant. Thus, there should exist a positive relationship between corporate gearing and the growth of GDP and the growth of aggregate investment, respectively, underpinned by intuitive investment-cycle theory. It may be argued that there is little existing literature underpinning the relationship between corporate gearing and macroeconomic activity factors as corporate gearing decisions and the determinants underpinning those decisions are probably themselves better considered determinants of macroeconomic activity (particularly investment expenditure) rather than the converse.

Overall, whilst the range of literature underpinning the potential impact of macroeconomic factors upon the corporate capital structure decision is clearly limited, there is some prima-facie theoretical underpinning and empirical evidence that such factors may constitute important inputs to that decision. However, it must be noted that such evidence focuses predominantly upon the impact of the macroeconomy on US corporate gearing decisions and thus contributes little to the European perspective.

Hypotheses

The objective of this paper is to determine the impact of the macroeconomic environment upon the European corporate capital structure, both in the short-run and the long-run. As the existing literature gives rise merely to the proposed sign of any relationship between corporate gearing and each macroeconomic environment factor, the hypotheses to be derived may reflect this information alone and therefore necessarily remain simple in nature. The more precise specification of gearing relationships, given by the nature of model components and the strength of cointegrating behaviour, must then be revealed by the analysis undertaken. The short-run and long-run time frames are differentiated in the analysis by means of the application of two different though complimentary econometric techniques, first differences time series regression modelling and cointegration analysis, the fundamentals of which are explained in the methodology. A key interest of the paper is therefore the fact that it broadens the analysis of macroeconomic influences upon the corporate capital structure to encompass two time-frames: the short-run (a state of disequilibrium) and the long-run (potentially a state of equilibrium).

The central hypothesis of the paper, hypothesis H1, states that macroeconomic environment factors significantly influence the European corporate capital structure. This hypothesis is addressed by testing five supporting hypotheses, H2 to H6. Hypothesis H2 states that the corporate debt-to-debt-plus-equity ratio (hereafter referred to as the corporate DDE ratio) is positively related to the rate of inflation. Hypothesis H3 states that the corporate DDE ratio is negatively related to stock market performance. The literature suggests that either a negative or a positive relationship may exist between the corporate DDE ratio and debt interest rates. However, a negative relationship appeals more strongly to intuition and may thus dictate the null hypothesis in this analysis. Therefore, hypothesis H4 states that the corporate DDE ratio is negatively related to the debt interest rate. Hypothesis H5 states that the corporate DDE ratio is positively related to the growth rate of GDP. Finally, hypothesis H6 states that the corporate DDE ratio is positively related to the growth rate of aggregate investment.

Data

The data set is drawn from the Datastream financial database and consists of annual time series corporate data for UK, Dutch, German and French quoted firms and annual macroeconomic data for each respective country, covering varying time-spans over the period November 1968 to November 1993. The UK corporate sample consists of up to 314 firms over the period 1968 to 1993, the Dutch corporate sample consists of up to 56 firms over the period 1978 to

1992, the German corporate sample consists of up to 204 firms over the period 1981to 1992, and the French corporate sample consists of up to 354 firms over the period 1983 to 1992.

The corporate data are weighted by the total assets employed by each respective firm, which is a widely used proxy for firm size. In so doing, the larger firms within each sample are given greater weighting, thus producing aggregated data points which are most representative of the firms which constitute them. The total assets employed measure is defined as the sum of all assets less all current liabilities.

The capital structure measure to be modelled throughout the analysis is the debt-to-debt-plus-equity ratio (or DDE ratio), the debt constituent of which (total loan capital) is defined as all loans repayable in more than one year, and the equity constituent is the historical market value of equity at a specified date. However, in addition to models containing this quasi market value ratio, the *book value* DDE ratio is also analysed when modelling the relationship between gearing and the debt interest rate measures. The reason for this additional modelling is definitional in nature: as debt interest rates rise, the cost of equity capital will also increase, thus reducing the market value of equity claims and in turn reducing the equity component of the quasi market value DDE ratio, producing a *positive bias* within the relationship between this ratio and interest rates. As the debt component of the quasi market value DDE ratio is measured in book value terms and the equity component is measured in market value terms, the definitional bias becomes further compounded. To account for this potential positive bias, then, both quasi market value and full book value DDE ratios are included as dependent variables in the interest rate models estimated.

The macroeconomic data are drawn to correspond to the time spans of the respective corporate samples for each country. The inflation measure employed is the retail price index for the UK, the consumer price index for the Netherlands and France, and the cost of living price index for Germany. The stock market index employed is the Financial Times All Share Index for the UK, the CBS All Share Index for the Netherlands, the Commerzbank Share Price Index for Germany, and the INSEE Industrial Share Price Index for France. The interest rate measures employed are chosen to correspond to 0-3 years (short-term), 3-7 years (medium-term), and over 7 years (long-term) in this analysis. These term definitions may or may not correspond to term definitions used in the analyses of other authors, but are defined as such to enable the modelling of quoted rates which are universal across country samples. The Gross Domestic Product is analysed for all countries except Germany, where the Gross National Product is examined. Finally, the aggregate investment data represent Gross Domestic Fixed Capital Formation for each respective country, which is the commonly quoted aggregate from each country's national accounts.

Methodology

Two econometric procedures are undertaken to determine the influence of the macroeconomic environment upon the corporate capital structure in the short-run and long-run. Firstly, simple bivariate time series regression models in first differences form are constructed and estimated to determine the sign and the significance of the response of corporate gearing to a change in each individual macroeconomic environment factor. Secondly, it is determined whether there exists any long-run equilibrium or cointegrating relationship between corporate gearing and each macroeconomic environment factor, a process which involves unit root testing and subsequent testing for the presence of a significant bivariate cointegrating relationship.

As most time series data are subject to either a stochastic or a deterministic trend, such data generally have to be de-trended before any sensible regression models may be constructed and estimated. Indeed, Charemza and Deadman (1992) note that such trends may otherwise lead to spurious regressions and uninterpretable statistics and diagnostics, thus leading to uncertainty regarding the robustness of resulting models. The most common method of removing trends in variables within time series bivariate models is to construct and estimate those models in first differences, that is, by computing the difference between successive observations and substituting these differences in place of the levels for each variable before estimation. However, whilst first differences time series modelling is clearly a far more robust method than regression analysis conducted upon variables in their levels, it is likely that such a modelling approach also removes any long-run properties of the underlying model, restricting the model's usefulness to explaining the relationship between the variables in the short-run alone. This restriction does not prove a problem in the analysis as examination of any long-run equilibrium relationship between the DDE ratio and the macroeconomic environment variables is left to the cointegration analysis to follow anyway. In this respect, the two econometric techniques are complementary.

To construct and estimate first differences time series regression models, the corporate DDE ratio is first differenced and the macroeconomic variable upon which it is to be regressed is also first differenced. The differenced DDE ratio thus becomes the dependent variable and the differenced macroeconomic environment variable becomes the independent variable as it is the reaction of the DDE ratio to changes in each macroeconomic environment variable which is of interest. A constant is also included in the estimated equation, so that the R-squared statistic may be easily interpreted and because there is no reason why the DDE ratio should take a value of zero where a particular macroeconomic variable takes a value of zero. Each first differences time series model thus conforms to the general structure of equation 1.

$$\Delta y_t = \alpha + \beta \Delta x_t + \varepsilon_t \tag{1}$$

where:

Δy_t = the first differenced corporate DDE ratio
Δx_t = the first differenced macroeconomic environment variable
α = the constant
ε_t = the model error

Equation 1 is estimated for the first differenced DDE ratio regressed upon each first differenced macroeconomic environment variable for each of the four country samples. Student t-tests are then computed at the five per cent significance level and the regression model R-squared statistics are computed. The significance and sign of the constant and the independent variable coefficient (the latter of which may be referred to as the sensitivity coefficient) are then examined so that the short-run perspective hypotheses may be tested. There are two requirements for any hypothesis to be given support: the sensitivity coefficient of the estimated model should conform to that stated in the hypothesis *and* the coefficient should be significant. If the former requirement is satisfied but the latter is not then only weak support may be given to that hypothesis.

Once the short-run perspective has been established by means of the construction and estimation of first differences time series regression models, it is necessary to determine whether there exists a long-run equilibrium or cointegrating relationship between the corporate DDE ratio and each macroeconomic environment factor. This is undertaken by means of the Engle and Granger (1987) approach to cointegration analysis. Firstly, the order of integration of the corporate DDE ratio and each macroeconomic environment factor is determined using the Dickey Fuller (1979) unit root test, hereafter referred to as the DF test. Secondly, those variables which are integrated of the same order as the corporate DDE ratio are further tested using the DF or Augmented Dickey Fuller (1981) tests (the latter hereafter referred to as the ADF test) to determine whether they are cointegrated with that ratio.

Before the unit root tests are undertaken, all of the variables in the analysis are tested for the presence of a deterministic trend. The null hypothesis is that there is no deterministic trend, and each variable is tested by means of an F-test of the estimated equation 2 at the one per cent level.

$$\Delta y_t = a + bT + cy_{t-1} + \varepsilon_t \tag{2}$$

where:

T = a time trend

If the F-ratio is greater than the Dickey and Fuller (1981) critical value then the null hypothesis of no deterministic trend is rejected, and thus a deterministic trend is present. Once the deterministic trend test is computed for each of the variables, the DF test is computed, as given in equation 3.

$$\Delta y_t = \delta y_{t-1} + \varepsilon_t \qquad (3)$$

The null hypothesis is that each variable is non-stationary. Each variable is sequentially tested and differenced until the order of integration is determined, that is, until the null hypothesis is rejected and the variable is found to be stationary. Critical values for the DF test are computed from Mackinnon (1991) response surface values. The null hypothesis of non-stationarity is rejected if the DF statistic is lower than the Mackinnon critical value for the relevant number of observations. If the DF statistic is higher than the Mackinnon critical value, then, the null hypothesis may not be rejected, and the variable must be integrated of some higher order. In cases where a deterministic trend is present within the variable, the DF unit root test is estimated with a trend in the right hand side of the test equation, as given in equation 4.

$$\Delta y_t = \mu + \alpha T + \delta y_{t-1} + \varepsilon_t \qquad (4)$$

The Durbin Watson (DW) test for autocorrelation is computed at each stage of the sequential DF testing. The null hypothesis is that there is no residual autocorrelation, and this hypothesis is rejected if the DW statistic is less than the lower bound DW critical value, accepted if the statistic is greater than the upper bound, and an inconclusive result is produced if the statistic lies between the bounds. To strengthen the result of the DF test, the null hypothesis must not be rejected, that is, insignificant autocorrelation supports a stationarity result.

Only those macroeconomic environment variables integrated of the same order as the corporate DDE ratio variable are tested in the second stage of the procedure to determine whether they constitute a cointegrating relationship with it. Firstly, the cointegrating vector is estimated by regressing the corporate DDE ratio variable upon each of the macroeconomic environment variables in turn, as given in equation 5.

$$y_t = \mu + \beta_1 x_t + v_t \qquad (5)$$

The estimated residuals are then tested for stationarity by means of the DF and ADF tests of equations 6 and 7.

$$\Delta\hat{v}_t = \delta\hat{v}_{t-1} + \xi_t \quad (6)$$

$$\Delta\hat{v}_t = \delta\hat{v}_{t-1} + \sum_{i=1}^{k} \delta_i \Delta\hat{v}_{t-i} + \xi_t \quad (7)$$

The ADF tests introduce as many lags of the estimated differenced residual as each sample requires to allow for autocorrelation. The null hypothesis that the residuals (also known as error correction mechanisms or ECMs) are non-stationary is rejected if the DF or ADF statistic is lower than the Mackinnon critical value for the relevant number of observations at the ten per cent level. Where ECMs are found to be non-stationary the relationship from which they are estimated is not a cointegrating relationship. In the context of this study, a non-stationary ECM signals that the bivariate relationship between the corporate DDE ratio and the particular macroeconomic environment variable tested does not form a long-run equilibrium relationship. The DW test is computed, for each DF/ADF test computed and acceptance of the null hypothesis of no residual autocorrelation is again the result required to lend support to a rejection of the null hypothesis of non-stationarity.

Therefore, if a macroeconomic environment variable is integrated of the same order as the corporate DDE ratio variable *and* it forms a cointegrating relationship with that variable, then the macroeconomic environment variable in question must exhibit a long-run equilibrium relationship with corporate gearing. If a significant cointegrating relationship is found between a particular macroeconomic environment variable and corporate gearing, then the related hypothesis may be supported for the long-run perspective, providing that the sign of the static long-run equation coefficient corresponds to the sign of the stated hypothesis.

Empirical results

The estimated first differences time series models describing the influence of the macroeconomic environment factors upon the quasi market value corporate DDE ratio are presented in Table 1. Table 2 presents the results of the first differences interest rate models with the book value corporate DDE ratio as dependent variable.

Hypothesis H2 is given some weak support as the majority of the inflation model sensitivity coefficients are positive, although they are all insignificant. Thus, by means of the interest rate effect of authors such as Corcoran (1977), the non-debt tax allowance effect of authors such as DeAngelo and Masulis (1980), or most probably a combination of both effects, an increase in the pace of inflation gives rise to an increase in gearing in the short-run.

Hypothesis H3 is given fairly strong support as all of the stock market index model sensitivity coefficients are negative and two of the four models exhibit a significant coefficient. Therefore, the reluctance of finance managers to issue equity unless equity markets are buoyant and price-earnings ratios are high, as discussed by authors such as Martin and Scott (1974), King (1977), and Marsh (1982), gives rise to a negative relationship between the stock market index and corporate gearing.

TABLE 1
First differences time series models of the influence of macroeconomic environment variables upon the corporate capital structure ratio

variable	sample	constant	constant t-value	Δsensitivity coefficient	coeffic. t-value	R-squared
ΔINFLATEchange	UK	0.00086173	0.048	-0.010485	-0.024	0.000028288
"	NL	-0.0075316	-0.340	0.44843	0.299	0.00807761
"	BD	-0.020540	-1.981	0.36716	0.419	0.0214737
"	FR	0.015185	0.753	1.8874	1.393	0.244319
ΔSMINDchange	UK	0.0000010012	0.000	-0.044952	-1.429	0.0925935
"	NL	-0.0078200	-0.508	-0.19704	**-3.455**	0.520358
"	BD	-0.021553	**-2.318**	-0.029723	-1.439	0.20564
"	FR	-0.0024489	-0.177	-0.11638	**-2.767**	0.560687
ΔSRINT	UK	0.0025636	0.154	0.0061028	1.220	0.0633388
"	NL	-0.00082247	-0.035	0.0043462	0.367	0.0132811
"	BD	-0.017798	-1.871	-0.0054066	-0.793	0.0652497
"	FR	0.0032251	0.195	0.019810	1.434	0.227071
ΔMRINT	UK	-0.0099177	-0.524	0.010494	0.883	0.0464998
"	NL	-0.0070718	-0.394	0.031155	1.968	0.243977
"	BD	-0.020191	-2.104	-0.0081842	-0.958	0.0925001
"	FR	0.011901	0.778	0.026737	2.225	0.414242
ΔLRINT	UK	0.00047486	0.032	0.030762	**2.643**	0.240958
"	NL	-0.0068832	-0.386	0.032729	2.020	0.253761
"	BD	-0.019450	-1.960	-0.0060647	-0.558	0.0334943
"	FR	0.019669	1.388	0.031066	**2.958**	0.555595
ΔGDP(GNP)change	UK	0.00012083	0.007	-0.55237	-0.893	0.0366142
"	NL	-0.0080082	-0.363	-2.1414	-1.456	0.174864
"	BD	-0.020164	-2.002	-0.43926	-0.811	0.0759727
"	FR	0.0024991	0.121	-0.33469	-0.238	0.00938747
ΔINVESTchange	UK	0.00087521	0.049	0.0017081	0.007	0.00000219707
"	NL	-0.0016922	-0.071	-0.44748	-1.349	0.168238
"	BD	-0.020427	-2.240	-0.18210	-1.571	0.235803
"	FR	0.0025961	0.126	-0.13828	-0.244	0.00986122

Note: t-values which are significant at the 5 per cent level are presented in bold
ΔINFLATEchange = the first difference of the relative change in the price index;
ΔSMINDchange = the first difference of the relative change in the stock market index;

Notes: continued

ΔSRINT, ΔMRINT and ΔLRINT = the first difference of the short, medium, and long-term

interest rates; ΔGDP(GNP)change = the first difference of the relative change in GDP (or GNP); ΔINVESTchange = the first difference of the relative change in gross domestic fixed capital formation.

Hypothesis H4 is rejected for the models containing the quasi market value DDE ratio as dependent variable, although the inference is less certain for the full book value DDE ratio models given in Table 2. For the quasi market value DDE ratio models, then, the coefficients are generally positive and insignificant, questioning the more intuitive negative relationship proposed by authors such as Marsh (1982). There are three possible explanations for this result. Firstly, it might be argued, on a bold and somewhat tenuous basis, that European debt markets are 'demand-driven', such that debt-purchasers appear to maintain a more powerful bargaining stance than debt-issuers. Such an argument is clearly contentious as it challenges an implicit assumption of many capital structure theoretical models which argue that financial markets are 'supply-driven' (and are therefore best examined from the corporate perspective). Secondly, it might be argued that the positive coefficient results from the increased tax incentive to debt which accompanies an interest rate rise as discussed by Corcoran (1977), thus encouraging greater gearing. Thirdly, the definitional bias discussed in the data section may account for much of the positive co-movement between gearing and interest rates. Although the first explanation may be easily dismissed when considering efficient financial markets, it is not possible to ascertain how far the positive coefficients observed are determined by the second or third explanations given.

However, the models presented in Table 2, which examine the relationship between the book value DDE ratio and various debt interest rate measures, do indeed allow some further consideration of the relative power of the competing explanations discussed. The models exhibit a mixture of positive *and* negative sensitivity coefficients. This result gives rise to a number of propositions. Firstly, at least *part* of the positive relationship observed between gearing and interest rates may be explained by the nature of the quasi market value DDE ratios modelled. Secondly, the influence of the macroeconomic environment upon the corporate capital structure is extremely sensitive to the type of gearing ratio analysed. Thirdly, there may indeed be some weak support for hypothesis H4 as negative sensitivity coefficients are observed in half of the interest rate models in Table 2, and thus managers appear more likely to issue debt when interest rates are lower, as proposed by Marsh (1982). Fourthly, as half of the models contain positive sensitivity coefficients even after the positive definitional bias has been accounted for, the debt interest effect, discussed as part of an inflation-to-gearing transmission mechanism by Corcoran (1977), may not be dismissed.

TABLE 2
First differences time series models of the influence of debt interest rates upon the book value capital structure ratio

variable	sample	constant	constant t-value	Δsensitivity coefficient	coeffic. t-value	R-squared
ΔSRINT	UK	0.0071032	0.410	0.0019030	0.366	0.00606401
ΔSRINT	NL	-0.010802	-0.387	0.012455	0.890	0.0734624
ΔSRINT	BD	-0.031520	-0.498	-0.0042010	-0.093	0.000952939
ΔSRINT	FR	0.031664	0.866	-0.0076273	-0.249	0.00879948
ΔMRINT	UK	-0.0083666	-0.435	0.019801	1.637	0.143518
ΔMRINT	NL	-0.0027450	-0.090	-0.0025740	-0.096	0.000769047
ΔMRINT	BD	-0.015406	-0.258	0.066864	1.257	0.149349
ΔMRINT	FR	0.018779	0.517	-0.029906	-1.047	0.135488
ΔLRINT	UK	0.0064058	0.374	0.010291	0.775	0.0265541
ΔLRINT	NL	-0.0027989	-0.092	-0.0016313	-0.059	0.000291145
ΔLRINT	BD	-0.016145	-0.266	0.074958	1.128	0.12377
ΔLRINT	FR	0.016299	0.413	-0.025466	-0.870	0.0975994

Finally, although there are significant sensitivity coefficients in two of the four long-term interest rate models with the quasi market value DDE ratios as dependent variables, none of the book value models contain significant sensitivity coefficients and thus the argument for a relationship between longer-term interest rates and corporate gearing remains essentially untested and thus unaddressed, at least for the short-run perspective.

Hypotheses H5 and H6 are clearly rejected as all of the aggregate income model sensitivity coefficients and the majority of the aggregate investment sensitivity coefficients are negative, whilst all of the model coefficients are insignificant. Both macroeconomic variables are indicators of an economy's position in the economic cycle. The negative relationships suggest that when firms are experiencing a contraction in their investment expenditure as a result of a decline in demand for their products, or aggregate demand more generally, they appear to increase their gearing ratios. It may be that the increased debt is used to bolster short-to-medium-term cash flows during the decline phase, in order that productive capacity may be *maintained* rather than *expanded.* When aggregate demand and investment start to improve, debt funding is relatively less important as firms will be more able to fund from the retentions arising from increased cash inflows and, additionally, as equity markets become more buoyant higher price-earnings ratios will encourage greater equity funding. However, the insignificance of the respective model sensitivity coefficients across the samples suggests that the cyclical nature of the economy is not a significant influence upon their preference for one form of external financial instrument over another.

Tables 3 to 7 give the results of the cointegration analysis to determine whether there exists any long-run equilibrium relationship between corporate gearing (measured in terms of quasi market value ratios across all models in addition to book value ratios in the interest rate models) and each macroeconomic environment factor. Tables 3 and 4 detail the results of the DF unit root tests which are subsequently summarised in Table 5.

TABLE 3
Stationarity tests conducted upon the corporate capital structure ratio and the macroeconomic environment variables

country	variable	F-test	DF (levels)	DF (1st diff)	DF (2nd diff)	DF (3rd diff)
UK	DDERATIO	4.2437	-0.7065	**-5.569**	-	-
NL	DDERATIO	2.6074	-0.6462	**-4.562**	-	-
BD	DDERATIO	6.491	-2.12	**-3.309**	-	-
FR	DDERATIO	2.4817	-0.2524	**-3.292**	-	-
UK	INFLATE	11.194*	-2.852	-2.248	-3.093	**-5.941**
UK	INFLATEchange	3.4339	-0.9444	**-4.533**	-	-
NL	INFLATE	2.5829	4.741	-0.5234	**-2.974**	-
NL	INFLATEchange	0.64828	-0.78	**-2.973**	-	-
BD	INFLATE	0.53825	5.289	-0.7471	-2.275	**-4.109**
BD	INFLATE change	6.215	-1.266	-2.44	**-4.054**	-
BD	INFLATEchch	4.8328	**-3.349**	-	-	-
FR	INFLATE	18.112*	-4.621	-	-	-
FR	INFLATEchange	4.2234	-2.507	-2.289	-	-
FR	INFLATEchch	4.0521	**-3.136**	-	-	-
UK	SMIND	3.3915	3.103	**-3.982**	-	-
NL	SMIND	3.8263	1.143	**-3.496**	-	-
BD	SMIND	2.6359	0.08977	**-3.419**	-	-
FR	SMIND	2.2303	1.149	-2.609	**-5.04**	-
FR	SMINDchange	8.4561	-2.274	**-4.838**	-	-
UK	SRINT	4.9822	-0.748	**-5.883**	-	-
NL	SRINT	1.069	-0.4438	**-4.193**	-	-
BD	SRINT	7.1631	-0.1963	**-2.916**	-	-
FR	SRINT	3.2687	-0.8089	-1.942	**-3.93**	-
FR	SRINTchange	3.7269	-2.171	**-4.223**	-	-

TABLE 3 (continued)
Stationarity tests conducted upon the corporate capital structure ratio and the macroeconomic environment variables

UK	MRINT	3.9764	-0.7221	**-3.747**	-	-
NL	MRINT	1.2282	-0.1138	-2.355	**-3.534**	-
NL	MRINTchange	2.1663	-2.298	**-3.493**	-	-
BD	MRINT	3.0024	-1.068	-2.412	**-3.765**	-
BD	MRINTchange	1.6458	-1.997	**-3.103**	-	-
FR	MRINT	2.4799	-1.517	-2.521	**-4.578**	-
FR	MRINTchange	4.9015	-2.892	**-4.715**	-	-
UK	LRINT	3.2936	-0.09284	**-3.726**	-	-
NL	LRINT	1.3285	-0.1257	-2.344	**-3.489**	-
NL	LRINTchange	2.1248	-2.28	**-3.389**	-	-
BD	LRINT	3.4121	-1.045	**-3.098**	-	-
FR	LRINT	2.7219	-2.115	-2.282	**-4.597**	-
FR	LRINTchange	5.2026	-2.469	**-4.771**	-	-
UK	GDP	1.2197	3.631	-2.308	**-5.531**	-
UK	GDPchange	5.3224	-2.5	**-5.818**	-	-
NL	GDP**	3.4678	4.35	-0.9631	-2.224	-2.628
NL	GDPchange	3.3791	-1.11	-2.273	-2.708	**-3.871**
NL	GDPchch	12.922*	-5.061	**-7.828**	-	-
BD	GNP	7.2415	10.13	0.01631	-2.125	**-2.974**
BD	GNPchange	2.3153	-0.2575	-2.572	**-3.644**	-
BD	GNPchch	4.7176	**-3.565**	-	-	-
FR	GDP	1.193	4.682	-0.6508	-2.043	-
FR	GDPchange	1.5094	-0.6622	-2.061	-	-
FR	GDPchch	2.8192	-2.474	-	-	-
UK	INVEST	2.1151	2.647	-1.751	**-3.542**	-
UK	INVESTchange	4.4418	-1.274	**-4.625**	-	-
NL	INVEST	2.399	3.857	-0.9125	-2.746	**-3.629**
NL	INVESTchange	0.2386	-1.225	-2.52	**-3.21**	-
NL	INVESTchch	5.1258	**-3.196**	-	-	-
BD	INVEST	4.4913	2.03	-1.75	-2.73	**-4.576**
BD	INVESTchange	4.8491	-1.929	**-4.157**	-	-
FR	INVEST	0.73487	1.839	-0.9624	-1.968	-
FR	INVESTchange	5.0329	-0.9925	-2.191	-	-
FR	INVESTchch	6.3174	**-3.853**	-	-	-

* deterministic trend found in variable and thus trend included in DF/ADF test
** DF for 4th difference = -3.847, which is statistically significant
Note: Figures in bold represent DF statistics which are significant when compared to Mackinnon critical values at the 1 per cent level

TABLE 4
Stationarity tests conducted upon the book value capital structure ratio

country	variable	F-test	DF (levels)	DF (1st diff)
UK	BVDDERA TIO	8.2882	-0.1722	**-5.782**
NL	BVDDERA TIO	9.3639	-0.3838	**-3.313**
BD	BVDDERA TIO	3.9247	-1.226	**-4.471**
FR	BVDDERA TIO	2.2912	0.7621	**-3.799**

TABLE 5

Summary table showing those macroeconomic environment variables integrated of the same order as the corporate capital structure ratio (figures in parentheses give the order of integration of the variable, and 'N' means that the variable may not be integrated)

	UK sample	Dutch sample	German sample	French sample
order of integration of the DDERATIO*	I(1)	I(1)	I(1)	I(1)
variables integrated of the same order as the DDERATIO	INFLATE change SMIND SRINT MRINT LRINT GDPchange INVEST change	INFLATE change SMIND SRINT MRINTchange LRINTchange	SMIND SRINT MRINT change LRINT INVEST change	SMIND change SRINTchange MRINT change LRINTchange
variables integrated of different order from the DDERATIO	GDP (2) INVEST (2)	INFLATE (2) MRINT (2) LRINT (2) GDP (4) GDPchange (3) INVEST (3) INVESTchange (2) INVESTchch (0)	INFLATE (3) INFLATE change(2) INFLATE chch (0) MRINT (2) GNP (3) GNPchange (2) GNPchch (0) INVEST (3)	INFLATE change (N) INFLATE chch (0) SMIND (2) SRINT (2) MRINT (2) LRINT (2) GDP (N) GDPchange (N) GDPchch (N) INVEST (N) INVEST change (N) INVESTchch (0)
order of integration of variables in unit root test including a trend	INFLATE (3)	GDPchch (1)		INFLATE (N)

* this applies to both the quasi market value ratio and the book value ratio

Table 5 shows that most of the macroeconomic environment variables in the analysis are integrated of orders 1 or 2, meaning that such variables have to be differenced once or twice, respectively, before stationarity is achieved. Additionally, it is noted that the quasi market value *and* book value corporate DDE ratios are integrated of order one in all four of the country samples. Therefore, certain of the macroeconomic environment variables must be expressed in relative change form (labelled with the suffix "change" in the analysis) before they achieve the same order of integration as the corporate DDE ratio and before they may be further tested for the presence of a cointegrating relationship with that ratio.
Those macroeconomic environment variables which are found to be integrated of the same order as the corporate DDE ratio either in levels or relative change form, are then tested for the presence of a significant cointegrating relationship with respect to that gearing ratio.

Tables 6 and 7 give the results of the cointegration analysis, showing that the majority of the macroeconomic environment variables *do not* exhibit a long-run equilibrium (or cointegrating) relationship with respect to the corporate DDE ratio. Indeed, the only variables which do exhibit such a relationship are the rate of inflation for the UK and Dutch samples and the medium-term interest rate for the UK and German samples, the latter of which occurs only for the book value DDE ratio relationships modelled. Why is it, then, that inflation and interest rates might be significant *long-run* or *strategic* determinants of European gearing whereas other macroeconomic environment variables are not?

TABLE 6

Cointegration tests to determine the existence of bivariate cointegrating relationships between the corporate capital structure ratio and the macroeconomic environment variables

sample	variable	DF lag 0	ADF lag 1	ADF lag 2	ADF lag 3	ADF lag 4	ADF lag 5
UK	INFLAT Echange	**-3.649**	-2.793	-2.171	-2.11	-1.753	-2.017
NL	INFLAT Echange	**-4.053**	-3.346	-2.067	-2.12	-	-
UK	SMIND	-2.86	-2.454	-2.137	-2.631	-2.312	-2.146
NL	SMIND	-2.144	-1.669	-1.065	-2.048	-	-
BD	SMIND	-1.825	-2.379	-0.07367	-	-	-
FR	SMIND change	-1.719	-	-	-	-	-

TABLE 6 continued
Cointegration tests to determine the existence of bivariate cointegrating relationships between the corporate capital structure ratio and the macroeconomic environment variables

UK	SRINT	-2.902	-2.587	-1.882	-2.067	-1.998	-1.846
NL	SRINT	-2.755	-2.789	-1.522	-	-	-
BD	SRINT	-2.203	-2.252	-0.2483	-	-	-
FR	SRINT change	-1.804	-	-	-	-	-
UK	MRINT	-2.673	-2.406	-2.113	-2.409	-2.29	-0.9632
NL	MRINT change	-2.384	-1.963	-1.604	-2.132	-	-
BD	MRINT change	-1.148	-0.9501	-	-	-	-
FR	MRINT change	-1.632	-	-	-	-	-
UK	LRINT	-2.801	-2.327	-1.839	-2.062	-1.807	-1.887
NL	LRINT change	-2.327	-2.007	-1.604	-2.122	-	-
BD	LRINT	-0.9484	-1.152	-0.5105	-	-	-
FR	LRINT change	-1.614	-	-	-	-	-
UK	GDPchange	-2.839	-2.432	-2.087	-2.449	-1.884	-2.05
NL	GDPchch	-2.413	-1.986	-2.121	-	-	-
UK	INVEST change	-2.997	-2.368	-2.064	-2.482	-2.233	-2.145
BD	INVEST change	-0.7097	-0.5265	-	-	-	-

Note: Figures in bold represent DF / ADF statistics which are significant when compared to Mackinnon critical values at the 10 per cent level

The rate of inflation exerts a significant influence upon the long-run or strategic capital structure decision of the firm due to the extremely pervasive impact of inflation upon corporate and financial economies. Whilst most macroeconomic environment factors exert an influence which is transparent, immediate and universal, thus exerting a significant impact in the short-run alone, the influence of inflation upon corporate gearing is so marked and continuous that it exerts a significant influence even upon the long-run or strategic capital structure decision. For example, changes in the rate of inflation influence: financial market returns, particularly the debt interest rate; the value of non-debt tax allowances, and thus the effective value of debt interest tax deductions; the values of all accounts items measured in nominal terms; and the confidence of investors in financial markets generally. All of these consequences of inflation, whether direct or indirect, are clearly capable of significantly influencing the extent of corporate gearing even in the long-run, as the transmission mechanisms through which they influence gearing are numerous, complex, and vary in time-span. Therefore, there is some support for hypothesis H2 in the long-run.

TABLE 7
Cointegration tests to determine the existence of bivariate cointegrating relationships between the book value capital structure ratio and the debt interest rate measures

sample	variable	DF lag 0	ADF lag 1	ADF lag 2	ADF lag 3	ADF lag 4	ADF lag 5
UK	SRINT	-3.096	-2.316	-1.64	-1.722	-2.459	-1.895
NL	SRINT	-0.8717	-0.07172	0.00425	-	-	-
BD	SRINT	-2.782	-2.587	-4.179	-	-	-
FR	SRINT change	-1.415	-	-	-	-	-
UK	MRINT	**-5.123**	**-3.318**	-1.931	-1.037	-2	-0.9631
NL	MRINT change	-1.149	-1.375	-0.5842	-0.3781	-	-
BD	MRINT change	**-3.514**	**-5.598**	-	-	-	-
FR	MRINT change	-0.5992	-	-	-	-	-
UK	LRINT	-2.877	-2.233	-1.587	-1.686	-2.642	-2.101
NL	LRINT change	-1.138	-1.374	-0.6124	-0.4106	-	-
BD	LRINT	-3.2	-2.94	-2.928	-	-	-
FR	LRINT change	-0.583	-	-	-	-	-

Medium-term interest rates appear to exert a significant influence upon the long-run or strategic capital structure decision of the firm. It was noted earlier that modelling the full book value DDE ratio upon the interest rate measures should remove the positive definitional bias, although positive sensitivity coefficients remained in half of such interest rate models describing the short-run perspective. Perhaps more surprisingly, such positive coefficients also appear in the static long-run equations which give rise to the significant error correction mechanisms identified. It is clear, therefore, that there may indeed exist a positive relationship between corporate gearing and interest rates, regardless of the positive definitional bias. This probably results from the debt interest tax incentive effect discussed earlier which appears to dominate

Marsh's (1982) proposition of a negative relationship. An explanation for this may be that whilst in theory lower interest rates should encourage increased gearing (greater debt in relation to equity funding), in the long-run the costs of debt finance and equity finance equilibrate so that the difference between them may relate *only* to differences in their relative merits. Thus, neither changes in the costs of equity or debt finance will exert a long-run influence, except where the latter is a result of a shift in inflation and merely represents part of an inflation-to-gearing transmission mechanism. Although interest rates appear to be a significant long-run determinant of corporate gearing, because their influence is probably best considered part of an inflation transmission mechanism and because the sign of the static long-run model coefficient is counter to that anticipated, hypothesis H4 is not supported in the long-run.

Conclusion

Overall, the central hypothesis that macroeconomic environment factors significantly influence the European corporate capital structure may be rejected in a general sense, both in the short-run and the long-run. However, this result masks the significant influence of certain individual macroeconomic environment factors upon the determination of corporate gearing. The only significant macroeconomic environment influences upon the operational capital structure decision appear to be the returns paid to external finance claimholders, that is, equity market returns and debt interest rates. More buoyant equity markets encourage a relatively greater use of equity whereas the influence of interest rates is complex, depending upon the precise gearing measure employed as well as the trade-off of the influence of lower interest rates directly encouraging greater gearing and lower interest rates indirectly discouraging greater gearing due to the resultant lower tax incentives to debt.

The only significant macroeconomic environment influences upon the strategic capital structure decision appear to be inflation and medium-term interest rates, although it is argued that the latter's influence is intrinsically bound together with the former's influence. Thus, higher inflation encourages gearing through higher tax-deductions on corporate debt interest, whilst also decreasing the real value of investment allowances, reducing the "crowding out" of debt interest tax-deductions and encouraging gearing. Clearly the interest rate impact upon gearing in the long-run is merely part of this inflation-to-gearing transmission mechanism.

References

Charemza, W.W. and Deadman, D.F. (1992). *New Directions in Econometric Practice*, Edward Elgar, Aldershot.

Corcoran, P. (1977). 'Inflation, taxes, and corporate investment incentives', *Federal Reserve Bank of New York Quarterly Review*, Vol. 2, pp. 1-9.

DeAngelo, H. and Masulis, R.W. (1980). 'Optimal capital structure under corporate and personal taxation', *Journal of Financial Economics*, Vol. 18, pp. 3-29.

Dickey, D.A. and Fuller, W.A. (1979). 'Distributions of the estimates for autoregressive time series with a unit root', *Journal of the American Statistical Association*, Vol. 74, pp. 427-431.

Dickey, D.A. and Fuller, W.A. (1981). 'Likelihood ratio statistics for autoregressive time series with a unit root', *Econometrica*, Vol. 49, pp. 1057-1072.

Engle, R.F. and Granger, C.W.J. (1987). 'Co-integration and error correction: representation, estimation and testing', *Econometrica*, Vol. 55, pp. 251-276.

Franks, J.R. and Broyles, J.E. (1979). *Modern Managerial Finance*, John Wiley and Sons, Chichester.

Holland, D. and Myers, S. (1977). *Trends in corporate profitability and capital cost*, Working Paper (MIT, Cambridge, MA).

Kim, M.K. and Wu, C. (1988). 'Effects of inflation on capital structure', *The Financial Review*, Vol. 23, pp. 183-200.

King, M. (1977). *Public Policy and the Corporation*, Chapman and Hall, London.

Mackinnon, J.G. (1991). 'Critical values for cointegration tests', in *Long-run economic relationships* (Ed.) Engle, R.F. and Granger, C.W.J., Oxford University Press, Oxford.

Marsh, P. (1982). 'The choice between equity and debt: an empirical study', *Journal of Finance*, Vol. 37, pp. 121-44.

Martin, J.D. and Scott, D.F. (1974). 'A discriminant analysis of the corporate debt equity decision', *Financial Management*, Winter 1974, pp. 71-79.

Modigliani, F. (1982). 'Debt, dividend policy, taxes, inflation and market valuation', *Journal of Finance*, Vol. 37, pp. 255-273.

Rudolph, P.M. (1978). 'The impact of price expectations and business conditions on the balance sheet structure firms', *Review of Business and Economic Research*, Fall 1978, pp. 61-73.

Schall, L.D. (1984). 'Taxes, inflation and corporate financial policy', *Journal of Finance*, Vol. 39, pp. 105-126.

Zwick, B. (1977). 'The market for corporate bonds', *Federal Reserve Bank of New York Quarterly Review*, Vol. 2, pp. 27-36.

16 The effect of simplifying approximations on the investment decision

Peter Atrill, Eddie McLaney and John Pointon

Introduction

When using either of the discounting methods of investment appraisal -net present value (NPV and internal rate of return (IRR) - it is cash flows and their timings which must be taken into account. This is because it is only when cash has to be invested in a particular project that the organisation starts to incur an opportunity cost. At that point, cash must be taken away from an alternative investment opportunity. Similarly, it is not until cash flows back from the project that it can be re-invested in other investment opportunities.

In practice, it appears to be common to use two approximations in order to derive the cash flows for a period. These approximations are widely discussed and often advocated in texts in accounting and finance. This paper will demonstrate, however, that these approximations can give misleading results when appraising investment projects, particularly when they are concurrently applied.

The approximations employed

When using NPV and IRR it is incorrect to use accounting profits as a substitute for cash flows. Profit represents the difference between revenues and expenses, which are not the same as cash received and cash paid. The realisation convention permits the recognition of revenue in a different period to that in which the cash is received (e.g. credit sales), and the matching convention permits the recognition of expenses in a different period to that in which the cash outlay occurs (e.g. depreciation). As a result, profit flows are likely to be chronologically out-of-step which cash flows.

However, the use of adjusted projected profits seems to be accepted as a valid basis for investment appraisal. There seems to be a paucity of formal empirical evidence on what happens in practice, however many of the leading UK and US business finance texts use this approach when illustrating NPV and IRR methods (e.g. Weston and Copeland, 1988; Brealey and Myers, 1988). The projected profit figures are usually adjusted by adding back significant non-cash items, such as depreciation, and dealing explicitly with cash flows arising from the acquisition and disposal of the capital asset involved.

In order to adjust for the timing difference between operating profit flows and their related cash flows, an allowance for working capital is typically made. The amount of working capital which is expected to be tied up in the project is treated as an initial outflow of cash and, at the end of the project, the release of working capital is treated as an inflow of cash. Adjusting for working capital in this manner would be unnecessary if a strict cash flow approach were adopted. Such an approach would automatically reflect the fact that credit sales achieved in one period may not generate cash until a subsequent period and stock acquired in one period may be not paid for until a later period etc. It is not clear why the projected profits adjusted for working capital approach is used in some texts; there may be an assumption that some managers prefer to think in terms of profit rather than cash flows. There seems to be an implicit assumption, however, that adjusted profits represent a reasonable approximation to the cash flows for the period.

The working capital adjustment is the first of the two approximations which are the subject of this paper. The second approximation relates to the point in time at which cash flows are treated as having occurred. In practice, operating cash flows (receipts from sales, payments for purchases of stocks, wage payments etc.) will normally occur throughout the year with bunching perhaps occurring at month ends as a result of the accounting routines of organisations which are geared towards settling bills towards the end of the month. Seasonal businesses will tend to have a less even cash flow pattern over the year than non-seasonal ones. However, the simplifying approximation seems frequently to be made that cash flows arising during a year will occur at the year end. This is presumably done in the belief that no significant distortion will result from using this approach. Again the empirical evidence for this is not strong; the many of the empirical studies on capital budgeting practices of firms which have been carried out over the years seem to have ignored this point. However, Corr (1983) surveyed 24 US and Canadian manufacturing firms of various sizes and found that all of them used annualised cash flows to deduce the net present value (NPV) or the internal rate of return (IRR). 11 of the 24 assumed that operating cash flows associated with a project occurred at the year end, 12 firms used a mid-year assumption and one firm varied its practice between these two approaches. Hodgkinson (1989) produced a series of case studies of the investment practices of nine UK commercial/industrial firms. Of these eight firms used the year-end assumption. Many of the leading texts seem to make the year-end assumption in their examples (e.g. Samuels, Wilkes and Brayshaw, 1990; Lumby, 1988 and Levy and Sarnat, 1988), even though few of them explicitly mention the assumption which they have applied.

Once again, the rationale for using the year-end assumption is not clear. It may be that it is used purely for ease of calculation. However, employing a mid-year assumption would also offer ease of calculation and may be a more valid assumption. This could imply that the year-end assumption is popular because it will tend to have a conservative effect on the resultant NPV or IRR.

A philosophical inconsistency or extreme conservatism?

The logic for the working capital adjustment is that cash flows tend to lag (in net terms) their accounting cash flow counterparts by a period which will vary from one project to another; perhaps a period of two or three months is typical. The value of the working capital associated with a particular project is the financial measure of this time lag.

If the year-end assumption is used purely for ease of calculation, there seems to be a philosophical inconsistency in concurrently applying these two approximations. On the one hand a 'broad brush' approach is taken by using a year-end assumption, yet on the other hand a fairly pedantic approach is taken to the fact that operating cash flows lag their accounting counterparts by a couple of months. This is particularly inconsistent in that both of these approximations will have an effect on the resulting NPV or IRR which is adverse to them.

It is probably valid to make simplifying approximations when making real investment decisions. After all, the data used in making such decisions is typically of dubious quality, based as it is on estimations of sales and costs for a number of years into the future. If year-end accounting flows are to be used, it seems likely that a more valid result will be generated by not making a working capital adjustment. This is because the distortion which will be caused by using unadjusted operating accounting flows will be opposite in effect (though not usually equal in value) to the distortion of making the year-end assumption.

If conservatism is the motive for using the year-end assumption, there is the danger that adding the working capital adjustment will make the outcome even more, perhaps excessively, conservative. It could be argued that since using these two approximations tends to understate the project's 'true' NPV or IRR, an allowance for risk for provided. This would however be a weak argument since the 'safety margin' generated by using the approximations would be generated without any reference to the perceived riskiness of the particular project under review.

In order to assess the error involved in using the two approximations, generalised expressions for the NPV based on various assumptions will be derived. A hypothetical example will then be used to illustrate the effect of employing the different assumptions on the outcome.

Derivation of the NPV using the approximations

Let us assume that an investment outlay of £J can be made immediately. The asset life is n years. Incremental production will start in month p. Finished goods will be held in stock for f months before sale. The selling price per unit will be £P and S units will be sold from month (p + f) to month 12n. Debtors will pay d months after delivery. The raw material content of each unit is estimated at £R. Raw materials will be held in stock for r months before use in production for months (p + r) onwards. During the first months they will be used as they are delivered and for months until month (p + r) the initial delivery in month p will be sufficient for production needs. Payments to suppliers of raw materials will be made u months after delivery. The direct labour content of each unit is estimated at £L. Labour will be paid at the end of each week in which the cost is incurred. Incremental production overheads, excluding depreciation, will be £H per month payable h months after they are incurred. The cost of dismantling the asset after n years will exactly cover its scrap value. The opportunity cast of capital is K per annum or m per month or w per week. Taxation is ignored.

Under the annual adjusted profits method, the working capital adjustment is given by four terms. These are:

- Raw materials stock ie a value of £rSR.
- Finished goods stock ie a value of £f(H + SL + SR).
- Trade debtors ie a value of £dSP.
- Trade creditors ie a value of £uSR.

Thus the value of the working capital adjustment is (in £s):

$$
\begin{aligned}
& rSR + f(H + SL + SR) + dSP - uSR \\
= \quad & (r + f - u)SR + fSL + dSP + fH
\end{aligned}
$$

During the first year there are 12 - (p + f - 1) = 13 - p - f months of sales so the first annual profit before depreciation is given by 13 - p - f months of profit ie £(13 - p - f)(SP - SR - SL - H) representing the difference between the value of the sales and the three elements of cost, raw materials, labour and overheads.

After the first year the annual profit, before depreciation, will be 12(SP - SR - SL - H).

The sum of the discounted annual profit figures, excluding the first and final years is:

$$\frac{12[S(P-R-L)-H]}{1+K} \left(\frac{1-1/(1+K)^{n-2}}{K}\right)$$

(See Appendix A for derivation).

With the working capital adjustment, the net cash flow at time zero under the annual adjusted profit method is:

- J - (r + f - u) SR - fSL - dSP - fH

ie the outflow comprises initial capital investment plus the working capital adjustment.

Conversely, in the final year the annual profit is increased by the working capital adjustment to determine the 'cash inflow', ie

$$\begin{aligned} & 12\,(SP - SR - SL - H) + (r + f - u)SR + fSL + dSP + fH \\ = \quad & (12 + d)SP - (12 - r - f + u)SR - (12 - f)(SL + H) \end{aligned}$$

It follows that the NPV under the annual adjusted profit method, denoted NPV (AAP) is given by:

$$\begin{aligned} \text{NPV (AAP)} = & -J - [(r + f - u)\,SR + fSL + dSP + f\,H] \\ & + (13 - p - f)(SP - SR - SL - H)/(1 + K) \\ + \quad & 12\left[\frac{S(P-R-L)-H}{1+K}\right]\left(\frac{1-1/(1+K)^{n-2}}{K}\right) \\ + \quad & [(12+d)SP-(12-r-f+u)SR-(12-f)(SL+H)]/(1+K)^n \end{aligned} \quad (1)$$

ie the initial capital investment and the working capital adjustment plus the discounted adjusted profits for the initial year, intermediate years and the final year and the final year's working capital adjustment discounted.

Let us now consider the 'correct' discounted values for the component cash flows. The present value of the receipts from debtors is given by discounting £SP per month from month (p + f + d), thus allowing for lags for production (p), sales (f) and credit (d), until d months after the end of the asset life ie until month (12n + d). Thus the discounted value of the receipts from debtors is:

$$\frac{SP}{(1+m)^{p+f+d-1}}\left[\frac{1-1/(1+m)^{12n-p-f+1}}{m}\right]$$

(see Appendix B for derivation).

Monthly payments to creditors represent (1 + r) months' supply initially and then one month's supply. The payments occur from month (p + u), p being the lag until the first month's production is complete and u being the lag for trade credit. The final payment is r months before the final month of the asset's life, ie month (12n - r). Thus the present value of the payments to creditors is:

$$\frac{SR}{(1+m)^{p+u}}\left[\frac{m(r+1)+1-1/(1+m)^{12n-p-u-r}}{m}\right]$$

(see Appendix C for derivation).

The monthly labour cost is £SL, the annual cost is £12SL and so the weekly labour cost is £12SL/52. The labour payments are weekly from the first week of month p to the end of week (52n - 4f), where 4f represents the gap in weeks between the last production for finished stock and the final sale. By discounting weekly, the present value of the payment to labour is:

$$\frac{(12SL/52)}{(1+w)^{4p-4}}\left[\frac{1-1/(1+w)^{52n-4f-4p+4}}{w}\right]$$

(see Appendix D for derivation).

The discounted value of payments for overheads at £H per month from month p until f months before the end of the asset life, ie month (12n-f), is:

$$\frac{H}{1+m}+\frac{H}{(1+m)^2}+...+\frac{H}{(1+m)^{12n-f}}$$

We can now formulate the true net present value which we denote as NPV(T):

$$NPV(T) = -J + \frac{SP}{(1+m)^{p+f+d-1}}\left[\frac{1-1/(1+m)^{12n-p-f+1}}{m}\right]$$

$$-\frac{SR}{(1+m)^{p+u}}\left[\frac{m(r+1)+1-1/(1+m)^{12n-p-u-r}}{m}\right]$$

$$-\frac{(12SL/52)}{(1+w)^{4p-4}}\left[\frac{1-1/(1+w)^{52n-4f-4p+4}}{w}\right]$$

$$-H\left[\frac{1-1/(1+m)^{12n-f}}{m}\right] \qquad (2)$$

A worked example

The specifications of a project are set out in Table 1. Although these specifications are hypothetical, they appear to be consistent with the type of investment profile which might be found in manufacturing industry. They include a large initial investment, the holding of stocks of raw materials and finished goods, and purchases and sales on credit. The relative sizes of the investments in plant and working capital seem reasonable (working capital represents 30% of the cost of the plant). Figures published by the Business Statistics Office show that working capital ie stocks plus debtors less creditors represents a significant value compared with that of fixed assets of UK companies over recent years. The 30% relationship used in the example may well be a reasonable approximation to many real-world investment proposals.

By substituting these figures into equations (1) and (2) we find that the NPV under the annual adjusted profit method is minus £4,640, compared with a true NPV of plus £16,581, a difference (error) of £21,221, an error of 128% of the true NPV or 7% of the initial asset investment.

Had the NPV been calculated using the year end adjusted profit method, but ignoring the working capital adjustment, the NPV would have been:

NPV = -300,000 + 110,000/(1.15) + 120,000/$(1.15)^2$ + 120,000/$(1.15)^3$ + 120,000/$(1.15)^4$

= £33,902

This gives an error of £17,321 (ie £33,902 - 16,581). This is a smaller error than is generated by using the annual adjusted profit approach with a working capital adjustment.

With mid-yearly discounting of adjusted profits, the NPVs will be:

NPV (with working capital adjustment)

$$= -390,000 + 110,000/(1.15)^{0.5} + 120,000/(1.15)^{1.5} + 120,000/(1.15)^{2.5} + 210,000/(1.15)^{3.5}$$

= £23,252

NPV (no working capital adjustment)

$$= -300,000 + 110,000/(1.15)^{0.5} + 120,000/(1.15)^{1.5} + 120,000/(1.15)^{2.5} + 120,000/(1.15)^{3.5}$$

= £58,070

TABLE 1
Project specifications

Asset outlay at time 0 (J)	£300,000
Asset life (n)	4 years
Commencement of production (p)	1 month
Selling price per unit (P)	£5
Units sold (S)	10,000 per month
Credit allowed to debtors (d)	1 month
Finished goods stockholding period (f)	1 month
Raw material cost per unit (R)	£2
Raw material stockholding period (r)	1 month
Trade credit taken from suppliers (u)	1 month
Direct labour cost of each unit (L)	£1
Production overheads per month (H)	£10,000
Credit period for overheads (h)	0 months
Annual cost of capital (K)	0.15
Monthly cost of capital (m)	0.011714916, ie $[(1 + m)^{12} = 1+k]$
Weekly cost of capital (w)	0.002691344, ie $[(1 + w)^{52} = 1+k]$

Consideration of results

The results may be summarised as follows:

Basis of calculation	**NPV (£)**	**Error (as percentage of initial asset investment)**
'True' basis, discounting monthly/weekly cash flows	+ 16,581	-
Annual adjusted profit with working capital adjustment discounting at year ends	- 4,640	-7
Annual adjusted profit without working capital adjustment discounting at year ends	+33,902	+6
Annual adjusted profit with working capital adjustment discounting at mid-years	+ 23,252	+2
Annual adjusted profit without working capital adjustment discounting at mid-years	+ 58,070	+14

The results listed above reveal significant differences between the NPVs derived using the simplifying approximations and the 'true' NPV. The reasons for these differences are not difficult to find.

With the year-end assumption and a working capital adjustment, a series of positive cash flows occurring at various stages during the year is being treated as if they occur significantly later. Introducing the working capital adjustment simply makes matters worse.

Though the error in the NPV when making no working capital adjustment is not much smaller than where the working capital adjustment is made, the results imply that making the adjustment does not give a more accurate result.

The most accurate of the simplifying approximations used in this example is mid-year discounting with a working capital adjustment. This is perhaps not surprising. Given the assumption in the example that cash flows occur evenly throughout the year, to assume that they occur at the mid-point will give a better result than assuming that they occur at the end of the year. Having made a 'mid-point' assumption, it seems logical to adjust the accounting flows for the working capital.

There is, of course, a real danger in trying to draw general conclusions from a particular set of circumstances. However, the example used, though hypothetical, does contain many characteristics likely to be found in a real-world situation, as was discussed earlier.

Summary and conclusions

When undertaking capital investment appraisal, future cash flows should be discounted at the point in time which they are expected to occur. However, it seems that in practice, many companies discount predicted profit flows (adjusted for depreciation) as if they occur at year ends. In the above example it was shown that the use of these two approximations can have significantly distorting effects. The distortion caused by the year-end assumption may, in some cases, be partially removed, albeit in a rough and ready way, by ignoring the working capital adjustment.

If some broad simplifying assumption is to be made it seems that taking mid-year accounting flows, adjusted for working capital, gives a reasonable approximation. Logic would seem to support this approach.

Undoubtedly it would be more accurate to discount cash flows on a monthly basis. In many cases, identifying monthly cash flows should not cause significantly greater problems than are posed by predicting annual cash flows. Similarly, discounting on a monthly basis should not pose a major burden for decision-makers particularly if a computer is used to do the calculations. It might be argued that the distortions caused by the year-end assumption should be accepted since they will typically err on the side of caution. However, this seems to be far too arbitrary an approach to risk analysis; it is surely better to be aware of the scale of the distortion and to deal with risk as a separate issue.

The point of the paper has been to show that combining a year-end assumption with a working capital adjustment is unlikely to lead to a more accurate result. This is in contrast to what conventional wisdom and many of the leading texts seem to be telling us.

References

Brealey, R and Myers, S 1988. *The principles of corporate finance* (3rd edition) McGraw-Hill International.

Hodgkinson, L 1989. *Taxation and corporate investment* (Chapter 7). The Chartered Institute of Management Accountants.
Levy, H and Sarnat, M 1988. *Principles of financial management*. Prentice Hall.
Lumby, S 1988. *Investment appraisal and financing decisions*. (3rd edition) Chapman and Hall.
Samuels, J M, Wilkes, F and Brayshaw, R E 1990. *Management of company finance* (5th edition) Chapman and Hall.
Weston, J F and Copeland, T E 1988. *Managerial finance* (2nd UK edition). Cassell.

APPENDIX A

$$12[S(P-R-L)-H]\left(\frac{1}{(1+K)^2}+\frac{1}{(1+K)^3}+\ldots+\frac{1}{(1+K)^{n-1}}\right)$$

$$= \frac{12[S(P-R-L)-H]}{1+K}\left(\frac{1}{1+K}+\frac{1}{(1+K)^2}+\ldots+\frac{1}{(1+k)^{n-2}}\right)$$

$$= \frac{12[S(P-R-L)-H]}{1+K}\left(\frac{1-1/(1+K)^{n-2}}{K}\right)$$

APPENDIX B

$$\text{SP}\left[\frac{1}{(1+m)^{p+f+d}}+\frac{1}{(1+m)^{1+p+f+d}}+\ldots+\frac{1}{(1+m)^{12n+d}}\right]$$

$$= \frac{SP}{(1+m)^{p+f+d-1}}\left[\frac{1}{(1+m)}+\frac{1}{(1+m)^2}+\ldots+\frac{1}{(1+m)^{12n-p-f+1}}\right]$$

$$= \frac{SP}{(1+m)^{p+f+d-1}}\left[\frac{1-1/(1+m)^{12n-p-f+1}}{m}\right]$$

APPENDIX C

$$\frac{(1+r)SR}{(1+m)^{p+u}}+\frac{SR}{(1+m)^{p+u+1}}+\ldots+\frac{SR}{(1+m)^{12n-r}}$$

$$= \frac{rSR}{(1+m)^{p+u}}+\frac{SR}{(1+m)^{p+u}}+\frac{SR}{(1+m)^{p+u+1}}+\ldots+\frac{SR}{(1+m)^{12n-r}}$$

$$= \frac{rSR}{(1+m)^{p+u}}+\frac{SR}{(1+m)^{p+u-1}}\left[\frac{1}{1+m}+\frac{1}{(1+m)^2}+\ldots+\frac{1}{(1+m)^{12n-p-u-r+1}}\right]$$

$$= \frac{rSR}{(1+m)^{p+u}}+\frac{SR}{(1+m)^{p+u-1}}\left[\frac{1-1/(1+m)^{12n-p-u-r+1}}{m}\right]$$

$$= \frac{SR}{(1+m)^{p+u}}\left[\frac{m(r+1)+1-1/(1+m)^{12n-p-u-r}}{m}\right]$$

APPENDIX D

$$(12SL/52)\left[\frac{1}{(1+w)^{4p-3}}+\frac{1}{(1+w)^{4p-2}}+\ldots+\frac{1}{(1+w)^{52n-4f}}\right]$$

$$= \frac{(12SL/52)}{(1+w)^{4p-4}}\left[\frac{1}{1+w}+\frac{1}{(1+w)^{2}}+\ldots+\frac{1}{(1+w)^{52n-4f-4p+4}}\right]$$

$$= \frac{(12SL/52)}{(1+w)^{4p-4}}\left[\frac{1-1/(1+w)^{52n-4f-4p+4}}{w}\right]$$

For Product Safety Concerns and Information please contact our EU representative GPSR@taylorandfrancis.com Taylor & Francis Verlag GmbH, Kaufingerstraße 24, 80331 München, Germany

Batch number: 10725935

Printed by Printforce, the Netherlands